Treasures for Scholars Worldwide

浙江省档案馆藏
中国旧海关瓯海关税务司与
海关总税务司署往来机要函

Semi-official Correspondence Between Wenchow Commissioners and the Inspectorate General of Customs in Zhejiang Provincial Archives

主　编｜赵伐　周彩英
本册编译｜何习尧

2

广西师范大学出版社
·桂林·

提 要

本册收录了浙江省档案馆藏1918年至1921年瓯海关税务司与海关总税务司署总税务司及代理总税务司、秘书科税务司、工程局总营造司等的往来机要函(亦称半官函)。信函如包含有附件,则用符号( )将附件名称列在该信函标题之后。为简化每封信函的标题起见,信函的责任者与受文人只写人名的中文译名,其英文原名、职务、供职单位集中在以下表中列出。

姓名	职务
安格联(F. A. Aglen)	海关总税务司署总税务司
包罗(C. A. V. Bowra)	海关总税务司署总务科税务司
	海关总税务司署代理总税务司
伟博德(W. H. C. Weippert)	海关总税务司署秘书科税务司
卢立基(L. de Luca)	海关总税务司署秘书科税务司
卓尔敦(K. E. Jordan)	海关总税务司署署襄办秘书科副税务司
丹安(B. Phillips-Denham)	海关总税务司署秘书科税务司
司徒达(L. T. Stodart)	海关总税务司署工程局总营造司
谭安(C. E. Tanant)	瓯海关税务司
阿拉巴德(E. Alabaster)	瓯海关税务司

Contents
目 录

1918 年

1月4日，谭安致安格联：汇报温州独立事件的涉事官员被撤职、私自出口大米的商人仍未提交罚金、天气状况等（S/O 111）（L060-001-0182-226） …………………………………… 3

1月8日，谭安致安格联：汇报 Poochi 号沉没的情况（S/O 112）（L060-001-0182-228） ……… 6

1月9日，谭安致安格联：汇报职员住所购置的选项及与总营造司的沟通情况并作建议（附税务司公馆周边地产草图）（S/O 113）（L060-001-0182-229） ………………………… 7

1月15日，安格联致谭安：说明可将米商仍未提交罚金一事告知都督（S/O）（L060-001-0182-227） ……………………………………………………………………………………………… 15

1月22日，伟博德致谭安：收到其第112、113号半官函（S/O）（L060-001-0182-230） ……… 16

1月22日，谭安致安格联：汇报英国发货人因拒绝向巡江吏交税导致其货物被扣留、就外国人能否包租中国民船在海关通关作请示（S/O 114）（L060-001-0182-232） ……………… 17

1月29日，安格联致谭安：就职员住所购置一事要求根据最低价选择并以公文汇报（S/O）（L060-001-0182-231） …………………………………………………………………………… 20

1月29日，安格联致谭安：说明外国人有权通过民船运输货物但在该种情况下不能享有协定税则或海关条例的保护、可发送公文索取相关文件（S/O）（L060-001-0182-233） ………… 21

1月31日，谭安致安格联：汇报批准帮办松原梅太郎赴沪治病、夹板船 Ting Hai 凭江汉关监督所发的牌照航行、商办轮船招商局的轮船尚未获得注册证书（S/O 115）（L060-001-0182-234） …………………………………………………………………………………………… 22

2月7日，谭安致安格联：说明已告知负责常关的帮办外国人使用民船运货的相关管理规定、已就外国人租用民船的相关问题提交呈文、关医Stedeford因病赴沪其职责由Dingly代替等（S/O 116）（L060-001-0182-236） …… 24

2月14日，伟博德致谭安：收到其第115号半官函（S/O）（L060-001-0182-235） …… 26

2月19日，安格联致谭安：认为其对常关职责的定义在通常情况下成立（S/O）（L060-001-0182-237） …… 27

2月28日，谭安致安格联：汇报与监督商讨其所收税款移交及与中国银行沟通手续费的情况（S/O 1 National Loans）（L060-001-0182-238） …… 28

3月6日，谭安致安格联：汇报帮办松原梅太郎请假返回日本治病、英领事因电影放映到访温州、商办轮船招商局打捞沉船、前两月税收情况、军队途经温州前往平阳等（S/O 117）（L060-001-0182-240） …… 33

3月12日，安格联致谭安：就监督移交其所收税款时扣除部分费用一事说明后续应逐步加强控制、授权其采用认为合适的方式上交税款（S/O）（L060-001-0182-239） …… 36

3月19日，伟博德致谭安：收到其第117号半官函（S/O）（L060-001-0182-241） …… 37

3月19日，谭安致安格联：汇报米商罚款一事在监督徐锡麒的帮助下得到解决、帮办松原梅太郎已在日本完成手术有望数周内返岗、关医Stedeford已返岗等（S/O 118）（L060-001-0182-242） …… 38

3月19日，谭安致安格联：汇报常关因查验的土布与厘局发行的免税放行文件描述不符而没收该货物、请示是否向税务处汇报此事（S/O 119）（L060-001-0182-244） …… 41

3月27日，包罗致谭安：就后续是购买还是续租Soothill夫人在温州的房产询问意见（包罗与Soothill夫人的往来函）（S/O）（L060-001-0182-246） …… 43

4月3日，安格联致谭安：对税务司在监督的帮助下解决米商缴纳罚款一事表示满意（S/O）（L060-001-0182-243） …… 48

4月3日，伟博德致谭安：收到其第119号半官函（S/O）（L060-001-0182-245） …… 49

4月4日，谭安致安格联：请示在第2733号及2793号通令修改了奖金支付的标准与方法后是否能根据第2334号通令向协助鸦片缉私的司法机构发放奖金（S/O 120）（L060-001-0182-249） …… 50

4月4日，谭安致安格联：汇报监督收到财政部指示其每月所收税款于次月最后一日移交给税务司（S/O 2 National Loans）（L060-001-0182-251） …… 51

4月8日，谭安致包罗：阐述Soothill夫人房产的详情并就购买该房产提出建议（S/O）（L060-001-0182-247） …… 53

4月10日，安格联致谭安：要求就是否向协助鸦片缉私的司法机构发放奖金一事以公文请示（S/O）（L060-001-0182-250） …… 59

4月10日，伟博德致谭安：收到其关于内债的第2号半官函（S/O）（L060-001-0182-252） …… 60

4月15日，谭安致安格联：汇报汇解内债偿债基金专款时使用鹰洋但汇丰银行以国币入账并询问在账目上应如何处理（S/O 3 National Loans）（L060-001-0182-253） …………… 61

4月15日，谭安致安格联：汇报税务处批准私运大米一案结案、就没收的土布及其罚款与监督的沟通情况、员工工作情况及动向、申请授权工程局为铃子手宿舍提供家具等（S/O 121）（L060-001-0182-255） …………………………………………………………………… 62

4月16日，谭安致安格联：汇报1877年与1878年港口界限条例的差异并请示以何为准（S/O 122）（L060-001-0182-257） ………………………………………………………… 66

4月24日，安格联致谭安：通知若有必要将与汇丰银行就汇解内债偿债基金专款的币种进行沟通并作调整（S/O）（L060-001-0182-254） ……………………………………… 70

4月24日，伟博德致谭安：收到其第121号半官函（S/O）（L060-001-0182-256） ……… 71

4月24日，安格联致谭安：指示将1877年与1878年港口界限条例的差异告知监督、建议以1878年条例为准并记录在案（S/O）（L060-001-0182-258） …………………… 72

4月25日，谭安致安格联：汇报雹暴的情况及遭受的损失（S/O 123）（L060-001-0182-260） …………………………………………………………………………………… 73

4月26日，谭安致安格联：汇报二等总巡雷达将其行李及家具寄往香港及相关开销、建议增加里程津贴的金额及为职员提供家具等（S/O 124）（L060-001-0182-262） ………… 75

5月7日，伟博德致谭安：收到其第123号半官函（S/O）（L060-001-0182-261） ……… 78

5月14日，伟博德致谭安：收到其第124号半官函（S/O）（L060-001-0182-263） ……… 79

5月17日，谭安致安格联：汇报收到官用物料凭单后允许军用大米装运、帮办金子四郎病后复职、关员调动及请假情况等（S/O 125）（L060-001-0182-264） …………………… 80

5月18日，谭安致安格联：汇报已购买Soothill夫人在温州的房产（S/O 126）（L060-001-0182-265） …………………………………………………………………………… 83

5月21日，谭安致安格联：汇报商会副主席申请使用运兵船将一批烟草运往厦门、说明商会副主席在购置关产事宜上对海关的帮助、尽管总税务司批准但该批货物最终未能通过运兵船运往厦门（S/O 127）（L060-001-0182-267） ………………………………………… 84

5月27日，谭安致安格联：汇报警察干扰鸦片缉私、将携带鸦片的罪犯交给监督徐锡麒、当地长官因温州独立事件被撤职等（S/O 128）（L060-001-0182-269） ………………… 90

5月28日，伟博德致谭安：收到其第125、126号半官函（S/O）（L060-001-0182-266） …………………………………………………………………………………………… 92

6月4日，安格联致谭安：同意使用政府运输工具将货物运往沿海港口、询问商会副主席的详情（S/O）（L060-001-0182-268） ………………………………………………………… 93

6月4日，伟博德致谭安：收到其第128号半官函（S/O）（L060-001-0182-270） ……… 94

6月4日，谭安致安格联：汇报监督徐锡麒处亦无1878年海关条例的副本、就修改港口条例提出建议、亚细亚火油公司询问港口界限、美孚石油公司不打算就储油槽向海关支付任何费用（S/O 129）（L060-001-0182-271） ················· 95

6月10日，谭安致安格联：说明协助购买关产的商会副主席Yang Chen-hsin详情、汇报温州正经历雨季（S/O 130）（L060-001-0182-273） ················· 101

6月25日，安格联致谭安：建议税务司着手海关条例的修改及更新并寄出其草案、告知条例修改无需领事同意（S/O）（L060-001-0182-272） ················· 103

6月25日，伟博德致谭安：收到其第130号半官函（S/O）（L060-001-0182-275） ······ 104

6月25日，谭安致安格联：汇报监督徐锡麒申请假期、在九龙关发现凭瓯海关收税单及监督委员所发收税单的走私事件、6月税收减少等（S/O 131）（L060-001-0182-276） ············ 105

7月1日，谭安致安格联：汇报监督徐锡麒因其父亲去世延长假期、收到鼠疫的误报并派医生进行检查、因难以制定防护染疫章程建议将其中的一些条例并入港口条例等（S/O 132）（L060-001-0182-277） ················· 107

7月9日，伟博德致谭安：收到其第131号半官函（S/O）（L060-001-0182-274） ········ 110

7月10日，谭安致安格联：汇报英国领事拒绝将所购关产登记在瓯海关税务司名下、购置Soothill夫人房产相关手续办理的进展（S/O 133）（L060-001-0182-279） ················· 111

7月11日，伟博德致谭安：告知对总税务司安格联的正确称呼方式（S/O）（L060-001-0182-281） ················· 114

7月16日，安格联致谭安：同意将简单的防护染疫规定并入港口条例内（S/O）（L060-001-0182-278） ················· 115

7月22日，谭安致安格联：汇报已就所购关产产权登记一事将授权书交给英领事、推迟购买邻近的房产、当地政府要求禁止谷物出口及就此事与道尹的交涉情况等（S/O 134）（L060-001-0182-282） ················· 116

7月23日，安格联致谭安：就所购关产产权登记一事寄出授权书并告知所有关产均登记在总税务司名下（S/O）（L060-001-0182-280） ················· 120

8月2日，谭安致安格联：请示常关巡役任命权的归属问题、汇报7月税收情况（S/O 135）（L060-001-0182-284） ················· 121

8月6日，安格联致谭安：就当地的谷物出口禁令说明此事应由各国使团与中央政府交涉、税务司只需保存好相关公文并将自己的意见记录在案（S/O）（L060-001-0182-283） ········· 123

8月13日，伟博德致谭安：收到其第135号半官函（S/O）（L060-001-0182-285） ······ 125

8月20日，谭安致安格联：就当地的谷物出口禁令表明已收到指示并照办、汇报扣押两艘共用同一份执照的民船并请示处罚方案、道尹请假赴沪等（S/O 136）（L060-001-0182-286） ··· ················· 126

8月22日，谭安致安格联：汇报监督坚持常关巡役的任命需要得到其同意、建议将常关巡役名单从职员录中撤除并以此取消监督的任命权、前监督坚持所有的请愿均需同时提交给监督和税务司等（S/O 137）（L060-001-0182-288） ……………………………………………… 129

8月27日，安格联致谭安：要求就两艘民船共用同一份执照一案以中英双语的公文详细汇报（S/O）（L060-001-0182-287） …………………………………………………………………… 131

9月2日，谭安致安格联：汇报所购Soothill夫人的房产已在领事处完成产权转移登记、邻近的中国房产购置问题尚未解决、在广济号商轮的舵室内缴获鸦片等（S/O 138）（L060-001-0182-290） ……………………………………………………………………………………… 132

9月3日，安格联致谭安：告知不会与税务处讨论常关巡役的任命权问题（S/O）（L060-001-0182-289） ………………………………………………………………………………………… 135

9月6日，谭安致安格联：汇报对误填转运执照的常关职员罚款、经交涉收回海警缴获的大米后将其拍卖（S/O 139）（L060-001-0182-292） …………………………………………… 136

9月10日，伟博德致谭安：收到其第138号半官函（S/O）（L060-001-0182-291） …… 140

9月12日，谭安致安格联：汇报谷物出口禁令在海关的实施情况、就该禁令导致的谷物以少量运输的方式走私请示应如何处理（S/O 140）（L060-001-0182-294） …………………… 141

9月23日，包罗联致谭安：就谷物出口禁令导致的走私建议与监督共同商议以达成处理方案（S/O）（L060-001-0182-295） ……………………………………………………………… 143

9月24日，伟博德致谭安：收到其第139号半官函（S/O）（L060-001-0182-293） …… 144

9月27日，谭安致安格联：就此前所提交的常关员工薪酬等级表建议将录事及二等验货的服务期限改为8年、汇报难以识别上海复出口货物提供的标记和号码、当地局势紧张贸易萎靡等（S/O 141）（L060-001-0182-296） …………………………………………………… 145

10月15日，伟博德致谭安：收到其第141号半官函（S/O）（L060-001-0182-297） …… 149

10月15日，谭安致安格联：汇报美孚石油公司的代理在公事房擅自搜查报单及就此事与其交涉的情况、当地报纸就常关扣押两艘共用同一份执照的民船的不实报道（S/O 142）（L060-001-0182-298） ………………………………………………………………………… 150

10月17日，谭安致安格联：汇报邮局被盗事件及调查详情（S/O 143）（L060-001-0182-299） ……………………………………………………………………………………………… 157

10月29日，伟博德致谭安：收到其第142、143号半官函（S/O）（L060-001-0182-300） ……………………………………………………………………………………………………… 161

11月4日，谭安致安格联：汇报当地政府通过颁发谷物出口护照谋取利益、浙江邮政司前来调查邮局被盗案件、当地流感病情严重、一艘遇难的日本汽艇获救等（S/O 144）（L060-001-0182-301） ……………………………………………………………………………… 162

11月18日，伟博德致谭安：收到其第144号半官函（S/O）（L060-001-0182-302） …… 165

11月26日，谭安致安格联：汇报Cordier教授索要一本职员录、当地在使用谷物运输护照上的不规范之处难以应对、和平庆典安排等（S/O 145）（L060-001-0182-303） ………… 166

12月17日，包罗联致谭安：就Cordier教授索要职员录一事要求向造册处税务司询问（S/O）（L060-001-0182-304） ……………………………………………………………………… 169

12月21日，谭安致安格联：汇报广济号商轮起火案的后续进展、当地道尹更换、民众反对前监督冒广生复职、监督来函允许广济号离港等（S/O 146）（L060-001-0182-305） ……… 170

12月31日，谭安致安格联：汇报广济号商轮起火案的后续处理仍在协商中、当年海关和常关税收情况、希望在税务司公馆修整期间申请假期（S/O 147）（L060-001-0182-307） …… 175

1919 年

1月6日，伟博德致谭安：收到其第146号半官函（S/O）（L060-001-0182-306） ……… 181

1月13日，伟博德致谭安：收到其第147号半官函（S/O）（L060-001-0182-308） …… 182

1月23日至2月11日，谭安与安格联：就是否给予美孚石油公司在港口装卸大批量油的特权及储油槽测量费收取作请示和指示（S/O 148）（S/O）（L060-001-0183-001） ………… 183

1月28日至2月11日，谭安与伟博德：就农历春节期间船只停运、广济号商轮的问题已基本解决、新任监督将在航运恢复后到任的汇报和答复（S/O 149）（S/O）（L060-001-0183-002）
……………………………………………………………………………………………… 190

2月10日至2月25日，谭安与安格联：就美孚石油公司准备用汽艇将油从上海直接运往瑞安一事作请示和指示（S/O 150）（S/O）（L060-001-0183-003） ……………………… 193

2月25日至3月11日，谭安与安格联：就洋员与华员在缉私奖金上的分配问题作请示和指示（S/O 151）（S/O）（L060-001-0183-004） ………………………………………… 198

3月4日至3月19日，谭安与安格联：就美孚石油公司用汽艇将油从上海直接运往瑞安的合法性及瓯海关新旧监督职权交接作汇报和指示（S/O 152）（S/O）（L060-001-0183-005） ……
……………………………………………………………………………………………… 201

3月22日至4月9日，谭安与安格联：就瓯海关与洋广局在查验和扣押货物事务上的交涉情况及河道测量作汇报和指示（S/O 153）（S/O）（L060-001-0183-006） …………………… 205

3月28日至4月15日，谭安与安格联：就常关华籍外班职员的加薪问题及河道勘测作汇报和指示（S/O 154）（S/O）（L060-001-0183-007） ……………………………………… 209

4月19日至4月30日，谭安与安格联：就内河航运的轮船在未开放港口造成的事故、统一港口内装卸油罐的限额、税务专门学校的招生流程、废除常关委员一职等事宜作汇报和指示（S/O 155）（S/O）（L060-001-0183-008） ……………………………………………… 212

5月20日，谭安致安格联：汇报缉获鸦片详情、当地可能抵制日货（S/O 156）（L060-001-0183-009） ………………………………………………………………………………… 218

5月26日至6月11日，谭安与安格联：就海关及港口法规修改、民众抵制日货情况、鸦片走私案件的处理作汇报和指示（S/O 157）（S/O）（L060-001-0183-010） ……………… 220

5月28日，安格联致谭安：说明自己对海关同人进修会持保留态度并要求其转告外班人员（L060-001-0183-011） …………… 226

6月10日至6月24日，谭安与伟博德：就当地抵制日货情况、财政部要求呈报贸易统计数据、鸦片走私案的结案情况作汇报和回复（S/O 158）（S/O）（L060-001-0183-012） ……… 227

6月28日至7月8日，谭安与安格联：就对海关同人进修会的态度、外籍职员的表现、内班华员的加薪申请作汇报和回复（S/O 159）（S/O）（L060-001-0183-013） …………… 232

7月2日至7月16日，谭安与安格联：就美孚石油公司在港界以外修建储油槽所用物料是否应征税作请示和指示（S/O 160）（S/O）（L060-001-0183-014） …………… 236

7月8日至7月22日，谭安与伟博德：就头等总巡后班阿理白要求辞职及其替换人选作汇报和回复（S/O 161）（S/O）（L060-001-0183-015） …………… 241

7月11日至7月29日，谭安与安格联：就鸦片走私案已上报至中央政府作汇报和回复（S/O 162）（S/O）（L060-001-0183-016） …………… 244

7月15日至7月29日，谭安与安格联：就当地反日活动升温作汇报和回复（S/O 163）（S/O）（L060-001-0183-017） …………… 249

7月19日至7月29日，谭安与安格联：就填埋并围圈海关前滩以备日后修建验货厂及当地反日活动的进展作汇报和回复（S/O 164）（S/O）（L060-001-0183-018） …………… 254

8月9日至8月19日，谭安与安格联：就总营造司对填围前滩空地的意见、当地反日活动降温、针对新子口税税则的请愿、鸦片走私案处理进展作汇报和回复（S/O 165）（S/O）（L060-001-0183-019） …………… 259

8月13日至8月26日，谭安与伟博德：就按指示对多征的进口货子口税退还税款作汇报和回复（S/O 166）（S/O）（L060-001-0183-020） …………… 263

8月20日至9月4日，谭安与安格联：就填围前滩空地的成本和谭安申请短期休假作汇报和回复（S/O 167）（S/O）（L060-001-0183-021） …………… 265

8月21日至9月4日，谭安与伟博德：就"Yung Shin"号货轮使用现金押款保结作汇报和回复（S/O 168）（S/O）（L060-001-0183-022） …………… 268

9月4日至9月18日，谭安与安格联：就监督与道尹同时离开、反日活动情况、勘查瓯海关前滩空地的计划作汇报和回复（S/O 169）（S/O）（L060-001-0183-023） …………… 271

9月15日至9月30日，谭安与伟博德：就申请短假赴上海补牙及引水管理章程修改作汇报和回复（S/O 170）（S/O）（L060-001-0183-024） …………… 275

9月20日至9月30日，谭安与安格联：就谭安因轮船班期调整申请推迟休假和海关监督更换作汇报和回复（S/O 171）（S/O）（L060-001-0183-025） …………… 279

10月6日至10月15日，谭安与安格联：就瓯海关前滩部分空地被占用、道尹已回但监督未归、瑞安和平阳的霍乱情况作汇报和回复（S/O 172）（S/O）（L060-001-0183-026） … 282

10月18日至10月29日，谭安与伟博德：就谭安请假赴沪作汇报和回复（S/O 173）（S/O）（L060-001-0183-027） ················ 285

11月4日至11月11日，谭安与伟博德：就谭安返回温州、副营造司查验瓯海关房屋状况、当地官吏外出及调任情况作汇报和回复（S/O 174）（S/O）（L060-001-0183-028） ········ 287

11月28日至12月9日，谭安与伟博德：就感谢为谭安加薪、当地新成立的船运公司倒闭、学生的反日活动、当地官吏近况、走私茶叶的民船倾覆作汇报和回复（S/O 175）（S/O）（L060-001-0183-029） ················ 290

12月16日至12月30日，谭安与安格联：就外班职员的不满情绪、是否向验货员印发有关机制洋式货物的通令、修正后的进口税则、当地官吏情况作汇报和回复（S/O 176）（S/O）（L060-001-0183-030） ················ 295

1920年

1月16日至1月27日，谭安与安格联：就帮办金子四郎患流感、去年底温州城区火灾频发、因扣留机制洋式货物与华企及浙江财政厅的摩擦、理船章程获外交使团认可有待税务处修改、当地官吏变动情况作汇报和回复（S/O 177）（S/O）（L060-001-0183-031） ················ 301

1月24日至2月3日，谭安与安格联：就总巡阿理白辞职后是否发给其关员履历表、是否为未注册商标的货物发放特别免重征执照作请示和回复（S/O 178）（S/O）（L060-001-0183-032） ················ 307

2月7日至2月17日，谭安与安格联：就总巡阿理白因故延期离职、英领事因进口煤油被征洋广捐到访、通往帮办宿舍的道路修建问题作汇报和回复（S/O 179）（S/O）（L060-001-0183-033） ················ 311

2月11日至3月2日，谭安与伟博德：就改进江海关装货证书的建议、查验到机制洋式货物的特别免重征执照不符实的情况、对运往厦门军需大米不予放行等事宜作汇报和回复（S/O 180）（S/O）（L060-001-0183-034） ················ 316

2月14日至3月2日，谭安与安格联：就对持有错误的上海所颁执照的货物予以处罚和向验货员印发关于机制洋式货物的通令作汇报和指示（S/O 181）（S/O）（L060-001-0183-035） ················ 321

3月11日至3月23日，谭安与安格联：就当地军阀走私大米、省樟木专卖局滥伐古树、硫磺硝石专卖局抬高价格等做法作汇报和回复（S/O 182）（S/O）（L060-001-0183-036） ··· 328

3月15日至3月23日，谭安与安格联：就新养老金和酬劳金方案的接受情况、建议通过总税务司任命录事和常关人员作汇报和回复（S/O 183）（S/O）（L060-001-0183-037） ······ 332

3月30日至4月9日，谭安与伟博德：就海关监督对录事和常关人员的任命权及放行一批军需大米作汇报和回复（S/O 184）（S/O）（L060-001-0183-038） ················ 336

3月30日至4月9日，谭安与伟博德：就希望造册处印发内债征收及汇解报表作建议及回复（S/O 4 National Loans）（S/O）（L060-001-0183-039） ………………………………… 339

4月5日至4月14日，谭安与伟博德：就在河口沙坝处设置航标一事作汇报和回复（S/O 185）（S/O）（L060-001-0183-040） …………………………………………………………… 341

4月10日至4月20日，谭安与伟博德：就洋广局扣留出口樟脑油一事作汇报和回复（S/O 186）（S/O）（L060-001-0183-041） ………………………………………………………… 345

4月14日，安格联致谭安：下发总税务司对江海关和总税务司署外籍职员的讲话并要求向瓯海关外籍职员集中传达（附总税务司讲话全文）（Confidential）（L060-001-0183-042） …… 349

4月15日至4月27日，谭安与伟博德：就平阳商人请愿减免常关所征茶税、海关监督近况、头等总巡职务交接作汇报和回复（S/O 187）（S/O）（L060-001-0183-043） …………… 364

4月24日至5月4日，谭安与伟博德：就洋广局扣留出口樟脑油的处理详情、帮办金子四郎的调离及后续接任作汇报和回复（S/O 188）（S/O）（L060-001-0183-044） ……………… 368

5月13日至5月21日，谭安与卢立基：就Yang Hsi-T'ung拟在瓯江入海口建造收费灯塔作汇报和回复（S/O 189）（S/O）（L060-001-0183-045） ………………………………… 371

6月3日至6月11日，谭安与卢立基：就德州石油公司未经许可在沿河仓库储存煤油、美孚石油公司申请启用其新建储油池作汇报和回复（S/O 190）（S/O）（L060-001-0183-046） …… 374

6月5日至6月17日，谭安与包罗：就谭安申请提前休长假作请示及回复（S/O 191）（S/O）（L060-001-0183-047） …………………………………………………………………… 380

6月19日至6月30日，谭安与包罗：就职员汉文学习所用报纸内含广告、帮办平野馨已到岗、茶叶出口情况、美孚石油公司和其他外国企业在海门购地修建储油池作汇报和回复（S/O 192）（S/O）（L060-001-0183-048） ……………………………………………………………… 382

7月8日至7月23日，谭安与包罗：就瓯海关与商办轮船招商局关于前滩地块产权的纠纷作汇报和回复（S/O 193）（S/O）（L060-001-0183-049） …………………………………… 386

7月8日，谭安致包罗：申请短假（S/O 194）（L060-001-0183-050） ………………… 390

7月10日，谭安致包罗：汇报浙海关监督误发官用物料凭单、由温州调往宁波的道尹请求免税放行其做书柜之木材（S/O 195）（L060-001-0183-052） …………………………… 392

7月10日至7月23日，谭安与卢立基：就外国企业和教会在海门的活动情况作汇报和回复（S/O 196）（S/O）（L060-001-0183-053） …………………………………………………… 396

7月13日至7月30日，谭安与卢立基：就海门的灯塔和码头建设、邮局电报局享受官用物料免税后应给予海关优惠、台风过境情况、新道尹就任作汇报和回复（S/O 197）（S/O）（L060-001-0183-054） ……………………………………………………………………… 400

7月15日，卢立基致谭安：就瓯海关前帮办金子四郎被举报勾结日商走私大米一事要求调查并汇报（附相关检举信）（S/O）（L060-001-0183-051） ……………………………………… 404

7月26日至8月6日，谭安与包罗：就谭安决定放弃其短假作汇报和回复（S/O 198）（S/O）（L060-001-0183-055） ……………………………………………………………………… 408

8月2日至8月13日，谭安与卓尔敦：就与商办轮船招商局关于前滩地块的产权纠纷、瓯江口灯塔修建、台风重创海门作汇报和回复（S/O 199）（S/O）（L060-001-0183-056） …… 411

8月8日至8月20日，谭安与卢立基：就瓯海关前帮办金子四郎涉嫌勾结日商走私大米一案的调查结果作汇报和回复（S/O 200）（S/O）（L060-001-0183-057） …………………… 415

8月11日，谭安致包罗：询问内港行轮执照的收费标准（S/O 201）（L060-001-0183-058） ………………………………………………………………………………………………… 421

8月14日至8月24日，谭安与卢立基：就与商办轮船招商局的土地纠纷作汇报和回复（S/O 202）（S/O）（L060-001-0183-059） ………………………………………………………… 423

8月24日至8月31日，谭安与包罗：就谭安请短假赴沪关务暂由帮办平野馨代管作汇报和回复（S/O 203）（S/O）（L060-001-0183-060） ………………………………………… 426

8月27日至8月31日，谭安与包罗：就谭安申请延长在沪假期作请示及电报批准（L060-001-0183-061） ……………………………………………………………………………………… 428

9月29日至10月9日，谭安与包罗：就瓯海关与商办轮船招商局的土地纠纷及谭安由沪返温作汇报和回复（S/O 204）（S/O）（L060-001-0183-062） ………………………………… 430

10月15日至10月26日，谭安与卢立基：就本月3日至7日温州受台风重创及对一批证照不全的军装征收关税作汇报和回复（S/O 205）（S/O）（L060-001-0183-063） ……………… 435

10月29日至11月5日，谭安与包罗：就瓯海关与商办轮船招商局土地纠纷的处置、内河行轮载运宁波货物由常关征税改由海关征税的实际效果、几起缉私案件作汇报和回复（S/O 206）（S/O）（L060-001-0183-064） …………………………………………………………………… 441

10月29日至11月5日，谭安与包罗：就因日籍帮办平野馨之妻即将生产建议将其调至上海一事作请示及回复否决（S/O 207）（S/O）（L060-001-0183-065） ………………………… 447

11月11日至11月23日，谭安与卢立基：就英领馆提议向瓯海关出售其在温州的房产作汇报和回复（S/O 208）（S/O）（L060-001-0183-066） ………………………………………… 449

11月24日至12月3日，谭安与包罗：就供事 K'o Yu-p'ing 领取养老金的起算日期、瓯海关税务司公馆的扩建、谭安请假回家作汇报和回复（S/O 209）（S/O）（L060-001-0183-067） ……………………………………………………………………………………………… 454

12月4日至12月14日，谭安与安格联：就各界对私人建造收费灯塔的反响、当地成立机构向出海捕鱼的民船收费、亚细亚火油公司购地兴建储油池、听闻道尹辞职作汇报和回复（S/O 210）（S/O）（L060-001-0183-068） ………………………………………………………… 460

12月9日至12月23日，谭安与安格联：就引水员的选拔和任命作汇报和回复（S/O 211）（S/O）（L060-001-0183-069） ……………………………………………………………… 465

12月24日，谭安致安格联：由于瓯海关税务司公馆维修和天气等原因申请提前休假（S/O 212）（L060-001-0183-070） ……………………………………………………………… 468

1921 年

1月21日至1月28日，谭安与安格联：就收缴鸦片的罚款数额、购置地产用于税务司公馆扩建等事宜作汇报和回复（S/O 213）（S/O）（L060-001-0183-071） …………………… 475

2月5日至2月17日，谭安与安格联：就收缴鸦片的后续处理、引水员选拔、批准帮办黄厚诚两周假期、帮办平野馨的夫人产下一子作汇报和回复（S/O 214）（S/O）（L060-001-0183-072） …………………… 480

2月28日至3月9日，谭安与安格联：就春节近况、拟没收从芜湖运来的赈灾米、瓯海关税务司公馆的维修进展、员工情况作汇报和回复（S/O 215）（S/O）（L060-001-0183-073） …… 486

3月4日至3月15日，谭安与安格联：就因暂无住处三等验货 S. R. Ambrose 需推迟上任、引水员考试选拔作汇报和回复（S/O 216）（S/O）（L060-001-0183-074） …………………… 490

3月11日，谭安致安格联：汇报购买税务司公馆扩建所需土地、建议由常关征收民船船钞、当地赈灾情况（S/O 217）（L060-001-0183-075） …………………… 494

3月16日至3月29日，谭安、司徒达与安格联：就建议工师 Sheridan 在瓯海关前滩围填工程完成后再离开作请示、签呈和回复（S/O 218）（S/O）（L060-001-0183-076） …………… 498

3月23日至4月6日，谭安与安格联：就工师在温州需多待至少1个月方能完成税务司公馆维修、谭安需提前离岗休假作汇报和回复（S/O 219）（S/O）（L060-001-0183-077） …… 503

3月24日至4月6日，谭安与卢立基：就谭安推迟离岗休假、帮办平野馨发烧、赈灾米运抵温州情况作汇报和回复（S/O 220）（S/O）（L060-001-0183-078） …………………… 507

4月1日至4月8日，谭安与卢立基：就常关司秤 Lin Yin-li 因吸食鸦片的不实指控被捕及被释放的过程作汇报和回复（S/O 221）（S/O）（L060-001-0183-079） …………………… 509

4月6日至4月12日，谭安与卢立基：就经检测司秤 Lin Yin-li 并未吸食鸦片作汇报和回复（S/O 222）（S/O）（L060-001-0183-080） …………………… 513

4月9日至4月20日，谭安与安格联：就司秤 Lin Yin-li 被诬告被捕一事未收到检察厅的解释作汇报和回复（S/O 223）（S/O）（L060-001-0183-081） …………………… 515

4月26日至5月11日，谭安与丹安：就阿拉巴德已抵达瓯海关接任谭安作汇报和回复（S/O 224）（S/O）（L060-001-0183-082） …………………… 519

5月11日至5月18日，阿拉巴德与安格联：就阿拉巴德到任后拜访当地官员、税务司公馆修缮尚未完工、常关税收方式可改进、收费灯塔建造情况、职员健康状况作汇报和回复（S/O 225）（S/O）（L060-001-0183-083） …………………… 522

5月27日至6月14日，阿拉巴德与安格联：就税务司公馆及验货员住宅修缮工作进展、与美孚石油公司就修建储油池的沟通、赈灾情况、职员情况等事宜作汇报和回复（S/O 226）（S/O）（L060-001-0183-084） …………………… 526

6月12日至6月24日，阿拉巴德与安格联：就税务司公馆及验货员住宅修缮进度、5艘轮船同时进港、Gull夫妇到访温州等事宜作汇报和回复（S/O 227）（S/O）（L060-001-0183-085） ······ 530

6月28日至7月16日，阿拉巴德与安格联：就瓯海关前滩填围及验货员住宅修缮的进度、与美孚石油公司就建造储油池的交涉情况、当地饥荒情况、进港轮船近况、与当地官员交往等事宜作汇报和回复（S/O 228）（S/O）（L060-001-0183-086） ······ 533

7月14日至7月29日，阿拉巴德与安格联：就统一常关的樟头捐征收标准、引水制度、6月海关税收减少、建议购置山顶土地、职员Gaylard申请改名等事宜作汇报和回复（S/O 229）（S/O）（L060-001-0183-087） ······ 539

7月31日至8月18日，阿拉巴德与安格联：就因省宪自治运动温州实施军管戒严、7月税收增加、海盗猖獗、验货员宿舍现状等事宜作汇报和回复（附浙江温处戒严正司令部布告第7号、第8号）（S/O 230）（S/O）（L060-001-0183-088） ······ 544

8月15日至9月3日，阿拉巴德与安格联：就省宪自治运动进展、民船遭海盗抢劫、台风登陆、工师Sheridan患痢疾等事宜作汇报和回复（S/O 231）（S/O）（L060-001-0183-089） ······ 555

8月25日，阿拉巴德致安格联：汇报浙江督军卢永祥近况和对选举的态度、台风导致温州与外界联系受阻、员工健康情况、工师Sheridan将返沪等（S/O 232）（L060-001-0183-090） ······ 560

9月12日，阿拉巴德致安格联：认同总税务司关于鸦片缉私奖金分配的建议方案、汇报税收稳定及存银行情况、瓯海夹板船商提交呼吁惩治海盗的请愿、8月税收下降的原因等（附夹板船商的请愿书）（S/O 233）（L060-001-0183-091） ······ 563

10月4日至10月31日，阿拉巴德与安格联：就当地民船关于船钞的抗议及处理情况、关产情况良好、9月海关税收增加作汇报和回复（S/O 234）（L060-001-0183-092） ······ 582

10月19日至11月2日，阿拉巴德与丹安：就商会已接受税务司有关民船船钞的建议、道尹返回、瓯海关在银行账户余额等事宜作汇报和回复（S/O 235）（S/O）（L060-001-0183-093） ······ 587

11月7日至11月28日，阿拉巴德与安格联：就民船船钞的征收情况、美孚石油公司派人来温接洽用地事宜、外班职员工作及中文学习情况、当地大兴土木修建道路等事宜作汇报和回复（S/O 236）（S/O）（L060-001-0183-094） ······ 590

11月25日至12月22日，阿拉巴德与丹安：就与民船和商会代表就民船船钞进行协商、帮办平野馨患流感、常关华班二等验货被人举报拟着手调查作汇报和回复（S/O 237）（S/O）（L060-001-0183-095） ······ 595

12月11日，阿拉巴德致安格联：汇报修改民船船钞暂征办法、帮办平野馨赴沪参加汉文测试、当地工程进展情况等（S/O 238）（L060-001-0183-096） ······ 598

12月28日，阿拉巴德致安格联：汇报当地船商反对修改民船船钞暂征办法的原因、瓯海关前关医Stedeford返岗、海关监督变动等（S/O 239）（L060-001-0183-097） ······ 600

1918 年

CUSTOM HOUSE,

S/O No. 111.

Wenchow, 4. January, 8

Sir,

WENCHOW INDEPENDENCE.

As a sequel to the Independence news has now been received of the removal of all the Officials who were then present, and who, like the Taoyin, had per force to sign the proclamation, or even, like the Chihshih, did not sign that document, but submitted to the ephemeral Government.

PADDY : EXPORTATION OF FROM NINGTSUN WITH POLICE CONNIVANCE.

The above news leads me to report that notwithstanding repeated entreaties to the former Supt, and again to his successor, I have not yet been able to obtain payment of the fine which I inflicted on the owner of the paddy removed with the Police connivance. (Vide August, September, October, November Summaries of non-urgent Chinese correspondence and my S/O Nos. 89, 90, 95, your S/O of 3rd October, and my 101, and 104.)

Since

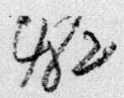

Since Mr. Hsü Hsi Chi assumed charge of the Wenchow Superentendency at the beginning of December I wrote him twice on this subject. The first time he had written to ask me at the Magistrate's request to deal leniently with a new seizure of paddy at Ningtsun - which request I acceded to at once - and I took the opportunity to revert to the former case and pointed out that the fine had not yet been paid. A few days later, upon hearing from the Ningtsun Examiner that the owner of the paddy was bargaining for the sale locally of his second crop upon which I had asked the Supt. to lay an embargo pending payment of the fine, I wrote again to report the news just received and urge speedy payment. The Supt. whom I saw on New Years eve told me he had written to the Magistrates and the matter rests there; but now that the Magistrate is removed from Office I am afraid that the case will never be settled satisfactorily and I beg to ask whether I must go on with it, or report to you officially and ask you to report to the Shui-wu Ch'u, or simply let the case drop. There would still be another way, and that would be by my reporting

reporting the case to the Governor direct. The case in itself is not very important but it shows an utter contempt of the Customs, and reporting to the Governor would at the same time draw his attention to the illegal prohibition to export cereals as actually enforced here.

Very cold these last few days.

Yours respectfully,

CUSTOM HOUSE,

S/O No. 112.

Wenchow, 8th January 1918.

SIR,

As you are aware the Poochi has been sunk and the event sad as it is is particularly felt here the ship being well patronised by the population. We have as yet received no details. The Postmaster had a telegram from the Shanghai Postal Commissioner advising the loss of the ship with mails so yesterday after receipt of the last mail by the Ningpo Steamer I wired to give you the numbers of your last correspondence received so as to facilitate the duplicating of documents supposed to have been lost, but everything seems to point that they must be few.

I am told most of the cargo is generally under insured and there may be a loss of over $100,000.

Political situation quiet.

Yours respectfully,

CUSTOM HOUSE,

S/O No. 113.   Wenchow   9. January, 18

Sir,

PROPERTY : ACQUIREMENT OF.

In your despatch No.758/66,552 of 26th September last you instructed me to find out whether sufficient land can be acquired near the Commissioner's residence for housing the whole Staff and report accordingly, adding that if it can be obtained for a reasonable sum the purchasing of the Commissioner's house will be then considered.

I acted accordingly and I wrote on 17th December the following letter to the Engineer-in-Chief to ask his advice:

" STAFF HOUSING ARRANGEMENTS.
" The question has made some progress,
" but is far from being settled, and before
" going further I would like to have
" your opinion. After a lot of writing
" and discussing I was informed verbally
" that I could not buy HaiTanShan, the
" Assistant's hill, as the Authorities cannot

" cannot see their way to sell the temple
" which undoubtedly is used for worship.
" However I am told I might buy TzuShan,
" the hill behind my actual house, that is
" only the top, the southern slope being
" reserved by the sellers on account of the
" graves of their ancestors. Once this top
" is levelled there would be a lot of room
" for a big house and plenty of ground all
" round. The price asked for is now $3,000.
" free of graves, and with a right of way
" for a path of access somewhere between
" Tzushan and Hai Tan Shan. This offer might
" perhaps be reduced to $2,800, but that is
" not sure. However as I am told by my
" intermediary, one of the heads of the
" Chamber of Commerce, that it is desirable
" to close the purchase before the New Year
" I think a firm offer would probably soon
" settle the matter. Now, do you think the
" property is worth it ? Of course we are
" in a special position : the land is not
" offered for sale but only available on
" account of my repeated requests to the
" Officials, and naturally the sellers take
" advantage of it.

As

As to the properties surrounding the Commr's House the owners of the two small lots to the East - A and B - are willing to sell for $ 1200 each which is preposterous. But it is again the same thing as with Tzu Shan. Besides, Mr. Southill formerly offered up to $300 for those properties, and I am afraid if we want to get them we shall have to pay at least twice that amount now.

I am also informed by the same intermediary that the land - C - South of those properties may be got for $2,000 which is also more than 3 times its value.

There remains in our immediate neighbourhood the lot - D - to the West opposite the entrance to the Commrs House. This so far cannot be got : only one half could be purchased, the owner of the other half refusing to sell.

Such being the case my proposals are :

1o. Buy Tzu Shan for Commr's House.
2o. Buy Southill's and two adjacent properties for Tidesurveyor.
3o. Buy the lot opposite those two properties though not very extensive for

Examiner's

" Examiner's house. Part of the two proper-
" ties to be added to the Southill property
" being given, if necessary, to the Examiner
" as garden.
" 4o. As to the Assistant we should cling
" to the actual quarters and as the temple
" cannot be purchased we should limit oursel-
" ves to our actual occupancy and may be a
" small side shrine and put up a two storied
" house facing North, East, and South and se
" separated from the temple by a good wall.
" If later on circumstances admit it then
" opportunity should not be lost to acquire
" the temple. Kindly give me your views
" about all this as I quite agree with my
" intermediary that it is advisable to settle
" the matter before the Chinese New Year.
" Otherwise it may mean another year's delay.
"   For more clearness I append a very
" rough sketch showing the properties round
" the Commr's House."
To this Mr. Dick replied :   28. Dec. 1917.
" In reply to your letter of the 17th
" instant there is no doubt that if the
" proposed houses are to be built in the
City

"City and not on the Island and, on the
whole, I think they should be in the City.
The Tzu Shan site is, after Hai Tan Shan,
the most suitable for the Commr's House. The
price asked is high, but not so very much
out of the way if the graves are removed
before it is handed over to us. It is a
most important point – getting rid of the
graves before we take possession. Of course
there will be a lot of levelling, but we
rarely get level sites to build on.

Generally I am entirely at one with you
in your proposals. Something must be done
regarding the housing of the Staff at Wenchow
and I see no other way of arriving at a
fairly satisfactory solution of the difficulty
except by the purchase of the sites that are
now obtainable."

To sum up the proposed expenditure would roughly amount to:

Tzu Shan	$3,000.
A and B properties	1,500.
C property	1,500.
Hai Tan Shan, uncertain, but not less than	1,500
Soothill property at least	7,500
(he wants Hk Tls. 6,000.)	Total $15,000.

This is evidently a big sum, but I am afraid there will not be any diminution by waiting. "Too many cooks spoil the soup" and this is true here again. There has been too much indirect and useless bargaining by all my predecessors - not that I want to blame them -, and as a result the people make us pay for our indecision. The Missionaries themselves, I believe, have been after Tzu Shan or Hai Tan Shan, but they missed - like the Customs - their chance after the 1884 riot. I would further point out that the property would be comparatively compact as it might perhaps be possible to arrange for a right of way from Tzu Shan to the Southill property. One of the advantages in buying A, B, and C lots (now gardens) would be to remove the intolerable stench from W.C. and liquid manure with which those gardens are cultivated.

There might perhaps be a chance to buy the whole lot D, half of which is already purchasable, and this would be to offer the owner to buy his whole property which consists of the garden shown under

D

D, a few shanties, and the Hsü house (a series of Chinese buildings) but it would amount to several thousand dollars.

Will you please take this question into consideration and give me your instructions.

Yours respectfully,

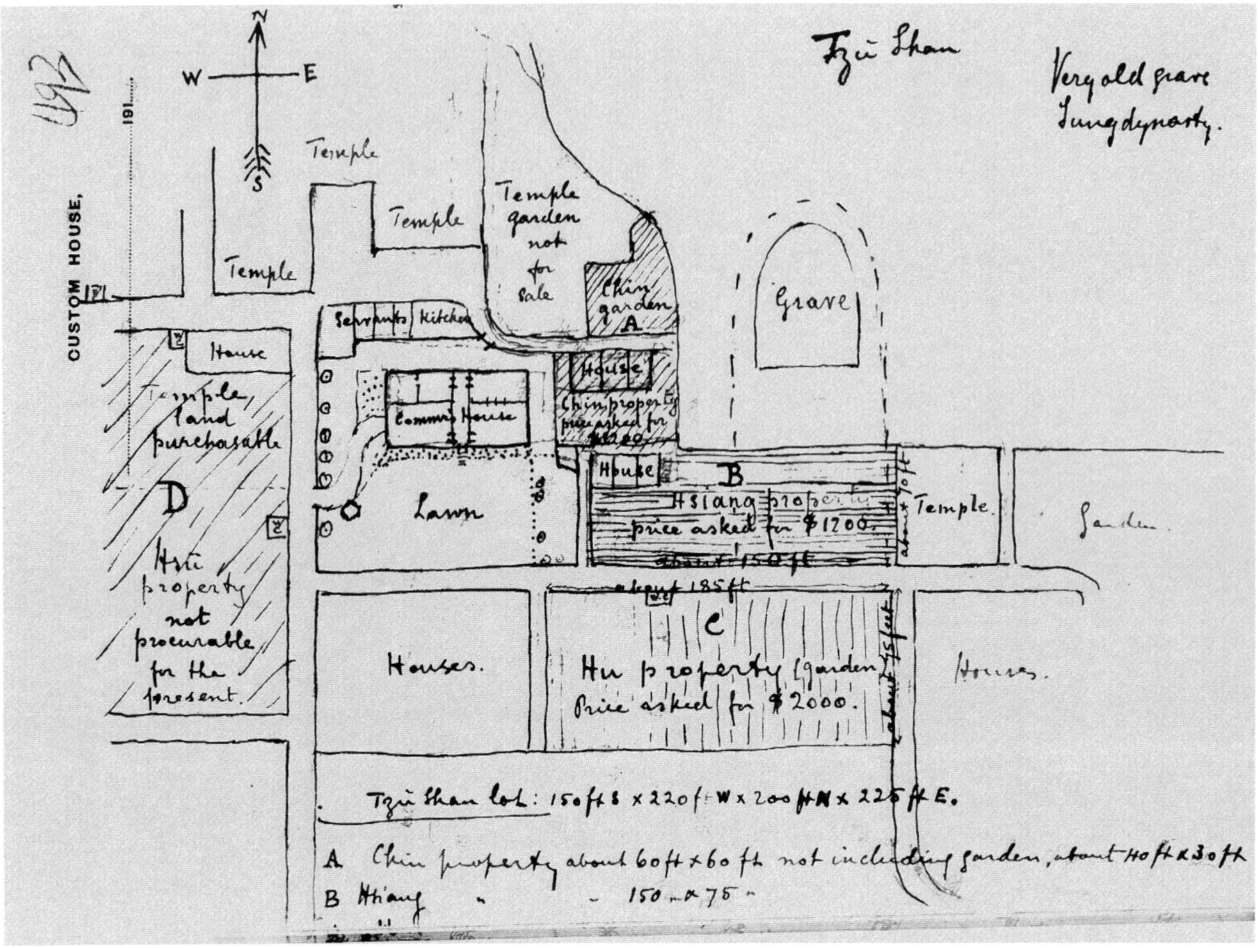

INSPECTORATE GENERAL OF CUSTOMS,

PEKING, 15th January, 1918.

Dear Mr Tanant,

I have duly received your S/O letter No. 111 of 4th January, 1918.

<u>Paddy exported from Ningtsun with police connivance: Commissioner unable to obtain payment of fine inflicted: proposal to report the case to the Governor.</u>

You may try the Governor.

Yours truly,

ant, Esquire,
NCHOW.

Inspectorate General of Customs,

PEKING,   22nd January,   1918.

Sir,

I am directed by the Inspector General to inform you that your S/O letter No.s 112 & 113 8th & 9th Jan. have been duly received. respectively

Yours truly,

W. H. Chapper

Private Secretary.

Tanant, Esquire,

Wenchow.

CUSTOM HOUSE,

S/O No. 114.

Wenchow, 22nd January 1918

SIR,

JUNKS CHARTERED BY FOREIGNERS: MAY THEY PLY FROM WENCHOW COASTWISE?

Mr. Wong Haiu Geng, the Assistant at the N.C. Office, reported yesterday that he had cleared a few days ago a Chinese junk loaded with 1173 poles for Chinkiang issuing papers in the name of the Chinese broker who had handed in the export applications. Later on he heard that the junk was detained by the River Police because the Shipper refused to pay the Haifeng tax. This shipper, a Mr. Ho Shu-fan, giving himself as a British subject also called to ask why his cargo was detained, to which I could only reply that I had heard he had not paid the Haifang tax and that this was out of my jurisdiction. He then asked whether there was any remedy and I said I did not think so as the the junk having been applied for and cleared under the name of the broker, a Chinese subject, he could

not

not claim being the Shipper and I advised him not to lose time and money to pay the tax. I also informed him that as foreign subject he could not ship goods by N.C. junks, the N.C. being reserved for Chinese, and Chinese junks, while foreigners had to ship their goods through the Maritime Customs. I think this is the proper definition of the Maritime Customs and Native Customs respective positions. But then the question arises can he charter junks and clear them at the Maritime Customs for other Treaty Ports along the coast or to Yangtze ports? Circular No. 924 emphatically says <u>no</u>. Circular No. 2076 allows of junk-borne trade in the Antung district under Maritime Customs control, but this is exceptional, and again Circular No. 1734, T.Q. settled, No. 264 says: "3º Chinese junks chartered by foreigners pay tonnage dues on the coast etc." The same Circular No. 1734 T.Q. settled No. 237 says: "Foreign merchants goods carried by junks are subject to exactly the same treatment as Chinese where part freights are

concerned;

concerned; a chartered junk's cargo pays foreign tariff duty". From this one might infer that chartering is permitted.

There is a want of clearness in all this, and as this Mr. Ho Shu-fan brought up his case to the British Consul at Ningpo, the question of his chartering junks may be raised shortly and I would be thankful for your opinion about its possibility.

Yours respectfully,

INSPECTORATE GENERAL OF CUSTOMS.

PEKING, 29th January, 1918.

Dear Mr Tanant,

I am writing this in further reference to your S/O letter No. 113 of 9th January, 1918.

<u>Question of purchase of property for Wenchow Customs.</u>

As the Staff housing question in Wenchow appears to be important from the sanitary viewpoint, you should obtain now at minimum prices first option on the contemplated properties and refer your proposals by despatch.

Yours truly,

Tanant, Esquire,
WENCHOW.

INSPECTORATE GENERAL OF CUSTOMS,

PEKING, 29th January, 1918.

Dear Mr Tanant,

I have duly received your S/O letter No. 114 of 22nd January, 1918.

<u>Respective positions of Maritime and Native Customs defined : foreigners said to be compelled to ship goods through the former, the latter said to be reserved for Chinese and Chinese junks.</u>

No. I don't think it is the proper definition. If a foreigner wants to ship by junk and pay the regular taxation to which junk trade is subjected, he has a right to do so. But he cannot of course claim any treaty tariff or Customs regulations for his protection.

<u>Ruling of Circular No. 1734 in regard to Chinese junks chartered by foreigners.</u>

There is a later ruling and if you will ask the question officially I will send you a copy of the correspondence with the port which raised the question.

Yours truly,

ant, Esquire,
CHOW.

CUSTOM HOUSE,

O No. 115.   Wenchow 31. January, 1917

Sir,

    STAFF : <u>Mr. U. Matsubara, 4th Asst., A. going to Hospital to Shanghai for treatment.</u>

    I regret to have to report that Mr. Matsubara's health is very unsatisfactory. At the end of October, although only absent from Office for two days, he was operated by Dr. Stedeford for a fistula in the rectum without apparent success, and of late he has again suffered very much, and taking advantage of the slack season of the Chinese New Year he has asked me for leave to go to Shanghai to be properly operated, and he will start within 5 or 6 days on the next ship's return. I am sorry for him for such an operation though simple always entails a certain amount of danger. I gave him leave to go but cannot fix him a time limit to return and it will be an affair for the Shanghai Doctor to state when he is again fit for duty. For the present I will do his work.

        Yours respectfully,

P.S. REGISTRATION OF VESSELS.

1o. Lorchas. With reference to my despatch No. 3277, now mailed, reporting registration of lorchas, it may interest you to hear that the Lorcha " Ting Hai " has been plying ever since 1894 with a Hankow Superintendent's P'ai issued in Mr. Moorhead's time giving as depth of the ship 10 chang instead of 10 feet, and breadth 28.7 " instead of 28.7 feet !

2o. Steamers. I also beg to report that the C.M.S.N. Co's steamers are as yet unprovided with Chiao-tung Pu's Registration Certificates. The instructions of your Circular No.2564 are evidently followed, but what about those of Circ. No. 2212 which gives 6 months to ships to be registered ?

CUSTOM HOUSE,

S/O No. 116.　　　　　　　　Wenchow, 7th February 1918.

SIR,

I beg to acknowledge receipt of your S/O letter of 29th January.

RESPECTIVE POSITIONS OF MARITIME AND NATIVE CUSTOMS DEFINED:

The definition I gave was based on I.G. Circular No. 1294, 1º "It is not Foreigners or Foreign Commerce that the N.C. deal with, but natives and native Trade, etc". Having received your letter I instructed Mr. Wong to act upon your definition and in future to accept foreigners applications making them understand at the same time that they must submit to the regular taxations to which junk trade is subjected.

CHARTERING OF JUNKS BY FOREIGNERS TO PLY TO AND FROM COAST AND YANGTZE PORTS:

The question is now referred to you in despatch No. 3280.

In despatch No. 3281 I also refer the question of treatment of junks trading
　　　　　　　　　　　　　　　　abroad

abroad as researches in Circulars about junks made me find out that Ningpo, Wenchow, Foochow and Amoy practice is at variance with Circular instructions.

MEDICAL OFFICER:

Dr. Stedeford has been unwell lately and is going to Shanghai and may be farther for one month. He obtained the assistance of Mrs. Doctor L. Dingly who already acted as Medical Officer here formerly. Owing to the difficulty to find Doctors in these war times and the short absence of the Doctor who is over worked, I did not raise any objection.

This is sent by the last steamer before the old New Year and we do **not** know what kind of communications we shall have with the outside world these 2 or 3 weeks.

Yours respectfully,

Inspectorate General of Customs,

PEKING, 14th February, 1918.

Sir,

I am directed by the Inspector General to inform you that your S/O letter No. 115 dated 31st January has been duly received.

Yours truly,

b. A. Chaipper

Private Secretary.

Tanant, Esquire,

Wenchow.

INSPECTORATE GENERAL OF CUSTOMS,

S/O

PEKING, 19th February, 1918.

Dear Mr Tanant,

I have duly received your S/O letter No. 116 of 7th February, 1918.

Respective positions of Maritime and Native Customs defined by Commissioner in his S/O letter No. 114 : definition was based on I.G. Circular No. 1294, § 1., "It is not Foreigners or Foreign Commerce that the Native Customs deal with, but Natives and Native Trade, etc.".

As a general statement this is quite correct.

Yours truly,

─── Tanant, Esquire,
─── NCHOW.

CUSTOM HOUSE,

Wenchow, 28th February, 1918.

S/O No. 1.
NATIONAL LOANS.

SIR,

As reported in my telegram of 15th instant the Superintendent informed me by despatch, on that day, that his collectorate collection for January amounted to $1,810.617 and that deducting Chingfei $180, and seizure rewards $5.119, the net amount he had to hand me for transmission to your National Loans Sinking Fund A/c. was $1,625.498 which sum he sent me at the same time. As your S/O Circular No. 21 does not mention anything about the Chingfei and Rewards deductions and says that the net revenue collection is to be handed over I must presume that the deductions are authorised by the Ministry and I did not raise any objection.

After receipt of your telegram and of your S/O Circular No. 22 I called on the Superintendent to fix a date for his remittances. He explained that for various causes,

causes, the clearest of which is the distance from some of his stations located in neighbouring Islands with which it is not always easy to communicate, he could not well remit regularly before the fifteenth and I agreed to it.

I then saw the Bank of China. Heretofore the Superintendent acting upon the Ministry's instructions handed over the funds to be remitted to the Bank which charged 10 per mille. I said this kind of remittance was finished and that I could only remit at the same rate as the public. The Banker finally came to this offer: remittances by drafts at 10 days sight, Bank Commission $5 per mille; or remittances by drafts at 15 days sight, Bank Commission $4.50 per mille. I said this is still too high as private remittances vary between $2.50 and 4 per mille. Indeed the China Merchants S. N. Co. for remittances of coins and bullion charge $1.60 per mille plus $1. for insurance, altogether $2.60. If to this we we add cost of boxes, their handling here and at Shanghai, the total cost of remittance should not exceed $3.50 per mille. The Banker added that there are wharfage dues to pay at Shanghai, which is true, but if we were to remit ourselves, the moneys being government funds, I do not think we should be called upon to pay these dues. Besides the Banker does not take into consideration the advantage he derives from the manipulation of the funds which in good banking business he would not have to remit so I told him that I could not make a fix arrangement unless I receive your approval. However as I had the January funds in hand I thought best to remit them at once by draft at 10 days sight and the remittance goes to Shanghai by this steamer. Please instruct me whether I am to accept the Bank's terms or whether I may ship the dollars to Shanghai through the China Merchants S. N. Co's ships.

    I must add that the sum remitted by

by the Superintendent was mostly made up of Chekiang Bank notes of the Bank of China - the Superintendent's N. C. Stations being to accept the Bank's Notes in payment of duties - and in case of trouble there would be a certain difficulty and consequent loss in cashing those notes, and on the whole there might perhaps be an advantage to employ the Bank at the condition that it will accept its notes at face value and deduct no commission for remitting their silver equivalent.

If you think I may accept the Bank's terms I intend, in order to simplify matters and save time, to ask the Superintendent to hand over the funds to the Bank direct and then transmit me the Bank's draft with his (Superintendent's) statement of collection. This would relieve my office from the trouble of shroffing dollars or examining Bank notes.

I should add that there is here a Branch Office of the Ningpo Commercial Bank (上海四明銀行) a bank which enjoys the public's public's confidence as much, if not more, than the Bank of China and it seems that the remittance of the funds might as well be entrusted to it, but until receipt of your instructions I am refraining from enquiring about its remittance rates.

Yours respectfully,

CUSTOM HOUSE,

No. 117.   Wenchow, 6. March, 1918.

Sir,

STAFF : Mr. Matsubara's sick leave.

In my S/O No.115 I informed you that Mr. Matsubara had to go to Shanghai to undergo an operation. I have now heard indirectly that he went to Japan for treatment.

British Consul visit.

Mr. W. Stark Toller, H.B.M's Consul for Ningpo and Wenchow has been here since the 25th with the object to show the " Battle of the Somme" cinematograph films. It went on allright, but the public did not seem to appreciate it much and would certainly have preferred more lively subjects. The Consul offered to the Officials to have a free night for the troops, but the offer was declined under pretext that the Province is under martial law and the troops cannot be out at night.

Shipping .

After the loss of the Poochi the China Merchants S.N.Co sent the Kwangchi to cruise round the wreck to try and pick up corpses. The weather was bad and the Captain could not go alongside the wreck. This was highly resented by the Wenchow population and there was a threat to boycott her. The matter, however, was reported settled at Shanghai; but when the ship arrived here on the 18th February the merchants refused to ship cargo and on the 20th she left in ballast for Foochow. The "Feiching" has since arrived and is taking an enormous cargo, but after all not so large considering that the last ship was the "Irene" on 8. February. No cargo for Shanghai was shipped by the Ningpo Inland waters steamers which resumed running on the 21st.

Revenue.

Our January collection showed increases as compared with 1917, but the February receipts were far below last year's figures. Adding up the two months we are still in advance of Hk.Tls. 826 (M.C.) and 1919 (N.C.) but I fear we shall have great difficulty to reach last year's March collection, viz.

Hk.Tls.

Hk.Tls. 6048 and 4419 respectively.

Otherwise the place is quiet. About 1,000 soldiers arrived from Ningpo and ~~Han~~ Hangchow at the old China New Year and ~~w~~ were sent by canal to Pingyang and beyond (Fookien frontier).

Yours respectfully,

INSPECTORATE GENERAL OF CUSTOMS.

S/O

PEKING, 12th March, 1918.

Dear Mr Tanant,

I have duly received your S/O letter No. 1 (National Loans) of 28th February, 1918.

Extra-50-li N.C. collection : Commissioner remarks that S/O Circular No. 21 makes no mention of deductions for Chingfei, Rewards, etc.

We have only to do with net receipts, but gradually we must try to secure some check on them.

Extra-50-li N.C. collection : question of method of remittance : Commissioner is of opinion that if shipped to Shanghai the collection, being government funds, will not be subject to wharfage dues.

You are at liberty to remit in any manner you choose provided it is safe. The collection will however have to pay wharfage dues at Shanghai I think!

Yours truly,

Tanant, Esquire,
WENCHOW.

Inspectorate General of Customs,

PEKING,　　19th March,　　1918.

Sir,

I am directed by the Inspector General to you that your S/O letter No. 117 6th March has been duly received.

Yours truly,

W. H. Chapman

Private Secretary.

Tanant, Esq.,

Wenchow.

CUSTOM HOUSE,

S/O No. 118.

Wenchow, 19th March 1918

SIR,

PADDY EXPORTED FROM NINGTSUN WITH POLICE CONNIVANCE:

References: Wenchow S/O Nos. 89, 90, 95, I.G. 3rd October 1917, Wenchow Nos. 101, 104 and 111 and I.G. 15th January 1918. I am glad to report that this case has at last been settled through the Superintendent, Mr. Hsu Hsi-chi's assistance in obliging the Yühuan Magistrate to press the paddy owner Yeh Chi Yin to pay up.

The case had hardly been settled that the Superintendent received instructions from the Shui-wu Ch'u to report as Yeh had sent a petition to complain of unjust treatment. The Superintendent sent me yesterday for perusal his reply to the Ch'u which says:

1º The paddy was not declared at the N.G. Station.

2º

2º No Huchao had been obtained although a new proclamation had been issued previously.

3º The paddy was removed surreptitiously. He did not mention, though, with police assistance.

However I hope this will settle the case. The Weiyuan who brought me the Superintendent's reply asked me whether I had informed you of the settlement of the case and I replied I would do so but not by despatch for after all the case is one of smuggling and need not be reported specially but that I had long ago acquainted you with all the particulars and that you would be glad to hear of the settlement.

STAFF: MR. MATSUBARA'S SICK LEAVE.
References: Wenchow S/O Nos. 115 and 117.

I have at last heard from Mr. Matsubara that upon his friends advice he decided not to be operated at Shanghai but went to Fukuoka where the operation was successfully performed, and that he hopes to return

return in a few weeks.

MEDICAL OFFICER.

    With reference to my S/O No. 116 I am glad to report that Dr. Stedeford our Medical Officer returned on the 14th much benefitted by his trip. Mrs. Doctor L.M. Dingly returned to Shanghai next day.

    Yours respectfully,

CUSTOM HOUSE,

S/O No. 119.   Wenchow, 19th March 1918

SIR,

SEIZURE OF NATIVE CLOTH.

  A big seizure of Native Cloth has just been made by the N.C.

  It was covered by free documents issued by the Haimen Likin Office in accordance with the Ministry of Finance instructions to pass free Native Cloth hand woven (I.G. Circs. 2666 and 2770); but some of it is machine made, some dyed in the piece, and some even not shirting weave. I have referred samples to the Shanghai Office to make sure of all those points. But I am afraid all that was passed by the Likin Office closing its eyes for a remuneration. This I cannot prove but this free issue of documents by the Likin Office will no doubt facilitate such malpractices and I beg to ask whether I should report you the case for transmission to the Shui-wu Ch'u. Of course the Likin will hide
itself

itself behind the shipper whom it will accuse of substitution upon shipment. Please wire me your decision. In any case I intend bringing the case to the Superintendent's notice.

Yours respectfully,

INSPECTORATE GENERAL OF CUSTOMS,

PEKING, 27 March, 1918.

Dear Mr Tanant,

I send you a letter I have received from Mrs Boothie about the house you occupy at Wenchow & also copy of my reply. I do not know how this matter stands exactly at present, but I suppose in view of the history of this house we shall be respective either to purchase it or to continue to lease it, even if you should be successful in obtaining other land for building purposes. I fancy also that there is not likely to be so much building land available at Wenchow that we can dispense with this house. My own idea is that it would be advisable to take advantage of the high exchange & purchase it. But as I am not sure what your views are on this point, I have been, as you will notice, non-committal in my reply to Mrs Boothie. I think it however only fair to her that she should be given a definite reply one way or the other.

Yours very faithfully,
A. V. Brown

Tanant, Esq.,
Wenchow.

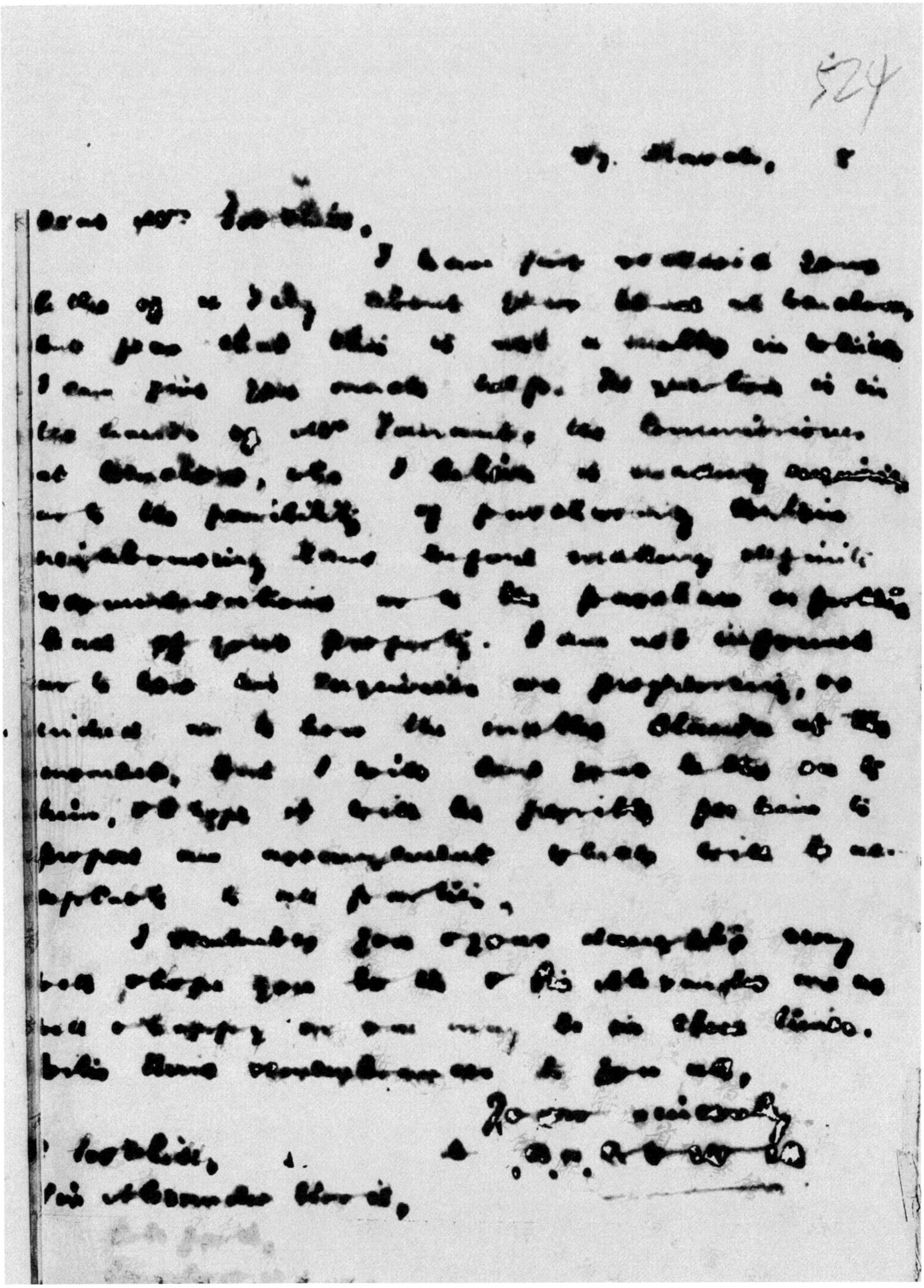

PERSONAL

C/o Sir Alexander Hosie,
Coleford,
Sandown, I.O.W.
4th Feb., 1918.

Dear Mr. Bowra,

I have distinct recollections of a chat with you, either at Peitaiho, or Peking, but cannot suppose you have done other than completely forget me. Possibly Mrs. Bowra may remember us, for my daughter and I were refugees in the British Legation during the Revolution and spent our Christmas evening under Lady Aglen's hospitable roof.

I must apologise for taking up your valuable time by writing to you, but I am in a little personal difficulty, and feel assured you will help me if you can.

I have a house in Wenchow which was built in 1892, at the request of the Customs, for Dr. Lowry. In 1904, at the request of the Commissioner, Mr. J.M. Moorhead, I practically rebuilt the house as he wished to occupy it himself.

occupants were always my friends, and know that anything I could do to make them comfortable would be done.

It would, therefore, be distressing, and a serious loss to me, if the premises were left empty.

The question of purchase by the Customs has been raised several times, and last by Mr. Tanant. I have always expressed my readiness to sell. When occupied by Mr. Moorhead he agreed that ten years purchase was a reasonable figure, but on Sept., 24, 1917, I wrote Mr. Tanant that if a sale could be effected while exchange was at the then high rate (4/10½) I would take less, to the mutual advantage of the Customs and myself.

My last letter from Mr. Tanant was written on 6th July 1917. He gives as his reason for not having signed the lease that "the house is too shaded from the breeze, and that there are bad smells from the neighbouring gardens".

In reply to this, I may say, the site was chosen by Dr. Lowry himself as the healthiest and coolest obtainable. The house is a good one with all the usual conveniences and

With kind regards to Mrs. Bowra and yourself,

I am,

Yours sincerely,

(Signed) LUCY SOOTHILL.

P.S. I am writing privately to you in the hope that you will be willing to take a kindly interest in the matter, which Mr. Paul King, whom I consulted the other day, thought you would be good enough to do.

I have head this evening from Lady Jordon, the sad news of her daughter's death. She died in her sleep, during the night, without any warning. It will be a terrible shock for poor Sir John.

True copy from original returned to Chief Secretary 8/4/18

INSPECTORATE GENERAL OF CUSTOMS,

S/O

PEKING, 3rd April, 1918.

Dear Mr Tanant,

I have duly received your S/O letter No. 118 of 19th March, 1918.

<u>Paddy exported from Ningtsun with police connivance: case at last settled with Superintendent's assistance.</u>

I am glad you have managed to settle it and that the Superintendent is a party to the settlement.

Yours truly,

Tanant, Esquire,
WENCHOW.

INSPECTORATE GENERAL OF CUSTOMS.

PEKING, 3rd April, 1918.

Dear Sir,

I am directed by the Inspector General to inform you that your S/O letter No. 119, dated 19th March, has been duly received.

Yours truly,

b. A. Chippeu

Private Secretary.

ーーーーー anant, Esq.,

ーーーーー Wenchow.

S/O No. 120.

CUSTOM HOUSE,
Wenchow, 4th April 1918

SIR,

SEIZURE REWARDS FOR OPIUM, ETC.

In view of the instructions of your Circulars Nos. 2733 and 2793 which grant $8 to Seizing Officers, $14 to informants, and $12 to Ship's Officers, per picul, for Poppy Seeds, to be paid out from Loan Service Accounts, I beg to ask whether the instructions of your Circular No. 2334 still hold good as regards the claim from the Judicial Authorities when culprits are handed over to them and how these amounts are to be treated when received.

Yours respectfully,

S/O No. 2.
NAT. LOANS.

CUSTOM HOUSE,

Wenchow, 4th April, 1918.

SIR,

With reference to your S/O Circular No. 24 <u>re</u> date for making remittances, I beg to report that after I had fixed with the Superintendent the 15th of a month for the handing over of the previous month's collection, as reported in my S/O No. 1 (Nat. Loans), he informed me, on 7th March of the receipt of the Shui-wu Chu's instructions to remit in future on the last day of the following month. As the Chu's despatch practically translated the instructions of your S/O No. 22 I made no reply thinking that I should soon receive new instructions from you on this subject, which indeed have come in your S/O Circular No. 24. So I hope everything will run smoothly in future.

The February collection has been

duly

duly received on 30th March and at once remitted to your Shanghai Account.

Yours respectfully,

CUSTOM HOUSE,

Wenchow, 8th April, 1918

S/O.

Dear Mr. Bowra,

Please excuse delay in not answering sooner your S/o Letter of 27th March. Matsubara has now been away for two months, and, alone, I have more to do than I can, at times.

As regards Mrs Soothill's letter on the question of renewal of lease or sale of her house, I must say she may feel annoyed that the matter has not progressed, but as I practically told her in my letter of 6 July 1917 – copy enclosed – that we would have either to renew the lease or buy the house, I don't think she need be so anxious. Besides, the Rev. Mr. J. W. Heywood of the same Mission who returned from leave a few months ago told me that Mrs Soothill had asked him to bargain if possible with me for the sale of the house, and she wrote herself to me to that effect – duplicate of her letter enclosed – so, what is the use my writing to her?

As to Mrs Soothill saying that the house was built in 1892, at the request of the Customs, for Dr. Lowry, I am afraid this is not exact. Dr. Lowry

. Bowra, Esquire,

Peking.

Lowry was then Assistant and Medical Officer, and would not live - and I sympathise with him - in the actual Assistant's quarters which are fit for one family but not for two as was then the case, and he was given a rent allowance. Someway or the other he asked his friend the Rev. Mr. W.E.Soothill, or Mr. Soothill proposed him, to build him a house, but certainly the original proposition did not come from the Customs. Here are extracts from a letter of 6 June 1892 written to Dr. Lowry by Mr. Soothill:
" In reference to our last conversation allow me to express in writing what I am prepared to do re house building. x x x . The whole would I expect be ready for occupation in four months from the acceptance of terms. The terms would be Hk.Tls 25 per month. Six months notice being required on either side. If the rentees would advance me two years rent it would ensure two years occupation and be a help to me. If not two, then one. As the house would be built with the ultimate intention of its being occupied by a member of this Mission it would call the more to my interest to make it an acceptable place of residence. x x x."
Once the question was settled between Dr. Lowry and Mr. Soothill it was referred to the Commissioner who finally obtained the I.G.'s sanction to the proposal,

In 1904, in Mr. Schoenicke's time, Mr. Soothill applied for a renewal of the lease for a further period of six years, promising to make some ameliorations and this was sanctioned by the I.G., but before the new lease was signed Mr. Soothill and Mr. Moorhead arranged to enlarge the house, and although - as stated by Mrs Soothill - Mr. Soothill may have hinted then that he would be willing to sell on the basis of 10 years rent which had then been increased to Hk.Tls. 50. a month, this has never been assented to officially by letter by the Customs to my knowledge. So much for the history of the house!

As regards available sites there are plenty. The only trouble as regards Customs is that nobody seems to have cared so far to enter into the tedious negotiations involved in the purchase of land in China. We butted ourselves from the beginning against that hill occupied by a temple half of which we rent as Assistant's quarters, and which would make an ideal residence site; but unfortunately it must be admitted that the temple is much frequented by worshippers and I don't see how we could oust them away from it. Anyhow the opportunity was lost after the 1884 riot. If we must therefore build on the flat we shall always be surrounded by neighbours, and that we build to the East or to the West it will be just about the same except that there is more available

available land to the west of the Custom House. I need not go into details over the question of smells, location, etc., which are objectionable, but I must mention that Mr. Dick was not at all enthusiastic over the purchase when he came here to give me his advice about the building question. However the house exists, and to finish with it I think myself that we might buy it, but the price asked for viz. Tls. 6,000. was outrageously too high. Mr. Dick without going into an actual examination of the quality of the materials, and simply judging from an external inspection, thought the house should not be purchased for more than $5,000, for he anticipated at least $1,200. in repairs and ameliorations. Such being the case I had, recently, a talk with Mr. Heywood and told him plainly what Mr. Dick and myself thought of the house, and we finally came to $6,000, but with this proviso that I could only recommend purchase at that price after thorough inspection by one of our Clerks of works for I am afraid there will be bigger repairs than anticipated on account of white ants. In fact I am nearly sure all the floors will have to be lifted in order to renew the supporting beams, as well groud as first floors.

Besides,

Besides I also told Mr. Heywood that I did not feel keen on asking the I.G. to purchase until I may make arrangements for the purchase of the two small neighbouring properties to the East, for the price asked for them is exorbitant, and if the owners were to hear of our purchase of Mrs Soothill's house at $6,000. they would not come down a cent. I don't think this conversation with Mr. Heywood has had time to reach Mrs Soothill, and no further progress has been made since, my Chinese intermediary having been absent.

Now there is of course the question of the good exchange and I find quite natural for Mrs Soothill to be anxious about the sale, and if you want to meet her wishes I have no other suggestion to make but to propose to buy outright and without Clerk of works inspection, but with a deduction of $500. for contingencies with repairs not anticipated, therefore offering $5,500. net. I would also suggest that you write to her and if she agrees that the money be paid at the rate of exchange of the day by Shanghai draft on London which would be handed over to her by the London Office in exchange for the title deeds. The property is registered at the British Consulate, and I presume you will require to have the transfer recorded, although there is no concession or settlement here, and a Chinese title deed would

would seem quite sufficient. I do not know what is customary about such purchases, whether the seller or the purchaser has to pay for registration. As regards Accounts the purchase once effected could easily be regularised by pro forma entries in our books and if possible a receipted vouchers made in the name of the Wenchow Customs.

I enclose 2 copies of this letter should you deem it advisable to transmit it to Mrs Soothill

Yours very faithfully,

INSPECTORATE GENERAL OF CUSTOMS.

S/O

PEKING, 10th April, 1918

Dear Mr Tanant,

I have duly received your S/O letter No. 120 of 4th April, 1918.

<u>Seizure rewards for Opium, etc.: revised scale and method of payment laid down in Circulars Nos. 2733 and 2793: can claim still be made on Judicial Authorities when culprits are handed over to them, as authorised in Circular No. 2334?</u>

I cannot go into such questions semi-officially. Please make your enquiry by despatch.

Yours truly,

Tanant, Esquire,
N C H O W.

INSPECTORATE GENERAL OF CUSTOMS.

PEKING, 10th Apr. 1918.

Dear Sir,

I am directed by the Inspector General to inform you that your S/O letter No. 2 (National Loans) dated 4th April, has been duly received.

Yours truly,

W. H. Chappell
Private Secretary.

E. Tanant, Esquire,

Wenchow.

S/O No. 3.
NAT. LOANS.

CUSTOM HOUSE,

Wenchow, 15th April 1918

SIR,

With reference to Audit Note No. 44 intimating that your National Loans Sinking Fund A/c. with the Hongkong & Shanghai Banking Corporation at Shanghai is kept in Chinese dollars, I beg to point out that my January remittance, $1,617.41, was made in a draft issued by the Wenchow Bank of China payable by the Shanghai branch of the same bank in Shanghai currency, which, as far as I know, is the Mexican dollar. The Hongkong & Shanghai Bank duly cashed the draft, but has not credited the account with the difference between Mexican and Chinese dollars and I beg to ask whether I am to claim it, and, if obtained, how I am to account for it in my monthly report.

Yours respectfully,

CUSTOM HOUSE,

S/O No. 121.   Wenchow, 15th April 1918.

SIR,

PADDY EXPORTED FROM NINGTSUN WITH POLICE CONNIVANCE.

With reference to my S/O 118 in which I mentioned that the Shui-wu Ch'u on receipt of the owner's petition had instructed the Superintendent to report, the Superintendent informed me a few days ago that the Ch'u had approved of the settlement of the case. I seized the opportunity to transmit your thanks for the Superintendent's assistance.

SEIZURE OF NATIVE CLOTH.

The case reported in my S/O 119 has been settled. After I had written to you we made 3 more seizures within ten days but since that time dutiable native cloth arrives duly covered by Ssu Lien Tan. I reported the case to the Superintendent pointing out the culpability of the Haimen N.C. Office and asking him to refer the

case

case to the Ningpo Superintendent and at the same time I sent him a bundle of samples with the Shanghai Customs appraisement. While calling on him I asked his opinion about the case and what kind of fine his own office would inflict in similar cases and on his replying 3 times duty I followed him and settled the case.

STAFF: OUT-DOOR STAFF TRANSFERS.

The removal of the actual Out-door Staff coming when I am overworked on account of Mr. Matsubara's absence led me to wire to ask permission to keep Mr. Lloyd until the Tidewaiter's arrival for I was afraid I might be sick and the Examiner would be left alone in charge of the office. Of course I have Mr. Wong Haiu Geng but he is now at the N.C. Office and it is not practical to come to and fro nor advisable to leave the N.C. Office without an Assistant. However, since I wired I heard from reports of the "Kwangchi" that our Tidewaiter had just arrived at Shanghai as she was leaving for

for Wenchow so he will come when she returns. Mr. Lloyd will have to wait for the same Kwangchi as his packing could not be ready to-day.

As to Mr. Matsubara I had a letter from him on 14th March from Fukuoka saying he had been operated at the College Hospital. One of my Clerks had also a letter asking for his pay, but since that time nothing has come. I have asked the Shanghai Commissioner to wire and enquire his whereabouts. My senior Clerk, Mr. Soh Ting-kong, whose father died in the country close to Chinkiang a few months ago, had then made arrangements for the funeral to take place on 18th April and I had promised to grant him leave, but owing to Mr. Matsubara's non-return I was unable to let Mr. Soh go. He does not complain but at the same time the poor man is very annoyed for he had to wire to postpone the ceremony.

TIDEWAITER'S QUARTER'S FURNITURE.

Your Circular No. 2790 having only been

been received quite recently and being rather busy to attend to a then non-urging question I had not had time to ask for instructions as regards furnishing the quarters, and as I heard the Tidewaiter had to wait a few days in Shanghai I thought better to wire and ask you to authorise the Works Department to provide him with furniture for bed, bath, and sitting rooms, and in the hope that you will approve of my suggestion I hurried up to write a letter to Mr. Dick to explain the case and ask him to do his best to provide the furniture at once if granted by you.

Yours respectfully,

S/O No. 122.

CUSTOM HOUSE,

Wenchow 15. April, 1918.

Sir,

REGULATIONS : CUSTOMS AND PORT.

I must apologise for referring again to the question of Customs and Port Regulations.

In my despatch No. 3245 I pointed out an error affecting Harbour limits in the printed volume of Customs Regulations (III Series, No.25). In your reply (No.766/66074) you said : " the latest sanctioned regulations are those in force". In my S/O No. 106 - which has been acknowledged but remained unanswered - I again pointed out that as regards port limits although there may not be an official sanction on record in our archives on account of the 1884 riot, we were faced by a "fait accompli", the port limits having been extended in 1878 (a fact then reported by Mr. Hobson to Sir Robert Hart, and again reported in 1882 by Mr. d'Arnoux without bringing forth any official objection) and I asked whether this non-objection could not be taken as a tacit sanction. Of course there is

against

against this the fact that since about Mr. Montgomery's time and the official publication of III. No. 25 we seem to have reverted to the 1877 port limits.

As the Statistical Secretary then pressed for the copies of up-to-date and accurate regulations I took leave to bring again the matter to your attention in the last paragraph of my despatch No. 3267 re Pilotage Regulations and in my S/o No.110, but although in your reply (I.G. No.783/67833) you referred me as regards Pilotage regulations to the port Pilotage Authority, not a word was added concerning the question of port limits, and my S/O also remained unanswered.

As I consider the Statistical Department just as much to blame as Mr. Montgomery for the error I referred the question to Mr. Taylor for his assistance, but he has just answered that " he cannot make any decision in the matter ".

Things were thus standing when the Asiatic Petroleum Co., Shanghai, wrote on 19th March to the Harbour Master :" We shall be pleased by your informing us whether the limits

limits of the port of Wenchow have actually been defined, and if so where they are situated I made him answer that he had handed me their letter and that I would reply, and the matter stands there. But, as you will see a decision must be taken.

As reported previously I was told by the former Superintendent, Mr. Mao, that the old Superintendent's archives are practically non-existant, and this though doubtful, is also the opinion of my Writer who says that during the Revolution there was practically no Supt. and archives may have been destroyed or muddled up.

I took advantage of the British Consul's recent visit to Wenchow to ask him for old Regulations without telling him my intention. He found the draft of the original Pilotage Regulations which we also have, but that is all. My opinion is that we should now when reprinting the regulations give the amended ones of 1878 which include the whole Harbour and thus give us authority over the whole City river frontage, for if we are limited to the North Water gate as per 1877 regulations all the Eastern suburb and the pontoons of the Haimen-Ningpo I.W.S.N. Steamers, the Standard Oil Co's City godown,

and

and other available properties for shipping would be out of our control, a very objectionable affair.

Without your instructions I refrained referring the question to the Supt., and I think we should not, for I consider the former probable acquiescement of 1878 sufficient, and if the question was now raised there is no saying when it would be settled.

Please give me your instructions so that I may furnish a copy of regulations to the Statistical Secretary, and be able to reply definitely to the Asiatic Petroleum Co.

Yours respectfully,

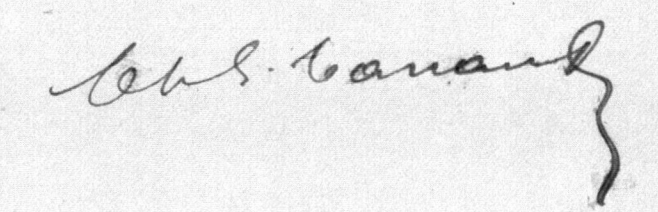

INSPECTORATE GENERAL OF CUSTOMS,

S/O

PEKING, 24th April, 19 18.

Dear Mr Tanant,

I have duly received your S/O No. 3 (National Loans) of 15th April, 1918.

<u>Wenchow remittance to National Loans Sinking Fund Account for January made in a draft payable in Mexican dollars : Hongkong & Shanghai Bank cashes draft but does not credit account with difference between Mexican and Chinese dollars, in which latter the Sinking Fund Account is kept.</u>

The matter will be adjusted here with the Hongkong & Shanghai Bank if necessary.

Yours truly,

Tanant, Esquire,
WENCHOW.

INSPECTORATE GENERAL OF CUSTOMS.

S/O.

PEKING, 24th Apr. 1918.

Dear Sir,

I am directed by the Inspector General to inform you that your S/O letter No. 121, dated 15th April, has been duly received.

Yours truly,

L. H. Chapper
Private Secretary.

E. Tanant, Esq.,

Wenchow.

INSPECTORATE GENERAL OF CUSTOMS.

S/O

PEKING, 24th April, 1918.

Dear Mr Tanant,

I have duly received your S/O letter No. 122 of 16th April, 1918.

Harbour Limits : discrepancy regarding between regulations of 1878 (which Commissioner regards as preferable but lacking definite confirmation) and original regulations of 1877 : instructions solicited as to which set is correct.

Consular assent not being required for the fixing or extension of Harbour Limits, I think your best plan will now be to bring the matter of the discrepancy to the Superintendent's notice and to suggest that the 1878 limits be now officially confirmed and placed on record.

Yours truly,

Tanant, Esquire,
ENCHOW.

S/O No. 123.

CUSTOM HOUSE,

Wenchow, 25. April, 1918.

Sir,

HAIL STORM.

Here is what I wrote to the Zikawei Observatory on the 22nd inst.

" I hasten to wite a few lines to infor you that we have just been visited by a terrible hail storm, something probably like you had in Shanghai a year or two ago. Hail stones of the size of an ordinary mother o'pearl button for summer white clothes were the smallest, while we had some bigger than pidgeon eggs, some of them of clear transparent ice. THe storm began by a violent thunder storm about 6 p.m. increasing in violence; then about 6.30 rain shortly followed by hail poured down for about 20 minutes. I am afraid if the storm was not local that it will have disastrous consequences in the country for the sesamum crop must have been hacked to pieces. Wind, hurricane force, for about 15 minutes. Direction about N.N.W."

Enquiries the next morning proved that

my description was not gloomy enough. The whole city was flooded by melting ice, hail stones having broken an enormous quantity of tiles. My house suffered like all others and there were 30 odd window glass panes broken. In the Methodist Hospital they had about 300 and about the same number at their College. At the China Inland Mission a small Chapel in the western suburb was partly blown down. The Custom House, I am glad to say did not suffer much though thdere were also a few glass panes broken, but the Tidesurveyor's gig was overturned by the wind and lost her rudder, but luckily we got it back by the next tide. About damage in the country it seems that the hail was not so strong to the North and down River, but sofar I have been unable to get an estimate of the disaster. A passenger boat running across the River disappeared with from 10 to 20 people and no trace has as yet been found of the wreck.

    Yours respectfully,

CUSTOM HOUSE,

S/O No. 124.　　　　　　　　Wenchow, 26th April 1918.

SIR,

  TRAVELLING EXPENSES:

  Mr. Lloyd shipped his luggage and furniture to Hongkong direct, the China Merchants S.N. Co., the only regular steamship Co. plying to this port, refusing to accept the packages for Wuchow. He had 49 packages which is not excessive for a married man in his position, and the Company after first claiming freight as per cubic measurement which would have amounted to about $300 finally charged $2 per package = $98. As the official mileage allowance granted him was $94 he is already short $4, and as I said this only as far as Hongkong.

  I think the errormous rise in freights calls for a revision of the Mileage Allowance, or else it might perhaps be advantageous for the Service to furnish all the Staff at least in the Out ports. My points

points are:

1º. you do not want the staff to be under obligation to the Steamer Companies. In this particular case the freight was paid no doubt, but a reduced one, which still leaves us under obligation and which does not allow the shipper to claim proper storage for his boxes, a third of which had to remain on deck.

2º. Had Mr. Lloyd sold his furniture by auction locally he could not have got more than one half its value, and perhaps less, and if he had to purchase again new furniture at Hongkong for use at Wuchow he would be in of his own packet for several hundred dollars, so his taking his furniture with him was certainly the wisest course for him.

3º. Should the Staff at Out ports be furnished, transfers could be effected more rapidly. In this case he had only 3 days at his disposal to hand over his office to the Examiner and pack up, and this was insufficient, and he had to wait a week for the ship's return from Shanghai. With
furnished

furnished quarters he could have been off within the 3 days.

I venture to subject my proposal for serious study for I think it would work to every one's satisfaction.

Yours respectfully,

[12]

S/O

INSPECTORATE GENERAL OF CUSTOMS

PEKING, 7th May, 1918.

Dear Sir,

I am directed by the Inspector General inform you that your S/O letter No. 123, dated 25th April, has been duly received.

Yours truly,

W. A Chappere

Private Secretary.

E. Tanant, Esq.,

Wenchow.

INSPECTORATE GENERAL OF CUSTOMS.

PEKING, 14th May, 19 18

Dear Sir,

I am directed by the Inspector General inform you that your S/O letter No. 124, ted 26th April, has been duly eived.

Yours truly,

Private Secretary.

Tanant, Esq.,

Wenchow.

CUSTOM HOUSE,

Wenchow 17 Aug 1918.

S/O. no. 125.

Sir,

MILITARY RICE and PROHIBITION TO EXPORT GRAIN. I have just posted Wenchow despatch No. 3295 reporting that the permission to export Rice for troops use granted by the Civil Governor and approved by the Peking Boards notwithstanding the local prohibition was practically a " coup de canif " in the Mackay Treaty, and asking you to have this matter of prohibitions duly gone into by the Shui-wu Ch'u.

If you take up the case I take leave to point out that the persons to blame are not the Superintendent, but the former local Taoyins and the Governors who have allowed this state of affairs to go on. As regards the actual Sup't, Mr. Hsü Hsi-chi, he has had nothing to do in this case and I must say for him that he is a vast improvement upon his predecessor Mr. Mao. On the 25th he called to say he had received

a

allow shipment of 900 Shih rice for troops use. I informed him that the prohibition was against it. He then said he had already informed the Governor and that the latter had promised to obtain the necessary authority. He then added that the troops had planned to mutiny and loot the City, and that the attempt had been checked, but that he could not guarantee that they would not begin again, and that it was useless to wait for further instructions. As there had been bad rumours already circulated I thought it prudent not to engage our responsibility for formalities sake and I said I would give the permit to ship on receipt of his Govt Stores Cert. It was brought in the same day, and part of the troops left at once for Amoy. In fact I heard afterwards that some of the soldiers had already begun pawning some bedding at their own valuation and it was time they were shipped away. For the same reason I did not make more objection afterwards to the shipment of their luggage reported in the same despatch No. 3295. Altogether 1361 men were sent away in two shipments (3 small steamers each time), and there now remains 500 men of the Luchün.
I

that previous to this case I was at last able, 40 years after the opening of this Office, to obtain a Govt Stores Cert. to cover the importation of the Military equipment authorised by your authority 34/7539 which arrived by an Inland waters steamer not covered by any Govt. Stores Cert. During Mr. Mao's tenure of Office I had once to ask for such a document but he would not issue it saying it was unknown in his Office, which may have been true. Mr. Hsu however, made no difficulty to issue one when I asked for it.

STAFF.

Mr. Matsubara returned on the 6th and looks in good health now.

The Out-door Staff transfers were completed by Mr. Ahlberg's arrival on the 8th and Mr. Ehtman left at once.

I am giving 4 weeks leave to Mr. Soh Ting-kong to go and bury his father.

Yours respectfully,

CUSTOM HOUSE,

No. 126.

Wenchow, 13. May, 1918.

Sir,

PROPERTY : COMMISSIONER'S HOUSE.

I hasten to write a few lines to let you know that Mrs Soothill has agreed to our offer of $5,500.00 which I transmitted by wire on 11th instant after consultation with Mr. Heywood her local representative.

At the same time I am glad to say that after endless bargaining with the Vice-president of the local Chamber of Commerce who had been directed by the former Superintendent to help me in the purchase of the adjoining Chin and Hsiang properties (lots A and B of the plan enclosed in my S/o No. 113 of 9. January last) we came to the final price of $1550.00 plus $93.75 for 25 cypress trees now standing on the property, and about $50.00 broker's fee at the rate of 3 li per tael. This makes practically $1700.00. It is very dear, but the Soothill and ourselves have been bargaining for it too long and in the meantime the owner's exigencies have grownes up. But dear as it is this acquisition will be more than repaid by the comfort it will bring to

to the occupants of the house. I shall inform you of all this by despatch on Monday. Yours respectfully,

CUSTOM HOUSE,

No. 127.   Wenchow   21. May,   18

Sir,

Application to employ Government Transport to carry cargo to Coast port.

I sent you the following telegram last night :" Government transport Ching an now here to carry 800 soldiers to Amoy may she on account of shortage steamers and delay transhipment Shanghai take 500 bales tobacco leaf to Amoy ? If so I presume she would have to pay Tonnage dues Tanant ". I think it is clear enough and does not require additional explanations. The permission was asked for by the Vice-president of the Chamber of Commerce, Mr. Yang Chen-hsin, the man who has acted as go-between in the proposed purchase of the two lots adjoining the Commissioner's house, reported in my despatch No. 3297, and although I did not see how his request could be granted, I thought as well to refer it to you. The fact is that trade at this port is entirely into the hands of the China Merchants S.N.Co. We suffer from shortage of steamers, the "Kwangchi" being the only steamer on the Shanghai run while before we

had

had both Kwangchi and Poochi. Occasionally a larger steamer is sent when too much cargo is accumulating. But again, admitting there be sufficient tonnage to take Wenchow cargo to Shanghai it is often the case that there is no available ship at Shanghai for immediate transhipment of cargo to Amoy, and the cargo has to go into godown, hence delays and, occasionally, pilfering. Besides, if any of the C.M.S.N.Co's staff engage in trade, knowing the difficulties caused by the shortage of tonnage, they may arrange to leave out certain cargo for certain ports, thus causing local dearth and rise in price, and then send cargo of their own giving it priority over other shipments. I therefore sympathize with the local shippers and I must say that the granting of the permission would greatly help our Revenue. We are now the 21st May and up to date we have collected Hk.Tl 3138. The "Taishun" is expected to-day and may take a good cargo of tea, the duty on which will not exceed Hk.Tls.2,000. We may also have again the Kwangchi before the end of the month and her cargo will bring us another 5 or 600 Tls duty.

All

All this, however, will make our Revenue about Hk.Tls. 6,000. against 8529 in 1917, and 9422 in 1916.

Mr. Yang told me that the Captain of the Transport is ready, the Authorities allowing it, to take his 500 bales at $ 4. per bale of 2 piculs. This is about the same freight as that of the C.M.S.N.Co, ~~Tonnage~~ , and he would have to pay Tonnage dues, but on the other hand there would be a saving of about one month time which means a lot for the big sum involved, about $25,000.

Purchase of property.

As stated in my despatch No. 3297 Mr. Yang's assistance is offered gratuitously, and although there will be brokerage payable to the broker who conducted the transaction, the whole affair passed through Mr. Yang who had to come repeatedly, and certainly exerted his influence, and for this I beg to ask whether it would not be advisable to make him a present ?

Yours respectfully,

P.S.   23. May.

<u>re</u> <u>Shipment of cargo by Government Transport.</u>

On receipt of your telegram of 21st saying you see no objection provided proper dues and duties are paid I sent at once for Mr. Yang and transmitted him the information for which he was very thankful. I thought prudent, however, to warn him that according to regulation 7 of the Regulations for Military and Police vessels (Circular No. 2518) such ships cannot carry cargo and that if any trouble should be raised afterwards the Captain would have to take the consequences. He replied that the Captain had already the permission of the Military Commander at Amoy to whom he had represented that he must take in some ballast and it would be as well owing to circumstances to take a cargo instead of ordinary ballast. Mr. Yang left me to go on board and fetch the Captain to show me his Register so as to calculate the Tonnage Dues payable, and while he was away I thought that I would have better to ask the Captain to hand me a statement explaining how he was empowered by the Amoy General to load cargo. But shortly afterwards Mr. Yang returned (it was then 5 p.m.) to say that the troops to be carried to
                                                            Amoy

the Captain to hand me a statement showing
the cargo just lost, was embowered by the Yoma Ceneral to count
but shortly. Any return (it wasthen
of a p.m.) yes that the troops to be carried to
Yoma

Amoy (local recruits not even in uniforms) had already been shipped and that the Transport (which I then heard was an old German man-of-war) would leave at daylight, and of course the idea of shipping the cargo had to be abandoned.

In the mean time there has been an atmospheric depression, the weather turned foggy and rainy and the ship is still in port. The Tobacco has been shipped per S.S. Taishun which takes this mail to Shanghai.

CUSTOM HOUSE,

S/O No. 128.   Wenchow, 27. May, 1918.

Sir,

OPIUM SEIZURE : POLICE INTERFERENCE.
On arrival of the Kwangchi from Shanghai on the 25th, Mr. Jönsson, our new Tidewaiter, standing on the pontoon, searched a man coming out from the ship and found one package opium in one of his pockets. While thus busy a Police Official rushed to the man, searched the other pocket and removed another packet. There was only one catty in all. Mr. Jönsson called for the Tidesurveyor who went to the pontoon and made the Police surender the packet. The owner was arrested. Later on the Police Official came and asked the Tidesurveyor to hand him over the culprit, which the Tidesurveyor refused pending report to me, and in order to stop this dual and simultaneous search I sent the culprit to the Sup't escorted by our boatmen, and I asked that in future the Police be instructed to wait until our examination be finished.

Change

Change of Magistrate.

The District Magistrate, the last of the Officials who were here at the time of the proclamation of Wenchow independence, last November, has finally been removed. He had not signed the proclamation of independence, screening himself behind the Taoyin his immediate chief, but nevertheless the Provincial Government found fault with him for not having warned it, and he had to go.

INSPECTORATE GENERAL OF CUSTOMS.

PEKING, 28th May, 1918.

Dear Sir,

I am directed by the Inspector General inform you that your S/O letter No. S125 & 126 ed 17th & 18th May respectively have been duly eived.

Yours truly,

C. H. Chiappe

Private Secretary.

Tanant, Esq.,

Wenchow.

INSPECTORATE GENERAL OF CUSTOMS.

S/O

PEKING, 4th June, 1918.

Dear Mr Tanant,

I have duly received your S/O letter No. 127 of 21st May, 1918.

<u>Commissioner receives an application for permission to ship cargo on a Government transport.</u>

I see no objection to the proposal provided proper dues and duties are paid.

<u>Purchase of property at Wenchow: gratuitous assistance given to Commissioner in negotiating the deal by a Mr Yang: proposal to give a present to the latter.</u>

Who is Mr Yang?

Yours truly,

Tanant, Esquire,
ENCHOW.

INSPECTORATE GENERAL OF CUSTOMS.

PEKING, 4th June, 1918.

Dear Sir,

I am directed by the Inspector General inform you that your S/O letter No. 128, 27th May, has been duly received.

Yours truly,

W. H. Chappell
Private Secretary.

Tanant, Esq.,

Wenchow.

CUSTOM HOUSE,

S/O No. 129.

Wenchow 4. June, 1918

Sir,

I regret to have to refer you again to the question of
CUSTOMS REGULATIONS AND PORT REGULATIONS :
On receipt of your letter of 24. April instructin me to bring the matter of the discrepancy in the Regulations to the Supt's notice and suggest that the 1878 limits be now officially confirmed and placed on record, I informed the Sup't personally that our archives were destroyed in the 1884 riot and I asked whether he could let me have a copy of the amended 1878 Regulations. He answered at once that he had practically no archives left since the Revolution. I was then going to put the matter in writing and ask him to confirm and place on record the 1878 Regulations, but it struck me that it would leave things in about as confuse a state as heretofore

Owing to the absence of steamers of large tonnage calling at this port, all ships, at least for the last twelve years, regularly came up to

the

the Wenchow Anchorage. In 1906 we withdrew the Tidewaiter originally stationed at the Lower Anchorage (Mao Chu Chiao) to board and accompany incoming ships to Wenchow, and finally in 1909 we abandoned the station and sold it in 1911. We would not be in position now to superintend shipping at the lower anchorage should any vessel elect to stop there, and therefore I think that if any change is to be made it should be towards modifying the Regulations contained in Customs and Port Regulations affecting port limits and anchorages (Vide III.- Miscellaneous Series : No. 25. Regulations, etc., 1859-99),

e Wenchow patches Nos. 6 and 2763.

    viz. CUSTOMS REGULATIONS (page 359)

    1o.- Limits of port.- they might perhaps be left as they stand.

    2o.- Anchorages.- the first sentence should be deleted.

    3o.- Boarding Officers.- should be deleted.

    PORT REGULATIONS, 1877 (page 364) - these are incomplete and were altered in 1878 so as to include under 6. and 7. respec- ~~tively~~ tively regulations 15o and 17o of the Customs Regulations -

    1.- Port limits.- already stated in Customs Regulations, should be deleted.

2.

2.- Limits of anchorage.- already stated in Customs Regulations, should be deleted.

3.- Vessel's number to be signalled.- obsolete, should be deleted.

4.- Rendez-vous flag to be hoisted, etc.- obsolete, should be deleted, although it might be found advisable to retain the second paragraph re boarding of vessels on arrival at Wenchow.

5.- Mooring; Shifting berth.- redundant, already included in Customs Regulations, 4o.

7.- Landing of passengers at lower anchorage.- obsolete, should be deleted.

In fact regulations 3. and 4. have been obsolete practically since the opening of the port (Vide Mr. Moorhead's despatch No. 2416). With the exception of those two regulations (Nos. 3. and 4.) regulations 1. 2. and 5. are redundant, and regulations 6. and 7. were originally in the Customs Regulations, and for this reason the whole code of Port Regulations might as well be abolished. But as it is necessary to distinguish between Customs and Harbour Regulations it seems it might be an opportune

occasion

occasion to modify the Customs Regulations, remove from them any rule concerning the Harbour viz : 4º.- Berthing ; 15o.- Discharge of ballast ; 16o.- Discharge of fire arms, and include them in Harbour Regulations adding any other regulations as may be thought advisable, such as the one concerning mooring of private buoys (Circular No. 1523), or even adopt the pro formâ Harbour Regulations of Circular No. 2060. This would have the advantage to include the local Notification re infectious diseases referred to in Wenchow despatch No. 2416. I must say, however that there would probably be objections to that part of the Regulations concerning Mineral Oils as the Standard Oil Co. owns a godown where it stores its products, fronting the River in the middle of the harbour, and the Asiatic Petroleum Co. owns a godown just at the upper limit of the Wenchow anchorage, but to all extents in just as bad a position for public safety as the one of the Standard Oil Co, as it is in the immediate vicinity of all the timber yards under the City walls. Besides, when the Port was opened in 1877, both Customs

and

and Port Regulations were submitted to and approved by the British Consular Authorities, and by them transmitted to the British Legation and I am afraid certain objections might be raised if we thus curtailed rights previously conceded, if not necessarily by the British Authorities, at least by other countries Consular Authorities, for the British Consul at Ningpo is bound to communicate any proposed change to his Shanghai colleagues in charge of their natinals interests in Chekiang ports, hence delays and possibly obstructions. I therefore thought better to ask your further instructions.

In this connection I should not omit to say that the letter of the Asiatic Petroleum Co asking to be informed of the limits of the port referred to in my S/O letter No. 122 gives me the idea that that Company is perhaps thinking to imitate the S.O.Co and build an Oil tank installation somewhere down river within the Port's limits of the Customs Regulations.

I

I should also add, while on this subject, that the Standard Oil Co's agent to whom I happened recently to mention that it might be in their interest to let us know officially what they are doing in the way of installation, so as to save time when it is ready, told me they did not expect to pay any fee, arguing of Ichang and Ningpo practice where, according to him no fee is paid for Customs supervision, which does not tally with Circular instructions.

Yours respectfully,

CUSTOM HOUSE,

s/o No. 130.   Wenchow, 10. June 19 18

Sir,

PURCHASE OF PROPERTY : GRATUITOUS ASSISTANCE GIVEN TO COMMISSIONER IN NEGOTIATING THE DEAL BY A MR. YANG : PROPOSAL TO GIVE A PRESENT TO THE LATTER.

In your letter of 4th instant just received you ask who is Mr. Yang. His name is Yang Chen-hsin, a native of Wenchow. He is one of the leading merchants dealing in what the Chinese call " Nan-huo ". He also farms the Sugar Tungchüan, and is, by election, Vice-president of the local Chamber of Commerce. My telegram of 20th May re possibility for a Government Transport to load 500 bales of Tobacco was sent at his request. Last winter when Wenchow independence was declared he was made Financial Commissioner, and was mulcted, I understand, of several thousand dollars when the independence was squashed. Of late I am told he is one of the 20 successful candidates whose names are submitted to the Civil Governor for appointment to the new Parliament, but I think nevertheless that his chances are poor.

He

He was asked by the former Superintendent, Mr. Mao, to assist me in the question of purchase of property (Vide October 1917 Summary of Non-urgent Chinese correspomdence, M.C. Subject 2) and I must say that he has shown the greatest oblingingness in this connection.

WEATHER.

We are now passing through a period of rain since over two weeks.

Yours respectfully,

INSPECTORATE GENERAL OF CUSTOMS.

S/O

PEKING, 25th June, 1918.

Dear Mr Tanant,

I have duly received your S/O letter No. 129 of 4th June, 1918.

<u>Customs Regulations and Port Regulations: question of Wenchow harbour limits, etc.</u>

If the Customs Regulations require modifying and bringing up to date you had better take it in hand and send up a draft for approval. Consular assent is not required.

Yours truly,

Tanant, Esquire,
W E N C H O W .

INSPECTORATE GENERAL OF CUSTOMS.

PEKING, 25th June, 1918.

Dear Sir,

I am directed by the Inspector General inform you that your S/O letter No. 130, ed 10th June, has been duly eived.

Yours truly,

W. H. Chappin

Private Secretary.

Tanant, Esq.,

Wenchow.

CUSTOM HOUSE,

S/O No. 131.   Wenchow, 25. June, 1918.

Sir,

SUPERINTENDENT'S ABSENCE.

The Sup't called on the 21st to inform me that he had been called by telegram to Shaohsing on account of his father's health and that he was leaving next morning. I hear however that, although this may be exact, he was instructed to arrange with the Ningpo British Consul for the settlement of the murder case of the British Missionary killed by pirates some weeks ago close to Santu. It seems that the pirates disposed of the stolen goods at Haimen, hence the transfer of the case from Fukien to Chekiang.

N. C. Smuggling.

I received recently a Kowloon Memo. reporting detection at Sanmun of two cases of smuggling by two junks from this district one covered by one of our D.P.C., and the

other

other by one D.P.C. issued by one of the Supt's stations. I investigated our case but could find nothing wrong here in passing the goods, and I requested the Kowloon Commr to deal with the case since the smuggling was detected in his district. As to the other case I reported it to the Supt., but I do not know what he will do, as, I understand, his stations are farmed to his Weiyuan.

REVENUE.

Although we are in June, our best month for duty collection on account of the exportation of tea, our monthly collection up to date only reaches 4300 Tls instead of Tls 12000 in 1917 and Tls 8700 in 1916. With the Kwangchi clearing to-morrow we may perhaps reach Tls.6000. The abnormal 5 weeks rains and consequent freshets, and the absence of one ship on the Shanghai run (Poochi not replaced) are no doubt the causes of this decrease.

I am having the whole Custom House repaited.

Yours respectfully,

/O
No. 132.

CUSTOM HOUSE,

Wenchow, 1. July, 1918

Sir,

With reference to my last letter, No. 131, reporting the <u>Superintendent's absence</u>, there is no doubt that it was caused by his father's state of health. He was granted two weeks leave by the Shui-wu Ch'u and told to place his Chief Secretary in charge, but on reaching Ningpo he heard of his father's death and wired for extension of leave and one month was granted, the Taoyin to be Acting Superintendent.

<u>Plague.</u> We have had a false alert of this disease. The N.C. Assistant, Mr. Wong Haiu Geng, reported on the 29th that a Fukien junk was rumoured to be attacked with plague, one man dead and four sick. When the Laopan was called for, he was said to have gone to Kanmen, a neighbouring station, and that the junk would leave for Kanmen by next tide.

I informed at once the Acting Sup't who wanted to wire to Peking for instructions

under

under the plea that we have no Quarantine Regulations. I replied that if the junk was really struck with plague there was not a minute to lose, and he finally agreed to my sending our Medical Officer on board. I think he was paricularly annoyed as he has few spare funds at his disposal. However the visit took place and Dr. Stedeford reported the crew all right and denying the rumour that one man had died. I therefore informed the Actg Sup't that the Junk would be allowed to clear as usual, and I claimed the Doctor fee, $10.

The Actg Sup't asked me since that time whether we could not establish Sanitary Regulations. I replied that up to now the question had been postponed on account of the difficulty to enforce them with the small staff at our disposal, and that it would be as well to take emergency measures when necessary. However as I saw that they would like to have some Regulations I think the best will be to incorporate them in the Port Regulations. Indeed it will be a good

reason

reason to insist on the revision of Customs and Port Regulations.

There is some kind of an epidemic raging here now, fever and gastric troubles, but fortunately it seems rather benign.

Yours respectfully,

S/O

INSPECTORATE GENERAL OF CUSTOMS.

PEKING, 9th July, 1918.

Dear Sir,

I am directed by the Inspector General to inform you that your S/O letter No. 131, dated 25th June, has been duly received.

Yours truly,

W. H. Chappell

Private Secretary.

Tanant, Esq.,

Wenchow.

CUSTOM HOUSE,

S/O No. 133.   Wenchow, 10th July 1918.

SIR,

PROPERTY PURCHASE: COMMISSIONER'S HOUSE.

In my despatch No. 3302 of 8th June I reported the British Consul's objection to register the property in the name of the "Wenchow Commissioner of Customs", and I asked for further instructions concerning the registration of the property in your official name, and also for the registration of the adjacent properties, but I have not so far been favoured with your reply. Meantime I received on the 8th the following letter from Mrs. Soothill, dated Sandown, Isle of Weght, 20th May, 1918:

"Dear Mr. Tanant,

In response to your cablegram saying

"Five thousand five hundred dollars final offer payable against deeds"

I have replied as follows.

"Terms accepted".

I now have pleasure in confirming the contract.

contract.

The deeds of the property are with the Hongkong & Shanghai Bank, Shanghai, and immediately after the Whitsun Holiday I propose to ask the Bank in London to cable its Shanghai Office to forward the deeds to the Rev. J.W. Heywood.

At the same time I will post to him a Power of Attorney, authorising him to sign any deed or instrument conveying to the Customs all my rights in the property.

I am cabling for the deeds to be sent to Mr. Heywood in order that if you wish to proceed with alterations to the house, you may feel at liberty to do so.

Hoping that all will turn out to your satisfaction.

I am, etc.

Yours faithfully,

(Signed) LUCY SOOTHILL."

As the Power of Atterney is thus likely to reach Mr. Heywood in about ten days I

would

would be obliged if you would send me a Power of Atterney as requested by the Consul or else in having instructions sent him by his legation to effect the transfer as first intended in the "Wenchow Commissioner of Customs" name.

As regards the two adjoining properties the owner of the Hsiang property is quite ready to settle his sale, but the owner of the other (Chin) lot has not returned from the country, and as the first property without the Chin lot would not be of much use to us being separated from us by an alley belonging to Chin, it is feared that this man on hearing of the purchase by us of the Hsiang lot would take advantage to raise his demand.

Yours respectfully,

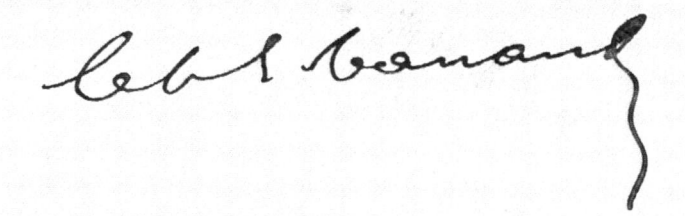

Inspectorate General of Customs,
Peking, 11th July, 1918.

S/O

Dear Sir,

I am directed by the Inspector General to inform you that his correct style is "Sir Francis Aglen, K. B. E.", and to request you to be good enough to make use of that style when addressing covers, etc. to him personally.

Yours truly,

(signature)
Private Secretary.

C. E. Tanant Esquire,
  Wenchow.

INSPECTORATE GENERAL OF CUSTOMS,

S/O

PEKING, 16th July, 19 18

Dear Mr Tanant,

I have duly received your S/O letter No. 132 of 1st July, 1918.

False alarm of plague: Superintendent asks if Customs could not establish sanitary regulations for the port of Wenchow.

Something very simple might be incorporated in Customs Regulations.

Yours truly,

Tanant, Esquire,
WENCHOW.

CUSTOM HOUSE,

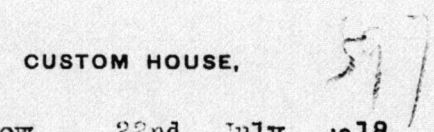

S/O No. 134.　　　　　　　Wenchow, 22nd July, 1918.

SIR,

PROPERTY PURCHASE: COMMISSIONER'S HOUSE.

　　　　Your Power of Attorney asked for in my last S/O letter crossed it and reached me on the 18th and I sent at once a copy to the Consul at Ningpo to ask him whether he is satisfied with it and when he will be able to come to effect the transfer on the Wenchow Register. In the meantime Mr Heywood received on the 15th his Power of Attorney and also submitted it to the Consul, so there is a hope that the matter will soon be settled. The Consul, I hear, is at Haimen on board the "Cadmus" to investigate the murder of the Rev. Graham close to Santu 2 months ago, so if he wants to come it would be easy to take the small steamer plying twice a week, which only stays over one night here.

　　　　As to the neighbouring Chinese properties I had some of the local Officials

for

for dinner on the occasion of the 14th July and Mr. Yang, of the Chamber of Commerce, told me he had been pressing Chin to conclude the sale but the latter has replied that he and his clan - it seems the property is undivided amongst about 40 people of that name - were trying to purchase another property to be used as a clan house or temple and could only part with the lot on completion of their own purchase. I am afraid this will postpone the purchase up to next Chinese New Year!

CEREALS: PROHIBITION TO EXPORT.

In view to check the rise in the price of cereals the Taoyin has obtained the Governor's sanction to prohibit the exportation of cereals, sweet potato included, to places within the province. This is all very well, but the terms of the prohibition saying that prohibition may in future be enforced when the price is above the average of the last five years, make it practically a perpetual prohibition. Besides there is a special clause allowing

small

small shipments up to 10 piculs. As it seems, useless to constantly call the local authorities to this disregard of Treaties, I was going to report the case at once and ask you to refer it to the Shui-wu Ch'u. It just happened, however, that the Taoyin, who had been sick and unable to call sooner after his taking over charge during Mr. Hsu's absence, came to call, and I took advantage to refer him to the prohibition. He pretended he was unaware of the ignorance of the Treaty and asked me to point out my grievances, which I did in a lengthy letter to the following effect:

1º. Any proclamation after being countersigned by the Governor should be notified at the Custom Houses by joint proclamations of the Superintendent and Commissioner.

2º. Prohibition though dealing with places within Province cannot be enforced as regards shipments to Ningpo through Maritime Customs, not having been established according to Treaty and not notified at

Maritime

Maritime Custom House.

3°. Prohibition does not refer to places outside province and yet all exports precedently allowed were for places in Fukien. Besides general prohibition to export dating from Ching Dynasty and renewed last year has not been repealed yet.

4°. A prohibition, with the exception of Army and Tribute rice, cannot make exceptions even in favour of small quantities, and besides the passing of small quantities would cover all sorts of smuggling.

Finally I took also exception to the exportation of cereals in normal times which the despatch said should remain subject to issue of Huchaos. I said that with the exception of Bonds to prevent the cereals from going abroad no other documents were needed.

I am waiting for a reply and will then transmit copy of the correspondence.

Yours respectfully,

INSPECTORATE GENERAL OF CUSTOMS,

S/O

PEKING, 23rd July, 1918.

Dear Mr Tanant,

I have duly received your S/O letter No. 133 of 10th July, 1918.

<u>Purchase of Property: British Consul objects to registering the property in the name of the Wenchow Commissioner of Customs: Commissioner asks for a Power of Attorney that the property may be registered in the Inspector General's name.</u>

A Power of Attorney has been sent you. All Customs property is registered in my name.

Yours truly,

Tanant, Esquire,
WENCHOW.

CUSTOM HOUSE,

S/O No. 135.

Wenchow 2. August, 19 18.

Sir,

NATIVE CUSTOMS : APPOINTMENT OF WATCHERS.

As you will see by my despatch No. 3314, there exists a difference of opinion between the Superintendent and myself over the question of appointment of N.C. Watchers, which, he says, should be referred to him for nomination of candidates. The matter as explained in the correspondence was raised quite accidentally as I was under the impression from former S/o correspondence between you and Mr. Acheson that yourself thought they were appointed by the Commissioner without reference to the Sup't, although Mr. Acheson in his letter No. 47 replied that he always asked the Sup't to nominate candidates. Besides, Circular No. 2213 seems to refer to " duty-collecting officers " only, and I do not think that Watchers should be included in that category. To me it is immaterial to apply or not to the Sup't, and as I have had so far very satisfactory intercourse with

Mr.

Mr. Hsü Hsi-chi, the actual Sup't, I am quite willing to do as he requests, but I thought nevertheless to first ask your instructions. Should you think that there is a principle to maintain in not applying to the Sup't, and should you deem it advisable to communicate with the Shui-wu Ch'u, I take leave to ask to put the matter in such a way so as not to affect Mr. Hsü's susceptibility.

While on the question of Native Customs I took advantage to refer you in a subsequent despatch queries concerning the classification and treatment of the staff generally.

REVENUE.

Our July duty collection was about the same as that of last year, but the Inland waters steamers gradually take away some of our Maritime Customs cargo, hence a final loss of revenue for the Government. The Wenchow N.C. Export duty and the Shanghai N.C. Import duty are altogether equal to our Maritime Customs Export duty. The Government therefore loses the Coast Trade Duty.

Yours respectfully,

INSPECTORATE GENERAL OF CUSTOMS.

S/O   PEKING, 6th August, 1918.

Dear Mr Tanant,

I have duly received your S/O letter No. 134 of 22nd July, 1918.

<u>Provincial authorities prohibit export of cereals: Commissioner, considering this a violation of the treaties, complains to Taoyin.</u>

The line for you to take is to point out the Treaty stipulations in the case of <u>grain</u> shipped through the Maritime Customs to other Treaty ports but if Provincial authorities nevertheless insist on prohibition to give effect to it, leaving it to the Treaty Power representatives to raise their own questions. You are not called upon to fight the battles of the foreign Treaty Powers and in any case the Central Government would not move unless the question were taken up by a Legation here. Where you are requested by high provincial authority to enforce a prohibition which you consider to be a violation of treaty see that you get the request in writing and that your

own

Tanant, Esquire,
Wenchow.

own opinion is duly placed on record for future reference. Article XIV of the Mackay Treaty has never been very strictly enforced and Legations will not move unless some big foreign shipping interest is involved.

Yours truly,

INSPECTORATE GENERAL OF CUSTOMS.

PEKING, 13th August 1918.

Dear Sir,

I am directed by the Inspector General to inform you that your S/O letter No. 135, dated 2nd August, has been duly received.

Yours truly,

C. H. Chappell
Private Secretary.

Tanant, Esq.,

Wenchow.

CUSTOM HOUSE,

O No. 136.

Wenchow, 20. August, 1918.

Sir,

Prohibition to export Cereals:

I beg to thank you for your reply of 6th August to my S/O Letter No. 134. I am now mailing my despatch No. 3319 reporting the prohibition and asking whether it should be enforced at the Maritime Custom House. At the same time I report a case of ignorance of the prohibition by the Juian Tungchüan Office in allowing wheat to be exported without Huchao. On the whole I hope you will see that my action follows pretty closely your instructions; but after having pointed out the unsatisfactory way the prohibition was established, I have had no reply and am still in the doubt about the passing of small quantities, a very loose way of establishing a prohibition, bound to facilitate smuggling and give all concerned endless trouble, and I therefore would be obliged if the Provincial Authorities could be made to cancel this tolerance

Junk entered with two sets of papers.

I have a curious case pending: A Native Customs broker entered 2 junks in ballast, one from

from Chekiang and one from Fookien, each provided with a Maritime Police Chih Chao. Upon sending a watcher to inspect them, it was discovered there was only one Junk covered by two Chih Chao. Fearing a case of collusion with pirates I did not seize the Junk not to give any alarm and I hurried up to report the case verbally to the Superintendent and ask for the immediate arrest of the Junk master. The Sup't, nevertheless asked me to write which I did at once. The Junk master, however, was not arrested, but the Police was evidently communicated with for I received petitions from 3 parties concerned with the Junk. But all their affairs do not concern me, and after waiting three days I wrote to the Sup't that I could not wait longer for the arrest of the Junk master and that I was giving instructions for the seizure and confiscation of the Junk for plying under two different Chih Chao, and I have had the Junk seized and brought to the Customs private anchorage. From what I hear of the case

case it seems that the Junkmaster is the former owner of the Junk and had again chartered her, and on his arrival in port he removed the Junk's name and hurried up to apply for freight to two different firms giving each a different Chih Chao to enter the Junk at the Native Customs. I think this should entail a heavy punishment, confiscation or fine, but our N.C. Regulations do not seem to provide for such cases, and I would be obliged for instructions.

The Taoyin has gone to Shanghai on three weeks leave.

Yours respectfully,

CUSTOM HOUSE,

S/O No. 137.

Wenchow, 22. August, 1918.

Sir,

Appointment of Native Customs Watchers.

I beg to acknowledge receipt of your despatch No. 823/70274/92 in reply to Wenchow despatch No. 3314/195 re appointment of N.C. Watchers.

As I said before I very much regret to have caused this question to rise, but I am afraid the Sup't is imbued of the opinion that he must be consulted. He has for him the local precedents when not only Watchers but even Office boys, etc., appointments were referred to his predecessor, and he expects me, if I do not apply for his candidates anyhow to ask his permission if I want to appoint a Watcher not recommended by him.

I only see one way to turn round the question, which I take leave to submit: The N.C. Watchers names are given in the Service List, while those of the M.C. Watchers are not. In view of uniformity, and on account of those men inferior position I do not think any distinction should be made, and the

general

general rule should apply to all Watchers and the names of the N.C. Watchers should be removed from the Service List. If this is done, advantage could be taken when forwarding the Service List to the Shui-wu Chü to point out the change and state that Commissioners are instructed to treat in future all Watchers alike, and, at the ports where it is still the local rule, to cease consulting the Sup'ts for their appointment.

As regards petitions the former Sup't has spread instructions that all petitions (Staff and Public) must be submitted to him as well as to the Commissioner, and it will take long to eradicate this habit, and it is rather difficult to know whether, when, or how he replies, or not, to petitions

Yours respectfully,

INSPECTORATE GENERAL OF CUSTOMS.

S/O

PEKING, 27th August, 1918

Dear Mr Tanant,

I have duly received your S/O letter No. 136 of 20th August, 1918.

<u>Case of Junk entered with two sets of papers.</u>

Report the case officially with full details and Chinese version.

Yours truly,

Tanant, Esquire,
Wenchow.

CUSTOM HOUSE,

Wenchow, 2nd September 18

S/O No. 138.

SIR,

PROPERTY PURCHASE: COMMISSIONER'S RESIDENCE.

  The Ningpo Consul having written recently he was unable to come for some time to effect the transfer of the Soothill property in his Register, Mr. Heywood, Mrs. Soothill's representative, wrote on the 21st to ask on account of the favourable exchange now ruling, whether we could not accept the title deeds duly endorsed by him and accompanied by his power of attorney, and pay him the fixed price.

  Though in ordinary circumstances I would not have acquiesced, I thought nevertheless owing to the moral standing of the concerned that we might act as requested, and I prepared a despatch to ask for your approval, and just as it was being posted I received a telegram from the Consul announcing his arrival, so I stopped the despatch and waited. The Consul arrived on the

the 27th; the transfer was duly recorded, and the title deeds, endorsed by the Consul, handed over to me by Mr. Heywood. So the question is settled, and I must thank you for the Staff, present and future. Once the house has been properly repaired it will prove a serviceable and not expensive, particularly for war times, acquisition.

As regards the purchase of the 2 neighbouring Chinese properties I regret to say that the matter is still pending. However I was promised that the owner would come at the end of the Chinese month, that is in a few days, and I delay reporting the Soothill purchase in the hope that I may have to report the other purchase together.

OPIUM SEIZURE.

We made, on information, a small seizure of 1½ catty of opium in the wheel house of the S.S. Kwangchi. There was of course nobody to claim it, but it is rather strange that the crew should not have smelt it, it, and as instructions are to hand over both opium and smugglers to the Authorities I mentioned the case to the Superintendent and asked his opinion. He thought the case rather small and proposed simply to speak to the China Merchants S. N. Co.'s agent to which I agreed.

Yours respectfully,
C.E. Carrall

INSPECTORATE GENERAL OF CUSTOMS

S/O

PEKING, 3rd September, 1918.

Dear Mr Tanant,

I have duly received your S/O letter No. 137 of 22nd August, 1918.

Appointment of N.C. Watchers: Superintendent maintains that he should be consulted: Commissioner suggests that Inspector General should take up case with Shui Wu Ch'u.

I don't want to take up this question with the Ch'u. You must do the best you can with tact and firmness to maintain your position!

Yours truly,

Tanant, Esquire,
Wenchow.

CUSTOM HOUSE,

S/O No. 139.   Wenchow, 6th Sept. 1918.

SIR,

I am now transmitting my August Summary of Non-Urg-Chinese Correspondence and I take leave to call your attention to the various N.C. cases it refers to.

DOCUMENT IMPROPERLY FILLED UP BY N.C. STAFF.

The Superintendent informed me that on account of a Transport Certificate issued by my Puchow N.C. Station, improperly filled up, his Juian Office had not recognised the validity of the document and had made the owner pay duty again, and he asked me to punish my Examiner and refund the duty. The Examiner's pay is only $16. per month and the duty claimed $11.55. After enquiries I could only prove negligence but no other malpractice, so I fined the Examiner one month's pay, out of which I repaid the Juian Office the $11.55 against due receipt of documents.

This

This is nothing by itself except that it has been caused by my asking for the punition of the Juian Tungchüan employés who issued documents for the exportation of wheat (prohibited) to which issue I objected in Append No. 3 of my despatch No. 3319 but while I complied with the request to punish my employé I have had so far no official reply to my letter complaining of those Tungchuan Officials caught red handed.
SEIZURE OF RICE BY MARITIME POLICE FROM JUNK WITHIN HARBOUR.

I have had again a case of interference by the Maritime Police with our shipping within the harbour. That Police received information that a junk on the point of clearing had on board 42 bags rice (piculs 65.43) and without asking for my permission searched the junk and was on the point of removing the rice when my N.C. Staff who said they also had received information repaired on board and wanted to take charge of the rice. But later on while

while the matter was being reported to me, the police removed the rice. I saw at once the Superintendent who had also been informed of the case, and he said, though he admitted the Police were wrong in not notifying us, he did not believe my Staff had had any information but had simply come on board on hearing of the Police being there. This may be so; but I didn't think worth while insisting and squabbling, seeing the trouble we have had in former cases, and as the Superintendent was willing to have the matter settled amicably at once I offered to give the Police the informants reward on the rice being handed over to me. This was on a Saturday afternoon. The Police, on my Staff going over to claim the rice, refused to hand it over. On the Monday morning I sent over my card with request to hand over the rice as arranged with the Superintendent and it was then delivered to me, short Pls. 1.20, but I waived this, and as we had an auction

the next day the rice was sold, fetched
$179.00,

$179.00, 3/10ths of which, $53.70 I sent to the Superintendent for the Police.

Yours respectfully,

INSPECTORATE GENERAL OF CUSTOMS.

PEKING, 10th Sept. 1918.

Dear Sir,

I am directed by the Inspector General inform you that your S/O letter No. 138 ted 2nd Sept. , has been duly eived.

Yours truly,

Private Secretary.

Tanant, Esq.,

Wenchow.

CUSTOM HOUSE,

S/O No. 140.

Wenchow 12. September 19 18

Sir,

PROHIBITION TO EXPORT CEREALS : TREATMENT OF SMALL SHIPMENTS.

I beg leave to refer you to my despatch No. 3319 / 198 on this question, in which, besides asking whether I was asking to give effect to the prohibition to export cereals at the Maritime Customs, I also asked whether I was equally to give effect to the exception mentioned in the prohibition in favour of small lots under 10 piculs. I gave as an instance of the trouble which this exception would put me to, the case of seizure of 88 bags of rice from an I.W.S.N. steamer claimed afterwards by the crew as each man's private property.

In your reply - No. 826 / 70414 / 95 - you instructed me to " give effect to the provincial prohibitions at both Maritime and Native Customs leaving foreign Consuls to take up the question if treaty rights are infringed ". I have done so; but this reply does not settle the smuggling possibilities open by the exception in favour

favour of small shipments. Indeed I am informed that I.W.S.N. steamers leaving Haimen all carry cargoes of rice. I do not know whether there is a prohibition at Haimen but if export is allowed to go on there it is evident that all available means must be taken by interested parties to ship rice, etc,, to that place, and they are bound to claim the advantage of the prohibition exception clause. I beg therefore to ask whether I am to recognize this exception or ignore it entirely. As reported in Append No.2 to my despatch No. 3319 I objected to it in my letter to the Sup't, but that letter has remained unanswered so far. In the meantime I have had the case of interference by the Maritime Police seizing rice from one of our junks within the Harbour (Subject No. 3, N. C. Summary (August) of non-urgent chinese correspondence) and it is highly desirable that we do not give any chance of interference to the Maritime Police which the passing of small shipments might create.

Yours respectfully,

INSPECTORATE GENERAL OF CUSTOMS.

S/O

PEKING, 23rd September, 1918.

Dear Mr. Tanant,

I have duly received your S/O letter No. 140 of 12th September, 1918.

<u>Prohibition to Export Cereals : smuggling possibilities open by the exception in favour of small shipments : Commissioner asks whether he is to recognize this exception or ignore it.</u>

This seems to be a matter in which you and the Superintendent might consult together, come if possible to an agreement, and make joint recommendations. It is quite clear that small personal shipments or carriage of rice will be very hard to stop.

Yours truly,

E. Tanant, Esquire,
    WENCHOW.

INSPECTORATE GENERAL OF CUSTOMS.

S/O

PEKING, 24th Sept. 1918.

Dear Sir,

I am directed by the Inspector General to inform you that your S/O letter No. 139, dated 6th Sept. 1918, has been duly received.

Yours truly,

W. H. Chapen
Private Secretary.

E. Tanant, Esquire,

WENCHOW.

No. 141.

CUSTOM HOUSE,

Wenchow, 27. September 1918.

Sir,

NATIVE CUSTOMS STAFF PAY.

With reference to my despatch No. 3324 submitting a proposed N.C. Staff scale of pay, it has now struck me that I should have made the last period of service of Lushih and Examiners 8 years instead of 7 so as to make their services finish at the same time as their duodecennial retiring third allowance becomes due. If you sanction my proposal please make the necessary amendment.

RE-EXPORTS FROM SHANGHAI CLAIMING E.C. OR N.E.C. BUT NOT IDENTIFIABLE.

I had in my despatch No. 3325 now mailed, to take up again this question, for it is for a large part what gives the local merchants a reason to complain. Slackness, to term it mildly, heretofore existed in examination, and notwithstanding Mr. Unwin's recommendations to re-examine all

Shanghai

Shanghai re-exports, the work, I feel convinced, was perfunctorily done. However, since Mr. Ehtman's arrival proper examination has been conducted. This has resulted in many lots of cargo being detained pending reference to Shanghai, and although I always advised importers to take delivery on deposit of sums varying from 1 to 3 duties, very often they refuse and of course afterwards complain of delays. Were we provided as I ask for it with marks and numbers reference to Shanghai in the majority of cases would not be necessary and there would be no reasons for delays. With the daily increasing production of imitation foreign goods it will become more and more difficult for our Examiners to distinguish between Foreign and Chinese goods, and in some cases I feel sure the original importation marks, and even the packing, will be factors in the Examiners decision, so much the more the reason for stating those marks now.

There is a last point which I might have added to my despatch and it is this : When goods

goods arrive from Shanghai, and this is the same at most small ports, Steamer Companies godown-keepers, not being to much in English, experience great difficulty in sorting the various lots, for the assistance given by Shipping marks badly written, most of the time with Chinese pens, is of very little use, and very often they must have recourse to Original marks, and when our Examiner refuses (in which I think he is right) to go and help to verify the lots delays must occur. An accident of that kind occurred here some time ago, some merchants clamouring that the Examiner refused to examine, but the fact was he refused to do the godown-keeper's work, and when I went to the godown and explained the case to the merchants and advised them to complain to the Company the trouble stopped. In any case all this shows that marks and numbers are useful, and because by slackness the Shanghai Office has gradually ceased to take notice of them it is is not proper that the ports of ultimate destination should be inconvenienced if they want to do their work correctly.

SITUATION.

There was a bit of excitement recently when news arrived that the Southerners were marching on Foochow, but it has now subsided. Trade is slack, though, and steamers few.

Yours respectfully,

C.A.S. Cananah

[42]

S/O

INSPECTORATE GENERAL OF CUSTOMS.

PEKING, 15th Oct. 19 18

629

Dear Sir,

I am directed by the Inspector General to inform you that your S/O letter No. 141, dated 27th September, has been duly received.

Yours truly,

W. H. Chapman

Private Secretary.

Tanant, Esq.,

Wenchow.

/Q No. 142.

CUSTOM HOUSE,

Wenchow 15. October, 1918

Sir,

DIFFICULTY WITH STAND'RD OIL Co's Agent. A few days ago, while going down to the General Office, I found the foreign Agent of the S.O. Co and his interpreter both on each side of our Returns Clerk leaning over him while he was searching applications on their behalf. I already had an opportunity a few months ago, while doing General Office work in Mr. Matsubama's absence, to tell that same S.O.Co's interpreter that I would not allow him to consult his former applications - which up to then seems to have been allowed So I was rather surprised this time to find both the agent and his clerk in the Office and I could not help saying :" What is all this, you know very well that this is not allowed ", or something like it, but rather on a tone of surprise than a comminatory one The two men without saying a word left at

once

once the Office. I should add that the agent had his hat on his head. Mr. Matsubara to my questions replied that he was rather busy when they came in and had not noticed them, and they never asked his permission s I did not say more intendimg to re-issue an old order of 1885 about the confidential nature of Customs work.

Within half an hour I received the following letter from the agent:

C.E.Tanant, Esq,
　　Commissioner of Customs,
　　　　Wenchow.

Dear Sir,

I wish to express to you my surprise at the way in which I was ordered, by you, out of the office room of the Customs this arternoon You may rest assured that had I known it was a private room I would not have been there and knowing me as you do I am surprised you did not take that into consideration.

　　　　　　　　　　　　　Naturally

Naturally you are quite right in enforcing rules of the Customs but considering that I am a foreigner and that the room was full of Chinese I certainly feel that merely as a matter of "face" and courtesy to me you might have either warned me in private or called me aside in a friendly way to explain the matter to me.

  Personally I consider the manner in which the thing was done about as near an insult as it could have been.

    Yours sincerely,

    (signed) T. A. Beall.

This document evidently called for an apology from me simply because the agent being a foreigner thinks he can do anything he pleases but this is out of question for the man placed himself entirely in the wrong, practically in sneaking information, and the proof of it is that when caught on the act he and his clerk vanished without saying a word not even trying to explain their presence. But even admitting that he (agent) did not know, his clerk knew, but probably did not

       tell

tell him what had happened previously, and had he remained there I would have told him. On the other hand he speaks of the "loss of face" by a foreigner in front of Chinese, but he does not take into consideration the loss of face of my Assistant whom he ignored, and incidentally the Service in going direct to the Clerk. Indeed I have noticed recently a tendency to ignore my Assistant probably because he is Japanese, but this cannot be withstood a minute. Admitting that the agent's status as foreigner entitles him to more consideration than the ordinary Chinese applicant why should he not conform himself to admitted foreign etiquette in asking the needed information from the Assistant and removing his hat in the Office ?

  I replied next day to ask whether he wanted the affair to be taken on officially :
" T. A. Beall, Esqre,
Agent, Standard Oil Co. of New York,
   Wenchow.
Dear Sir,
  I duly received your yesterday's letter.

letter. I did not intend taking up the matter officially with my Administration, but the tone of your letter is such that it seems you want me to do so. I therefore write to ask whether this is your real intention for I must tell you frankly that in this case I consider myself the aggrieved person.

    Yours truly,

   (signed) C. E. Tanant

    Commissioner of Customs.

The reply as as follows:"

Dear Sir,

  In answer to your letter of even date would advise that I most certainly think that you should do as you see fit about the matter under discussion.

  My stand is, even will continue to be, that inasmuch as I was ignorant of the privacy of the office and as there was, so far as I could see, no sign stating that the Office was private, the manner of my being ordered out was exceedingly discourtious and un-called-for.

  Frankly, I had considered it a matter
         between

between us personally if you chose to make it official it is distinctly "up to you". It makes no difference to me one way or the other."
    Yours sincerely,
  (signed) T. A. Beall

The matter stands there and I do not expect further developments, but I thought better to report it, seing how newspapers are prone to seize such affairs, and it would not do to appear to hide an incident which I have no reason to keep secret from you.
NEWSPAPERS.

  About newspapers this is a good opportunity to call your attention to the fancy letters from " our own correspondent " appearing in the N.C. Daily Press and the N.C. Herald. There is in the latter paper of 28 September, page 747, column 3, a long letter about " Illegal rice export " in which a wrong reference is made to the Junk with two sets of papers which is being detained pending instructions asked for in my despatch No.3324 This detention has nothing whatever to do
        with

with rice smuggling, but as the correspondent has to issue so many letters a year so as to obtain his free copy of the paper, and as there is very little worth while reporting from this quiet place any subject is good evidently.

Yours respectfully,

CUSTOM HOUSE,

O No. 143.

Wenchow, 17. October, 1918.

Sir,

THEFT AT THE POST OFFICE.

There has been a rather important theft at the Post Office, committed a few nights ago: Some $1,600. worth of 10 and 20 dollars stamps, $200 odd cash, and the titledeeds of the newly purchased property for the building of a Central Post Office in the City,

Our night-watchman and the Post Office own night-watchman declared they heard nothing which may be true. Fortunately after a few days the Postmaster was able to have one of his letter carriers arrested, and this man confessed he was terrorised by two regular thieves which on his indications were also arrested. They further indicated a fourth man either as plotter of the theft or receiver of the goods. This man was also arrested, but so far denies all charges.

In

In this connection the Postmaster asked me a week or so afterwards to stop the China Merchants S.N.Co's S.S. "Kwangchi" in the middle of the stream on arrival from Shanghai, and to allow a party of detectives and policemen to go on board and arrest the fourth man who is one of the ship's employés. I replied I would do so on the written request from the Tribunal or the Sup't, and I advised him to hurry up to obtain the necessary document as the Kwangchi was due shortly afterwards. But no written request came and when the ship arrived I let her go as usual alongside the Company's pontoon. The Police were waiting there and before the ship had made fast they were on board, caught the accused and took him ashore.

Later on the man when tried gave as an alibi that he slept on board the night of the theft, and the Court again instructed the Postmaster to request me to arrange with the Captain for the production of some of his crew as witnesses, notably a ship's carpenter who, it was said, was in the Captain's employ. But

I refused again to act on any verbal request and I added that the ship being Chinese, and the ship's carpenter being an employé of the Company and not of the Captain personally, the simplest for the Court would be to apply to the Company. The advice was apparently followed for the man went to Court, and gave his deposition.

From all this it appears to me that there seems to exist some doubt in the Court's mind about its rights which I believe are undeniable in the case of Chinese subjects on board Chinese ships. I do not think the Captain's nationality can make any difference, and I shall be thankful for your opinion for future guidance, for I do not think we need be consulted about the lawful arrest of any Chinese subject on board any Chinese ship?

If it is not abusing too much of your time it may perhaps interest you to hear about this man's biography. He was first employed on board the Kwangchi as coolie of the steward for Chinese passengers body here and gradually became the transmission agent for all parcels of money, opium, and other valuables, all this under the very eye and nose of the Company, and, I regret to say, the Customs. About Opium we could not catch him, and as regards treasure, it has always been the rule to allow packages of silver to go to him freely. As a result he built up last year a foreign style house which with land cost him over $3,000. and when arrested he was still doing the same business and at the same time had become the owner of a Chinese hotel in Shanghai, and such rapid fortune cannot have failed to create jealousy which will help the Court to establish his guilt.

    Yours respectfully,

64/

INSPECTORATE GENERAL OF CUSTOMS.

PEKING, 29th Oct. 1918.

Dear Sir,

I am directed by the Inspector General to inform you that your S/O letter No.s 142 & 143 dated 15th & 17th Oct. respectively have ~~has~~ been duly received.

Yours truly,

W. T. Chappen

Private Secretary.

— Tanant, Esq.,

Wenchow.

CUSTOM HOUSE,

S/O No.144.

Wenchow, 4. November, 1918.

Sir,

IGNORANCE OF CUSTOMS BY PROVINCIAL AUTHORITIES.

My last two despatches, viz., No. 3333 :

Cereals : prohibition to export to be absolute at Commr's N.C. stations while subject to exceptions at Supt's N.C. stations :

and No. 3334 :

Wenchow Magistrate and Maritime Police proposals to search vessels for Opium and Rice :

are typical instances of the actual state of affairs in this country. Our local Officials see high Officials in Peking trying to grab the Governmental power, and acting upon the same principle, or rather want of principles, they similarly try to pick up all they can. But nevertheless I think the prohibition case should be objected to officially, for without caring whether it is properly established and liable to objection by foreign powers, it simply comes to an utter disregard of our N.C. As said in my despatch a Huchao for 100 piculs costs $40. which go into the

pocket of the issuing Official, and on

presentation

presentation the Supt's N.C. stations are obliged to let the lot go, and what is not said, but is admitted usual practice, is that at least one third more than the stated quantity is shipped; and worst of all the same Huchao when properly handled is used several trips. In this connexion I reported in my September Summary of non-urgent Chinese correspondence: N.C. subject 1, the non return of certain Certificates of cargo under Bond sent to a neighbouring N.C. station of the Ningpo Superintendent. The Supt. himself said he was taking up the case as it savoured of malpractice, but over a month has elapsed and no satisfactory explanation has been received and may not be received, for the Ningpo Superintendent is the brother of H.E. Sun Pao-chi, and it would be rather risky for the Wenchow Sup't to attack any one so closely related to such a high personage.

  The Chekiang Postal Commissioner, Mr. Arlington, paid Wenchow a brief visit to investigate

investigate the P.O. robbery reported in my last S/O.

INFLUENZA is still raging here. I had a mild attack ten days ago and have been more or less well ever since. My Clerk, Mr. Ko Yu-ping has now got it and passed it on to his neighbourhood. The R.C. Orphanage and the C.I.M. girls school have also been good spreading ground; three fourths of their children caught it.

JAPANESE MOTOR BOAT IN DISTRESS. A Police Junk has just towed into port a small Japanese motor boat which had left Formosa for the Liu Kiu Islands with a cargo of coal. She encountered a bad blow her rudder gave way and she was blown towards Chekiang. The crew were nearly starving when rescued.

Yours respectfully,

P.S. I just heard of the death of Mr Ko's only child, a 9 years boy Ni Tsing Chin, a very good N.C. Exam. also reported dead. Particulars in the week.

645

INSPECTORATE GENERAL OF CUSTOMS.

PEKING, 18th November 1918

Dear Sir,

I am directed by the Inspector General inform you that your S/O letter No. 144 ted 4th November, 1918, has been duly eived.

Yours truly,

Private Secretary.

C.E. Tanant, Esquire,

WENCHOW.

CUSTOM HOUSE,

S/O No. 145.

Wenchow 26. November, 1918.

Sir,

APPLICATION FOR SERVICE LIST.

Professor Henri Cordier, the compiler of Bibliotheca Sinica, has asked me a copy of the Service List which it is not in my power to distribute, and I take leave to enclose his letter - which kindly return - in the hope that you may perhaps satisfy his desire.

MALPRACTICE AT TSUMEN N.C. STATION.

With reference to my last S/O letter re Ignorance of Customs by Provincial Authorities, I have now recorded in despatch No. 3339 the Ningpo Superintendent's refusal to deal further with the case. As you will see by the documents it is admitted by the Tsumen Weiyüan that a cargo of wheat destined to Tsumen and covered by Huchao and our Bond Certificate was allowed to be landed at another place and was finally relanded at Tsumen 5 months afterwards. Why were the Junks allowed

allowed to land their wheat Inland and not at Tsumen, and what did the Junks from the moment of landing to that of relanding at Tsumen 5 months later ? No mention of it is made in the official explanations but it is notorious that landing and shipping of cereals, although prohibited here goes on at all the N.C. Stations outside of my 50 li radius for the greatest benefit of the Weiyüan concerned, and when one is caught it seems we could expect that some punishment be meted out. The Wenchow Sup't is straight enough, but admitting he be willing to help me, I cannot well ask him to fight against the brother (as is the Ningpo Sup't) of the Shui-wu Ch'u Minister!

PEACE FESTIVITIES.

14th Nov. Custom House closed (telegram of 13th)

16th " Tea party offered by Taoyin and Sup't to Foreign Community, all Chinese Officials, gentry, etc., ~~present~~

21st " Lunch offered by Foreign Community to 20 Officials and gentry.

22nd Hoisting of Belgian flag in honour of King Albert's return to his capital.

28t]

28th, 29th, 30th, days fixed by the Provincial Authorities for local celebration. I had a set of flags made more or less according to shape, several hundred small lanterns to hang above the compound wall and a festoon of electric lamps in front of the verandahs

Yours respectfully,

S/O

INSPECTORATE GENERAL OF CUSTOMS.

PEKING, 17th December, 1918.

Dear Mr. Tanant,

I have duly received your S/O letter No.145 of 26th November, 1918.

<u>Application from Professor Henri Cordier, Compiler of Bibliotheca Sinica, for Copy of Service List.</u>

You might write to the Statistical Secretary and ask if Mr. Cordier receives regularly the Customs publications, including the Service List.

Yours truly,

E. Tanant, Esquire,
   WENCHOW.

CUSTOM HOUSE,

S/O No. 146.   Wenchow, 21st Dec. 1918.

SIR,

ATTEMPT TO SET FIRE TO S.S. "KWANGCHI".

With reference to my despatch No. 3342 reporting the attempt to set fire to the S.S. Kwangchi I beg to explain that I thought better to inform you first by despatch so as to give you at once an official report in case of enquiries by the Shui-wu Ch'u.

I have now to add that the body of Mr. Hsü Hsiang-fan was left in the wrecked offices of the China Merchants Co. by his followers when they fled. The Hsu family repaired afterwards but up to now refuse to bury him, insisting on the immediate settlement of the case. The papers of the Company having been scattered or destroyed the Chief clerk, in the Agent's absence, opened offices in his own house, but no cargo has been passed for the Kwangchi which is detained by order of the

Authorities

Authorities. Yesterday the son of the deceased sent me a petition asking for the detention of the Kwangchi. I andorsed his petition saying that his business did not concern the Customs and added that if he wanted to have the ship detained he should apply to the Authorities.

As there is no saying when the Kwangchi will be allowed to clear, and as there have been renewed threats of arson against the ship, I think it would be well if she could be sent away soon, and as I received these last few months various Superintendent's despatches transmitting the Ministry of Communications instructions to protect the Company against threats of the deceased Hsu, I thought it as well to take advantage of these instructions to write to the Superintendent and ask for an early clearance of the ship which would be advisable as well in the interest of the Company as in that of the mercantile community anxious to ship its cargo, and particularly in in the Customs interest, the enforced idleness of the ship preventing free movements of cargo and causing consequent loss of duties (of which we are much in need as we are now over 8,000 Tls. short of last years collection). My despatch cannot fail to be an argument for the prompt clearance of the ship. Up to now nothing has been done and the Captain has simply been requested by the Agent the morning after the trouble not to leave the ship for fear of accident.

CHANGE OF OFFICIALS - TAOYIN AND SUPERINTENDENT.

Mr. Huang Ch'ing-lan, Wenchow Taoyin is transferred to Ching Hua (Chekiang) while the Ching Hua Taoyin Mr. Chao is transferred to Wenchow. This Mr. Chao - a brother in law of ex Viceroy Li Han-chang, I am told - was Wenchow Taoyin when local independence was proclaimed a year ago. He was then like all other Officials recalled to Hangchow and subsequently appointed Ching Hua Taoyin. I understand that the change now announced will

will only be effected on paper, both Mr. Huang and Mr. Chao remaining at their actual posts and practically acting for each other.

As to the change of Superintendent the sudden appointment of Mr. Mao Kwang-sheng has been decidedly unwellcome and a strong campaign has been started against him resulting in numerous telegrams to Hangchow. and Peking against the appointment. Mr. Mao who had arrived at Shanghai is said to have been recalled to Peking to answer the charges now brought against him.

Yours respectfully,

P.S. 23/XII/18.

A despatch has now been received from the Superintendent informing me that the Kwangchi's affair would be investigated by the Judicial Authorities and that the

ship

ship would be cleared without delay, as there is no other ship available for the Shanghai-Wenchow service. A good cargo is being now passed and she takes this letter.

CUSTOM HOUSE,

Wenchow 31st December 1918

S/O NO. 147.

SIR,

ATTEMPT TO SET FIRE TO THE S.S. "KWANGCHI".

The ship left on the 24th with a good cargo, but will not return until settlement of the case which is very prejudicial to business generally. The Chamber of Commerce are agitating for the early despatch of another steamer but nothing definite has as yet been reported. The whole affair now seems to be one of face saving as well for the family of the deceased Mr. Hsü as for the China Merchants S.N. Co. The people generally and most officials side with the Company but the General and some gentry side with the Hsü family and some arrangement satisfactory to both parties is being discussed.

YEARLY REVENUE COLLECTION.

I regret to say that our M. C.

Collection

Collection is 8,466 Tls. short of the 1917 Collection. The N. C. is plus Tls. 2,993. This deducted the total loss is Tls. 5,472.
SHORT LEAVE.

Circular No. 2,866 calls for applications of those whose long leave is due. There is none due here. However in view of Staff arrangements I take leave to mention that after the new year holidays I shall have to report the purchase of the Commissioner's House and ask that it be properly repaired and I would deem it a **favour** if whole repairs are effected - which may take from 2 to 3 months - I could be granted a short leave which I intend spending in Japan. I cannot fix any time but the Summer would be the best time. I have repaired the Custom House and revarnished it completely (Offices and Tidewaiters' Quarters) and it took 5 to 6 weeks to have each floor properly dried (Ningpo varnish) so I compute it won't take much less than 3 months to do my house properly. I shall
apply

apply officially when reporting the purchase of the house.

Yours respectfully,

1919 年

INSPECTORATE GENERAL OF CUSTOMS.

PEKING, 6th January, 1919.

Dear Sir,

I am directed by the Inspector General inform you that your S/O letter No. 146 ed 21st December, 1918 has been duly eived.

Yours truly,

Private Secretary.

E. Tanant, Esquire,

WENCHOW.

INSPECTORATE GENERAL OF CUSTOMS.

PEKING, 13th January 1919.

Dear Sir,

I am directed by the Inspector General to inform you that your S/O letter No. 147 dated 31st December, 1918, has been duly received.

Yours truly,

W. H Chappere
Private Secretary.

E. Tanant, Esquire,

WENCHOW.

CUSTOM HOUSE,

Wenchow, 23. January, 1919.

S/O No. 148.

Sir,

STANSARD'OIL Co's INSTALLATION & TANK STEAMERS.

I am afraid my despatches Nos. 3349 and particularly 3350 will brig you new undesired work, but I hope you will admit that I have done my best to settle the question, though I did not succeed. The fact is that the Company wants to force its ships on us probably in view to turning round the difficulties created by the local Authorities. At a safety point of view there is nothing to say against the installation. The Company selected a bare hill spur in a remote, practically uninhabited corner, and this causes no danger. The only objection could be the distance. It may be that the Company did not pay the usual fees and douceurs, but this has nothing to do with us. I said in my despatch that the seller of the land had been imprisoned. I really believe it was not for selling but for having removed graves. Nevertheless we have all the trouble and the

Company

— 183 —

Company wants to force our hands. 2

Strictly speaking the Company having no tank lighter into which to discharge the Oil in bulk we should not grant it any facility and if necessary let it take the Oil back if it cannot land it, but this is preposterous nowadays and we must therefore try to deter it from sending its ships until the installation be sanctioned, and the only way I can suggest is to impose high fees for the various operations, one by one, say Tls 5. for unloading outside of harbour limits, plus Tls. 20. for examining, i.e. verifying gauges, etc., plus Tls. 20. for supervision of repacking. I am afraid my Tls. 20. fee will not act as a deterrent as the work could easily have been done in two days with 3 or 4 pumps instead of one.

I should add that after the Oil had been landed and just as the ship was ready to change her moorings and come into harbour to load exports, the Agent again called and asked for permission to first send her to the installation to help testing the pipe line and pump water into the tank, the

installation

installation pump being unsuitable and sent back to Shanghai. I refused to comply with this request and my decision was received with dismay, I may say. But how could I act otherwise when I have just received the Authorities instructions to direct the Company to first fulfill the formalities ?

I have also to add that my decision to moor the ship outside of Harbour limits was not well received as it was argued by the agent that heretofore lorcha with cargoes of oil had been allowed to anchor within the Harbour. This is correct, but lorcha cargoes are easily landed in 2 or 3 cargo boats, but in this Meinan case she had a big quantity of oil (Agent's own words), 45840 gallons as per Manifest = 4584 cases, plus 500 cases, plus 4000 tins, altogether the equivalent of 7000 odd cases, and I said this quantity was too large. It happened that a lorcha consigned to the Company arrived while the Meinan was outside harbour limits, with a cargo of 2000 cases Oil and 360 tins phosphorus matches. I also ordered her to anchor outside harbour limits and collected the Tls. 5. fee, and I issued a Notification that in future all boats with more than 1000 cases of Kerosine Oil will have to anchor and discharge outside harbour limits.

I might also mention that the very matches which formed part of that lorcha's cargo had hardly been landed and stored in one of the Company's agents stores when they caught fire. How, I cannot find out; possibly on account of the coming New Year settlement but nevertheless it shows that my precautions are not absolutely useless. The fire occurring shortly after noon in broad daylight was soon put out, otherwise it might have been more serious.

To sum up this S.O.Co's tank steamers case it simply comes to this : The Company, though it may have the right to employ tank steamers has not yet been permitted to put up an installation and go alongside to discharge oil. Are we therefore bound to grant it special facilities when, knowing this, it persists sending its steamers here? If we do it, it opens a precedent for other industrial concerns to claim similar
privileges,

privileges, and this I do not feel authorised to grant without reference to you.

OIL TANKS MEASUREMENT FEE.

There is a further point with this case which does not seem - at least as much as I can find out by Circulars - to have been settled, viz. the collection of a fee by the Customs for measuring and certifying the capacity of the tanks as well ashore as on board ships. We claim a measurement fee for the ships which we measure for Tonnage; why not then also for measuring and certifying the capacity of oil tanks? Of course we do not collect measurement fees for Foreign Ships as we accept Treaty Powers own ships measurements Certificates, but in the matter of Oil tanks and ships built in China the case is different, the place of construction of the ships and of the installations being in Chinese territory. May be the measurement fee forms part of the Bonding license fee? But as unbonded tanks need not be measured there would nevertheless remain the question of a fee for specially measuring and certifying the capacity of certain holds of ships used as tanks, which is quite different of Ships ordinary Tonnage measurements.

Yours respectfully,

INSPECTORATE GENERAL OF CUSTOMS.

S/O

PEKING, 11th February, 1919.

Dear Mr. Tanant,

    I have duly received your S/O letter No.148 of 23rd January, 1919.

<u>Standard Oil Company's Installation and Tank Steamers: Commissioner thinks that, strictly speaking, the Company having no Tank Lighter into which to discharge the Oil in Bulk, we should not grant it any Facility.</u>

    I don't agree with this. We are only concerned to see that the oil is safely discharged, in circumstances which protect the revenue. The arrangements proposed appear to me to give adequate safety and protection and the fee to be sufficient. The question of the oil tanks on shore is another matter. We do not touch it

C.E. Tanant, Esquire,
    W E N C H O W.

it until the local territorial authorities are satisfied.

<u>Query whether Customs ought not to claim a Fee for Measuring and Certifying the Capacity of Oil tanks.</u>

The supervision fee includes all this, I think.

Yours truly,

CUSTOM HOUSE,

S/O No. 149.   Wenchow, 28th January 1919.

SIR,

OLD CHINESE NEW YEAR.

The last steamer is leaving to-morrow morning, with a poor cargo, and we may not have another steamer for a fortnight on account of the old Chinese New Year Holidays, so I write a few lines to inform you of my enforced silence.

The China Merchants trouble is apparently settled but no details of the settlement have come out. The Company sent here the "Tungwah" these last three trips as she cannot run north now, while the Kwangchi is in dock; but we do not know which ship will return after the New Year. The Company only sent the Tungwah by order of the Governor who, on hearing of pourparlers for a contract with a Japanese Ship to run here, telegraphed to the Tao Yin to stop the pourparlers.

The new Superintendent, Mr. Chou Ssu-p'ei, has not arrived yet, and is only

expected

expected when steamers resume running.

Yours respectfully,

[A.—42]

S/O

INSPECTORATE GENERAL OF CUSTOMS.

PEKING, 11th February, 1919.

Dear Sir,

I am directed by the Inspector General to inform you that your S/O letter No. 149 dated 28th January, 1919, has been duly received.

Yours truly,

Private Secretary.

C.E. Tanant, Esquire,

WENCHOW.

CUSTOM HOUSE,

S/o No. 150.

Wenchow, 10. February, 1919.

Sir,

STANDARD OIL CO'S IMPORTATION OF KEROSENE OIL IN BULK PREVIOUS TO OBTAINING PERMISSION TO USE ITS TANK INSTALLATION.

In his letter of 7th January embodied in the Wenchow despatch No. 3350, pages 10 to 13, the local Agent of the S.O.Co objected to my levy of a Tls. 20. *per diem* fee for examination and supervision of repacking of Kerosene Oil in bulk on board the importing steamer, and in the second paragraph of that letter he asked me as follows to submit you the case: "Of course after arrangements are made to have our tank bonded all of this difficulty will be finished. As it is very uncertain when this will be accomplished, and it will be necessary for us to receive bulk cargos from time to time, we earnestly request that you obtain the Inspector Generals instructions in the case".

I

I now have to report the receipt on the 8th instant from the same Agent of the following letter: "Our Shanghai Office has advised that they will make no further shipments to Wenchow of bulk oil without containers until we can use the tank at our new installation. This will serve to cancel the request outlined in the second paragraph of our letter of January 7th.

This comes to say that they do not desire to have the matter reported to you. However I think it as well that I did report so as to expose what I may call a piece of bluff to try and force my hand to establish a precedent against which the Chinese Authorities could have no recourse.

S.O.Co's INTENTION TO RUN LAUNCHES TO JUIAN: QUERY CONCERNING.

I hear now verbally from the S.O.Co's Agent that they wish to send Oil in barrels or cases, presumably covered by Transit Passes direct from Shanghai to Juian by steam launch Considering the distance and the small quantity that can be carried on board a steam

launch

launch, I have an impression that the said steam launch may mean heir S.S." Meinan" (153 tons), for the Agent inquired whether there was any map showing the depth of water at the entrance to the Juian River (Fei Yün Chiang 飞云江). I told the Agent that we have no such particulars, and that as regards plying Inland, Juian though along the Coast is not yet a recognised place of call for steam launches, and that permission to go there will have to be asked for regularly. He then replied that there is a very small steam launch plying across that River - which is exact - and if she is allowed to ply there he claimed that their launches may also go. The fact is that there is a very small launch, the Hui Chang, 5 tons, acting only as ferry and towing one or two passenger boats between Juian and Nan an on the opposite River Bank where passengers tranship to an Inland Canal leading to PingYang. How was she allowed to run there ? There are no traces in our archives. She arrived here from Shanghai in 1907 and is registered at the Chiao-tung Pu. Her Certificate issued by that Ministry allows her to run between Yoching

on

on the Coast, North East of Wenchow, to Heng Tu Ta Shui Chiang ching kuo Fei Yun Chiang 起樂清訖橫渡大水港經過飛雲江 and therefore it remains to decide whether the issue of that Chiao-tung Pu Certificate of Registration creates a precedent which other launches may claim to trade at Juian, and I would like to have your opinion on this point.

STEAMERS.

The Ningpo small steamers plying under S. I. W. S. N. Certificates resumed plying shortly after the old New Year, but there is no sign yet of a China Merchants S. N. Co's steamer.

Yours respectfully,

INSPECTORATE GENERAL OF CUSTOMS.

S/O

PEKING, 25th February, 1919.

Dear Mr. Tanant,

I have duly received your S/O letter No.150 of 10th February, 1919.

<u>Standard Oil Company wish to send Oil in Barrels or Cases direct from Shanghai to Juian by Steam-Launch: One small Steam-Launch, the "Hui Chang", already acting as a Ferry and towing Passenger Boats across the Juian River: Query whether the granting of a Chiao-tung Pu Certificate of Registration to this Vessel creates a Precedent, which other Steam-Launches may claim, to trade at Juian.</u>

I think the rule is that launches may not trade exclusively between inland places without permission.

Yours truly,

C.E. Tanant, Esquire,
    WENCHOW.

CUSTOM HOUSE,

S/O No. 151.   Wenchow, 25. February, 1919.

Sir,

SEIZURE REWARDS.

As I hear you are settling Out-door staff grievances there is one point which I must refer you.

It has been local practice to divi[de] Seizure rewards equally between the Tidewaiter the Watcher, and all the boatmen forming a Searching party, and this is well founded, I think, for, while the Tidewaiter searches passengers and their luggage, the boatmen search the ship and prevent passengers escaping in sampans and drive them to the Tidewaiter.

Now, our Tidewaiter has objected to thi[s] on the plea that it is a lowering of positio[n] for a foreigner to accept the same reward as a Chinese. I told him I would not alter the practice which is fair, but that if he object[s] to sharing the result of seizures he must st[ate] state separately his own seizures.

Mr. Jönsson says it is Canton practice to give

give more to foreigners than to Chinese; but it may be that there are many foreign Tidewaiters and that they do all the searching including crew's quarters, coal bunkers, etc., all very nasty jobs. But here the Tidewaiter is alone and this part of the work falls on the boatmen with most of the time no result.

The CHINA MERCHANTS S.N.Co. have at last resumed their steamer service to and from Shanghai and the " Feiching" arrived on the 22nd.

Yours respectfully,

INSPECTORATE GENERAL OF CUSTOMS.

S/O

PEKING, 11th March, 1919.

Dear Mr. Tanant,

I have duly received your S/O letter No.151 of 25th February, 1919.

<u>Seizure Rewards and Outdoor Staff Grievances: Commissioner says local Practice is to divide Seizure Rewards equally between Tidewaiter, Watcher and Boatmen: Mr. Tidewaiter Jönsson objects to this, on the ground that it is a Lowering of Position for a Foreigner to accept the same Reward as a Chinese.</u>

This, so far as I know, is not one of the Outdoor Staff grievances, but if your practice were changed, on the lines desired by Mr. Jonsson, it might quite well become a Chinese grievance.

Yours truly,

C.E. Tanant, Esquire,
WENCHOW.

CUSTOM HOUSE,

S/O. No. 152.   Wenchow 4. March, 19

Sir,

STANDARD OIL CO'S CLAIM TO SEND STEAM LAUNCHES FROM SHANGHAI TO JUIAN.

I beg to acknowledge receipt of your S/o letter of 25th February in reply to my S/o No. 150 in which I enquired whether the issue of a Certificate of Registration by the Chiao-tung Pu to the small steam launch "Huichang" acting as a ferry and towing passenger boats across the Juian River, entitled the S.O.Co to claim the right to send steam launches from Shanghai ti Juian.

In your reply you tell me :"

> " I think the rule is that launches may not trade exclusively between Inland places without permission ".

Yes, I know it, but the launch if not authorised has nevertheless been tolerated by my predecessors to ply there, and she obtained through the Superintendent her Chiao-tung Pu Certificate of Registration. She has been

plying

plying there for several years and I think that we must recognize the "fait accompli" for I do not see how we could now stop her without raising hostilities with all the local Officials, gentry and people. A few months ago I had to insist on her coming to Wenchow for her annual inspection instead of allowing one of the China Merchants Ships Engineer to go and inspect her at Juian. The Company made a lot of fuss against being obliged to send the launch here; the case was even referred to the Superintendent by the owners, but finally they sent the boat and subsequently her passenger boats for inspection (Vide Summaries of Non-urgent Chinese correspondence : September, M.C. Subject 3 and October, M.C. Subject 1).

But the question now raised by the S.O.Co demand is not the same. That Company's point is : there is a steam launch allowed to ply across the river at Juian; why then, following established precedent, should we not be permitted to send our launches from Shanghai to Juian ? My argument is that the launch now plying across the Juian River is specially allowed to

ply

ply there as a ferry boat for public convenience and is not trading, i.e. carrying cargo and this makes a difference with the status of other steam launches plying between a Treaty port and an Inland place with cargo, and what I asked in my last S/o is whether you agree with my reply that Juian is not a recognised place of call for steam launches and that permission to go there should be asked for through the Consul, or whether acting on the precedent of the steam ferry boat plying at Juian we may without reference to the Chinese Authorities allow other launches to repair there
SUPERINTENDENT.

Mr. Chou Ssu-pei, the new Sup't arrived only on the 22nd, and as your telegram had then been received saying that the monthly allowance could only be issued in advance with the successor's consent, the departing Sup't, Mr. Hsu Hsi-shi, changed his mind and only handed over charge on the 1st March. He had all his accounts squared up and also remitted me his net collection for February. He left this morning for Shaohsing, his home, where he intends to spend some time until the political horizon be more clear.

      Yours respectfully,

INSPECTORATE GENERAL OF CUSTOMS.

S/O   PEKING.   19th March, 1919.

Dear Mr. Tanant,

I have duly received your S/O letter No.152 of 4th March, 1919.

Standard Oil Company's Claim to send Steam Launches from Shanghai to Juian: Commissioner says that what he asked in his last S/O letter was whether the Inspector General agreed with his Reply to the Company that Juian is not a recognised Place of Call for Steam Launches, or whether, acting on the Precedent of the Steam Ferry Boat plying at Juian, we may, without Reference to the Chinese Authorities, allow other Launches to repair there.

It seems to me that a place to which a steam launch has been running for years must be a recognised place of call within the meaning of the rules.

Yours truly,

C.E.Tanant, Esquire,
WENCHOW.

S/O No. 153.

CUSTOM HOUSE,

Wenchow, 22. March, 1919.

Sir,

DETENTION OF EXPORT CARGO BY YANG KWANG CHÜ.

In my despatch No: 3332 I reported this Office practice to allow the Yang Kwang Chü to station a Lushih in my General Office to copy all particulars from Applications so as to facilitat the collection of its dues.

In your despatch in reply (No.838/71296) you instructed me to stop the practice. The Sup't had then been informed of his removal and it was agreed with him I would wait to give effect to your instructions till his departure. Neverthe less I informed privately the Yang Kwang Chü Director with whom I have always had pleasant intercourse that I had received instructions to stop the practice.

The Sup't's departure was delayed and finall on the arrival of the new Sup't I informed the Yang Kwang Chü (Subject 4, Maritime Customs, February Summary of Non-urgent Chinese correspondence).

The

The Lushih did not return, but since that the Yang Kwang Chü has had men in the street in front of the Custom House weighing cargo. This, I do not think I can object to so long as it does not interfere with our work. But the Tidesurveyor also informs me that a Yang Kwang Chü employé watches examination of cargo in the China Merchants godown, and I now beg to ask whether I should object to his presence there.

Now another question has arisen with the same Yang Kwang Chü. In order to enforce the payment of several thousand dollars still over-due the Director of that Office did not see better, but to stop 4 cases pig intestines - valuable exports - and some coarse paper on their way from the Custom House to the steamer This was reported the next day and the shipper sent in a petition to claim assistance. I sent my Chinese Assistant, Mr. Wong Haiu Geng, to infor the Director of the Yang Kwang Chü that failing to have that cargo released I would have to take up the case officially. He promised to release it within two or three days when there would

would be a steamer, but I said no it must be released at once, and shortly afterwards it was released. This morning I saw the Sup't and reported the case about which he had already heard and he told me he agreed with my decision.

The R.C. Likin has arrived and is re-surveying part of the channel.

Yours respectfully,

INSPECTORATE GENERAL OF CUSTOMS.

S/O

PEKING. 9th April, 1919.

Dear Mr. Tanant,

I have duly received your S/O letter No.153 of 22nd March, 1919.

<u>Employe of the Yang Kwang Chu is watching Examination of Cargo in the China Merchants Godown: Commissioner enquires whether he should object to his Presence there.</u>

If the China Merchants don't object, you need not do so!

Yours truly,

C.E. Tanant, Esquire,
    WENCHOW.

CUSTOM HOUSE,

o. 154.   Wenchow, 28. March, 1919.

Sir,

MARITIME CUSTOMS NATIVE OUT-DOOR STAFF : increase of pay of.

Some of my Maritime Customs Native Out-door staff have not had their pay increased for 3 years or more, and before attending to this question I was waiting for your reply to my proposal re increase of pay of the Native Customs staff. This question has been settled and now reported in my despatch No. 3365, N.C.210.

I was then taking up the Maritime Customs Native Out-door staff case, but I have now received your Circular No. 2912 re Foreign Out-door staff reorganisation, and as it is rumoured that the Chinese staff at Shanghai has also petitioned for an increase of pay I thought that these claims might lead to further instructions re Chinese staff pay and it might be better to postpone issuing any increase in case a general one be contemplated, and I therefore beg to ask whether I may issue the usual increase to deserving Native O.D. men or
whether

whether I should wait for further instructions

SURVEY OF RIVER.

The " Likin " has been hard at work re-surveying approaches to the harbour, and by what I saw of the new map they did good work. The rainy weather unfortunately is very much interfering with the work. By a strange coincidence a Chinese gunboat from Foochow ran aground on one of the sand banks three days ago and has remained there in the absence of a tide sufficiently high to enable her to float. This accident may have been due to bad navigation but nevertheless shows the necessity to keep the channel properly surveyed and charted. I am afraid, though, with sand banks continually moving that it will be necessary to re-survey part of the river at least once a year, which will perhaps entail more work on the Marine Department.

Yours respectfully,

INSPECTORATE GENERAL OF CUSTOMS.

s/O

PEKING, 15th April, 1919.

Dear Mr. Tanant,

I have duly received your S/O letter No.154 of 28th March, 1919.

Maritime Customs Native Outdoor Staff: Commissioner in doubt whether to issue the usual Increase to deserving Native Outdoor Men, as he thinks a general Increase of Pay may be contemplated.

I do not propose to take the initiative in regard to the pay of Native Outdoor Staff - i.e., whose names are not in the Service List.

Yours truly,

C.E.Tanant, Esquire,
  WENCHOW.

CUSTOM HOUSE,

S/O No. 155.   Wenchow, 19th April 1919

SIR,

ACCIDENTS CAUSED BY I.W.S.N. STEAMERS AT NON OPEN SEA PORTS: QUERY RE JUDICIAL SETTLEMENT OF.

The Superintendent told me a few days ago that accidents had occurred in his predecessors time and recently at K'anmen, a small port of Yühuan Island close to the mouth of the Wenchow River, caused by the small Ningpo-Wenchow steamers not anchoring and simply reducing speed to take in or land a few passengers, and he asked me what steps should be taken to have the cases settled. I replied on the spot that I thought the territorial official should be the proper authority but in case of difficulty it would be better to have the cases transmitted to the Ningpo Superintendent as the steamers port is Ningpo where their I.W.S.N. Certificates are issued.

I have now written to give him the

text

text of Art. 8 and 9 of the S.N. Inland Regulations (amended) 1898; and at the same time I added that circumstances are not quite the same at K'anmen, a sea port, on account of tides, weather, etc. as inland, and that for this reason it might be better to have the cases settled by the Ningpo Superintendent and Commissioner, — So much the more as cases concerning foreign steamers would have to be referred to Ningpo, and it seems that Chinese steamers should be treated similarly.

LIMITATION OF NUMBER OF CASES OF KEROSENE OIL ALLOWED TO BE HANDLED WITHIN HARBOUR:

In my despatch No. 3358 I reported having had to fix at 1,000 cases the limitation of the quantity of kerosene oil allowed to be handled by one ship within Harbour, and that the Asiatic Petroleum Co. had objected on the plea that lorcha, on account of dangers, difficulties, and delays, were refusing to take cargoes of oil from Shanghai to Wenchow, which threatened to stop its trade.

The

32

The Coast Inspector whose opinion I thought well worth having replied that at Shanghai only 50 cases of kerosene oil are allowed to be handled by one boat at a time, so the Company should not grumble. However the Ningpo Agent called a few days ago and finally asked that lorcha coming in with more than 1,000 cases and obliged to anchor outside harbour, be allowed to come into Harbour when all oil above 1,000 cases has been landed. He lays stress on the fact that I allow a vessel to come in direct when arriving with less than 1,000 cases, and on the fact that at Ningpo vessels are allowed to enter Harbour with several thousand cases, it being left to the Harbour Master's discretion to fix a limitation when he thinks fit. I replied that I had submitted the case to Shanghai and that my limitation had been found too liberal, but that I would not alter it for the present until they (A.P.Co.) have got a regular installation, but that at the same time I would not do anything to make my

limitation

limitation ineffective in view of possible future limitations.

    We have a very small staff and cannot possibly man any vessel with Watchers and we must practically take the ships' word for the cargo they have on board, and if a vessel that has been ordered to anchor outside would apply for permission to enter Harbour when she has discharged part of her oil cargo we could not send sufficient men on board to check whether the quantity left on board is or not within 1,000 cases, and even with the staff handy it would be rather difficult to check the cargo left on board without moving it, which is preposterous. Such demands are the result of laxity in the rules enforced at all the ports. It seems however that the danger created by kerosene oil on board a vessel is the same at all ports and therefore there should be uniformity of practice in the limitation.

    I promised the A.P.Co.'s Agent I would submit you his case and I will be thankful for instructions if you think

advisable

advisable to alter my decision.

CUSTOMS COLLEGE : ADMITTANCE TO.

I have been asked by a local photographer who has a son for whom he wishes to find a position as Clerk what are the conditions of admission to the Customs College, and I would be obliged, if a programme exists, for a few copies so as to be able to reply to demands of particulars. The young man in question has been a student at the local Methodist College.

NATIVE CUSTOMS WEIYUAN.

I am now mailing my reply to Circular No. 2920, in which I suggest the abolition of the post. While speaking to the Sup't, a few days ago, I mentioned I had been instructed to report on the usefulness of the Wei-yüan and he admitted he is rather superfluous. There is none for the Maritime Customs as used to be the case formerly and things work as smoothly. As to the Allowance to copy Notifications I hope that you will sanction its discontinuation. It is nothing but a squeeze. I did not mention anything about it to the Sup't.

Yours respectfully,

INSPECTORATE GENERAL OF CUSTOMS.

S/O   PEKING, 30th April, 1919.

Dear Mr Tanant,

    I have duly received your S/O letter No. 155 of 19th April.

<u>Cases of accidents caused by I.W.S.N. steamers at ports not opened to trade: Commissioner enquires what is the proper authority empowered to make judicial settlement.</u>

    The question is one for the local authority to deal with.

<u>Limitation of number of cases of kerosene oil which may be handled in harbour: Commissioner suggests uniform regulation for all ports.</u>

    Uniformity in local regulations is desirable of course but in a country of the size of China where conditions vary so much it can be overdone.

<u>Customs College: what are conditions of admittance?</u>

    The examinations are held at centres such as Shanghai and Canton. The young man should apply to the Shui-wu Ch'u College for particulars. An examination is to be held next month.

          Yours truly,

E. Tanant, Esquire,
Wenchow.

CUSTOM HOUSE,

S/O No. 156.

Wenchow 20. May, 1919.

Sir,

SEIZURE OF OPIUM AMONGTS PACKAGES OF TREASURE (Wenchow despatch No. 3375 (N.C.No. 213).
I would have liked to report this case complete, but it has already lasted two weeks, and I do not know when it will be settled, so I thought better to report facts up to date and to ask for instructions.

As explained in my despatch the second batch of 18 packages (about $ 21,000) owned by 6 men has been released on the owners being found innocent by the Court. As to the first batch of 10 men owning also 18 packages, value about $25,000, the Superintendent who called yesterday is of opinion that that part of the treasure belonging to the man who may be convicted, or the whole lot, if the whole batch of men is found guilty, should be confiscated, for he agrees with me that it is impossible to admit that the box of opium was introduced by a stranger. With one exception

the

the men had only one or two packages to look after, in fact they had practically no luggage; how then could a stranger introduce a suspicious box amongst these packages ? There are two men, it appears, on whom the Court suspicions lay : one who had some boxes about similar in appearance to the old candles box, and one well clad giving the impression of a well to do merchant He had three round baskets containing also, as an exception, some clothing. The Sup't, says that the Court and the Taoyin are glad that these men were caught as it is surmised that though Fookienese they trade with Formosa, and that this large sum of money which they carried with them represents the proceeds of sales of Formosan Opium at various places along the Coast, and they are accused with that money to pay for the smuggling of a quantity of rice and wheat. So, on the whole, confiscation on our part would not be disapproved, but I presume the Officials would rather prefer to confiscate themselves.

JAPANESE BOYCOTT.

I am told a Japanese boycott has been declared but, if enforced, it seems to go on quietly.

Yours respectfully,

CUSTOM HOUSE,

S/o No. 157.

Wenchow, 26, May, 1919.

Sir,

REVISED CUSTOMS REGULATIONS and
PROPOSED HARBOUR REGULATIONS.

I mailed two days ago through the Coast Inspector my despatch No. 3376 submitting Revised Customs Regulations and Proposed Harbour Regulations. According to Circular instructions only questions concerning Harbour and not Customs Regulations should be submitted through the Coast Inspector, but in this case the two questions being so connected owing to repetitions in the original Regulations, I could not help submitting the two questions together.

I now beg to point out how redundant it seems to give harbour limits in each set of Regulations, and I would suggest that they be eliminated from the Customs Regulations.

While searching the old correspondence and trying to understand why the 1878 Amended Regulations (ignored by Mr. Montgomery) were

either

either not approved or not objected to, it struck me that all Inspectorate despatches from 1st March, 1878, to Feb, 1879, were signed either by Messrs R.E.Bredon and W.Cartwright or R.E.Bredon and J.M.Dane, for the I.G.; that was one of the few times Sir Robert Hart went home, and it may be inferred that the Regulations when received at the Inspectorate were not replied to pending the Chief's return, and were practically forgotten by the time of his return. On the other hand most of the Inspectorate despatches for 1883, the year in which the Amended 1878 Regulations were again sent in reply to Circular No. 201, are signed :"E.McKean" Chief Secretary, which corroborates the statement in my despatch relative to Mr. McKean's correspondence in 1899 - when Statistical Secretary - with Mr. Montgomery.

  I hope you will excuse my insistence in taking up again this question, but the present uncertainty is too unsatisfactory. I should have added to my despatch that the actual Harbour limits (those of 1877, down to the Water Gate) are too narrow, and, in practise, have become
         obsolete

obsolete by the fact that the I.W.S.N.Companies have been allowed, without our being questioned, to purchase land and establish pontoons (Vide Wenchow despatch No.3245), so the Chinese Authorities could not much raise objections to our claim that the lower harbour limit is that of the 1878 Amended Regulations.

BOYCOTT.

There are placards at the City gates advising the people to boycott Japanese goods and regard Tsao Ju-lin as a treator. There was a meeting of about 1000 school students on Sunday and afterwards they paraded the most important streets with boycott flags and occasionally rested to make speeches and explain the idea of the boycott.

A fire took place at 9 p.m. in the center of the City on the 24th just in front of the Tungling's residence, but fortunately it was accidental and not due to the boycott. A large oil and groceries shop was burnt down. During the fire some 50 onlookers standing on a bridge were thrown into a canal through the falling of a stone railing. Nobody was drowned.

Seizure

SEIZURE OF OPIUM AMONGST PACKAGES OF TREASURE.

    I have to add, with reference to my despatch No. 3375, N.C. No.213, and my. S/o No.156 that another judge sent by the Shenpan t'ing (the first one had been sent by the Chiencha t'ing) called on the 24th to inspect the tins of Opium and enquire generally, and I accompanied him to the Bank to have the bags containing cases opened. From conversation it seems that the case has not made any progress, and this gentleman mentioned the possibility of the case being passed on to a higher court. He also said that of the 10 men owning the 18 packages still detained 8 have so far been released on guarantee.

    I fear that this release of 8 men who know probably as much as the others to whom the Opium belongs to is only an excuse to allow the whole gang to settle between themselves whom they will choose as scape goat so as to avoid the possible confiscation of the whole 1£ of dollars or the conviction of the head man who has the appearance of a well to do merchant. The Official delays, though perhaps
                             technically

technically explainable, cannot have any other result and, of course, are profitable to Courts underlings, if not to higher Officials. About the culpability of the whole lot I cannot but repeat that at my Office they denied knowing the owners of the box of Opium as well as of the tin concealed in the 800 dollars package, while once locked up in the Court's gaol they soon found out the owner of that tin. Now I wonder whether it would not be time for you to intervene and press the Shui-wu Ch'u to give instructions to the Court to either withou further delay find the culprit or throw the responsibility on the whole gang ?

    Yours respectfully,

INSPECTORATE GENERAL OF CUSTOMS.

S/O

PEKING, 11th June, 1919.

Dear Mr Tanant,

I have duly received your S/O letter No. 157 of 26th May.

Revised Customs Regulations and Proposed Harbour Regulations.

I forget where this question had got to. If you can succeed in laying it to rest it will be a good thing!

Seizure of opium amongst packages of treasure: culprits detained by Chinese court but no judgement pronounced as yet: suggestion that the Shui-wu Ch'u be moved to instruct court either to pass judgement on one of the culprits or make all of them responsible.

I am afraid the Ch'u is not competent to give instructions to the court.

Yours truly,

E. Tanant, Esquire,
Wenchow.

Inspectorate General of Customs

Peking, 28th May, 1919.

Dear Mr. Tanant,

A movement to form a Customs Association at Shanghai, in the preliminary proceedings of which the Shanghai Commissioner and two of his Deputy Commissioners have taken some part, is now, as I daresay you have heard, on foot and the ports are to be canvassed on the subject.

Now I don't want it to be assumed that Indoor participation at Shanghai, for which there were reasons that I sympathise with and understand, necessarily means that I approve of the movement.

I have already stated officially my views on the subject of Customs Associations and I see no reason to modify them nor any necessity to restate them. Any movement which promotes esprit de corps, mutual benefit and good-feeling between all members of the Service has my hearty sympathy. But it is obvious that I must at this stage maintain an attitude of reserve towards any particular movement promoted by only one section of this cosmopolitan Service of which the objects have not been defined.

If you are given reason to believe that your Outdoor Staff assumes that I approve of the movement because of the Shanghai Indoor Staff participation, I authorise you to correct this assumption. On the contrary I regard the movement as ill advised and dangerous to the Service.

Yours sincerely,

CUSTOM HOUSE,

S/O No. 158.

Wenchow, 10. June, 1919.

Sir,

BOYCOTT.

The boycott goes on. One of the members of the Provincial Assembly who had run away from Hangchow when there was trouble at the Provincial Assembly, returned a few days ago and was accused of having bought on the sly at Shanghai 40 packages - 58 piculs Japanese seaweed valued at about $850.00. A mob of about 300 students took him to the Chamber of Commerce and wanted to parade him through the streets clad in woman's dress. Finally the boycotters fined him $20. for purchase of Kerosene Oil to burn his seaweed which, it is said, will be burnt down publicly in a few days.

On top of all this telegrams arrived announcing the closing of shops at Shanghai and other places, and this rather perturbs the local Officials. I was informed verbally by the Sup't that the local General in charge of the Chin Pei Tui refuses, under pretext of illness, to side with the Civil Officials in case of troubles, and they were instructed by the

the Governor to rely, ~~in case of trouble,~~ on the 300 Luchün troops quartered here, which is rather dangerous as the Chin Pei Tui number about 2000 men.

This General Mei who has always been a great freind of the Hsü family, a member of which was killed when attempting to set fire to the S.S.Kwangchi last December, is now said to have given if not permission anyhow tacit approval to his freind Hsü's project of burning the ship, and this would explain why no proceedings were taken against his followers while the China Merchants S.N.Co. obtained practically no redress for the sacking of their Office.

Of late some freinds of that family wanted to erect in front of the Magistrate Yamen a stone column with a tablet to the memory of the head of the family who was drowned in the Poochi, but some other gentry made opposition and finally the matter has been reported to Hangchow for decision. This would be quite enough to turn the General against the Civil Officials

STATISTICS

STATISTICS OF TRADE FOR MINISTRY OF FINANCE.

In my despatch No. 3380 I reported the Ministry of Finance's demand of Statistics of Trade. It seems strange that we should be asked constantly statistics of this or that. It may be that the Officials of the Boards are not aware of our publications, or even possibly wilfully ignore them on account of their being produced more in a foreign than a chinese form; but nevertheless the result is the same.

Now that the Tariff is going to be changed giving the names of dutiable articles numbered in a consecutive series, based not on alphabetical order as the 1902 Tariff, but on Categories, it will perhaps be found advisable to change the order in which goods are stated on our Import and Export tables of quarterly and annual Statistics, and in this view I take leave to suggest that the Tariff nomenclature be followed, each article named therein being summarised separately and being given a separate entry on our Import tables. If more or various particulars are subsequently asked for we would then be in a firm position to refer the Office asking for

for them to our printed statistics based on the Tariff, and we could decline further researches.

SEIZURE OF OPIUM AMONGST PACKAGES OF TREASURE. (Reference to Wenchow despatch No. 3375 and S/O Nos. 156 and 157).

The case has been settled and I have just received a Supt's letter transmitting the Shenpanting's verdict. After release of two gangs of 8 men each there remained two accused: one who had a tin of opium in his package of dollars: found guilty and given 1 year gaol & fined $100. and to have his package (about $800) confiscated; and one who had $4,100. in 3 wooden boxes about similar to that in which the 5 tins and 3 packages opium were packed up. This man still denies his guilt, but has nevertheless been sentenced to 2 years gaol & $400. fine, and confiscation of $100. out of the 4,100, as the Judge accepts his story that the dollars were not his property.

Yours respectfully,

[A.-42]

S/O

INSPECTORATE GENERAL OF CUSTOMS.

PEKING, 24 JUN 1919.

Dear Sir,

I am directed by the Inspector General to inform you that your S/O letters Nos 156 & 158 dated 20th May & 10th June, have been duly received.

Yours truly,

W. A. Chapman
Private Secretary.

C. E. Tanant, Esq.,
Wenchow

CUSTOM HOUSE,

S/O No. 159.

Wenchow, 28, June, 1919

Sir,

STAFF : ASSOCIATION MOVEMENT.

I duly received your Circular Letter of 28. May authorising me to correct any possible assumption by the O.D. Staff that you approve of the Customs Association movement recently started at Shanghai, and, in reply, I beg to say that the matter had been mentioned to me long before receipt of your letter by my Assistant and by the Tidesurveyor, and that I also received the Association prospectus, and at the time I told them I did not see much the use of such association which gave me the impression of being started by some men desirous to create to themselves some kind of positions analogous to those of Secretaries of Labour Associations, in the hope to derive some private advantages such as practical permanent residence at Shanghai, etc., and I added that for such a reason alone I could not belong to the Association

Association as it is impossible to tie your hands as regards Staff movements, and that it would not be fair to the Staff to keep the same men at Shanghai permanently.

I have had no other opportunity nor did I think advisable to revert to the matter.
My Foreign Staff are not dissatisfied:
Mr. Matsubara, my Assistant, waits quietly and does not complain although I presume an increase of pay would satisfy him like all young men.
The Tidesurveyor, Mr. Ahlberg, was glad of his promotion and now awaits anxiously the promise of pension. His health is not very brilliant and he would, I think, be glad if he could retire to his holding at Altadena, California, whose dry climate particularly suits him and his wife. From hearsay he has an idea that he may be entitled to resign at once if the O.D. Staff term of Service entitles them to a pension after 25 years Service.

As to the Tidewaiter, Mr. A. Jönsson, he is a very quiet man and apart that I do not find him lively enough for a young man of his age, I can speak well of him. He has learnt a lot of examination work from Mr Ahlberg, and the latter is not over glad to see him transferred for he will

will have again to educate Mr. Jönson's successor.

CHINESE ASSISTANT AND CLERKS.

Speaking of Staff, I should say that the only ones who evince some kind of disappointment are the Chinese Clerks, but even this very mildly. They asked me several times whether I had no reply to their petition (Wenchow desp. No. 3357), and I referred them to your reply to their Shanghai colleagues' petition which they had shown me, and I advised them to wait as you would surely take up all those questions one after the other.

Yours respectfully,

INSPECTORATE GENERAL OF CUSTOMS.

S/O   PEKING, 8th July, 1919.

Dear Mr Tanant,

I have duly received your S/O letter No. 159 of 28th June.

<u>Chinese In-door Staff: petition for improved pay and prospects: no answer received as yet.</u>

Their petition will be replied to but as I have to take all decisions I cannot decide everything at once and at the same time do my other work which increases every year!

Yours truly,

C. E. Tanant, Esquire,
   Wenchow.

CUSTOM HOUSE,

S/O No. 160.

Wenchow, 2. July, 1919.

Sir,

STANDARD OIL Co's INSTALLATION OUTSIDE PORT LIMITS : QUESTION OF DUTIABILITY OF TO INLAND DUES? QUERYING.

When I wrote my S/O No. 148 and despatches Nos. 3349 and 3350 re S.O.Co's installation and Tank steamers, the Company's agent was still living in the Constable's house of the British Consulate which had been rented by the Company since a few years as its Foreign Staff quarter and at the time the question of Staff quarters on the installation site and incidentally that of dutiability to Inland dues of materials sent from Wenchow to the installation for building purposes was overlooked.

That property of the S.O.Co. is situated on the left bank of the Wenchow River, about 3 miles below, and on the opposite side of, the City (Vide Marine Department Chart No. 11), and the question is to know whether it is located Inland or within the port as open for residence to Foreigners, and whether materials

sent

sent there for erection of houses, etc., should have been passed free or should have paid either Tungchüan or Transit Dues or particularly Native Customs Export Duty.

I should mention that regulation 1o. of the old Customs Regulations for the port of Wenchow (suppression of which I advocated in my despatch No. 3376 submitting a Revised set of Customs Regulations and a new set of Harbour Regulations) states :" 1o.- Limits of Port.- Vessels shall be considered to have entered the port of Wenchow on passing a line drawn from the Outer Battery at Lungwa to the Fifteen-gun Battery at P'an Shih". (These places are far below the S.O.Co's installation). But it may be argued that this regulation established limits for the movements of vessels and has nothing to do with territorial limits of the place opened to trade.

As regards the erection of the installation nothing was mentioned about it until it was well advanced. The materials either arrived from Shanghai duty-paid, or occasionally paid import duty here on arrival, but that is all and on leaving Wenchow for the installation

they

they were not declared as well as I know either at the Maritime Customs, Tungchüan-chü or Native Customs, though strictly speaking all goods leaving the Harbour in tha direction should pay Native Customs duty unless covered by Transit Passes.

What is the value of those materials is not easy to ascertain, but nevertheless could be well fairly well estimated by looking over all our Import applications for the last three years, date within which th installation has been put up, and unless wrongly valued on importation or Shanghai documents should reach a few thousand Tael when it comes to taking into consideration a 30 ft. Iron tank, a large godown well cemented, a medium size foreign house with new furniture throughout, and some of the roofs covered with machine-made tiles.

I had been thinking of referring the question to the Superintendent, but seeing the difficulties how created to the Company over the ownership of the installation, I thought better to wait and not make thing worse; on the other hand were I to claim payment of N.C. Duty, the Company might pay and

and argue of this payment as a right to establish itself there. In the doubt I thought better to refer you the question. The points are :

Is the place an Inland place or can it be considered as part of the port ?

If it is Inland, the place being below Wenchow, and all goods for that direction being liable to payment of N.C. duty whether foreign or native and having originally paid duty, even if imported originally through the Native Customs, can we now claim payment of duty? There was no declaration made at the time the goods were taken to that place.

If we are to claim duty are we to claim it now while the question of permit to use the installation is still under discussion or should we ask the Superintendent to make this payment a <u>sine qua non</u> to the issue of permit ?

Besides if the place is to be considered Inland, and N.C. Duty on materials to be collected, I presume the same rule should be adhered to once the installation is licensed, and all goods, including agent's stores, should be dutiable with the exception of Tank Oil !

Yours respectfully, COS Canaux

INSPECTORATE GENERAL OF CUSTOMS.

S/O

PEKING, 16th July, 1919.

Dear Mr Tanant,

I have duly received your S/O letter No. 160 of 2nd July.

<u>Standard Oil Co.'s installation situated outside Port limits as defined by old regulations: are inland dues leviable on building materials, etc., for installation?</u>

Harbour limits are one thing, Port limits another. We don't know what the Port limits are and I am inclined to think they have never been defined. Don't raise any question or levy any transit dues or N.C. duties!

Yours truly,

C. E. Tanant, Esquire,
  Wenchow.

CUSTOM HOUSE,

S/O No. 161.

Wenchow, 8. July, 19 19.

Sir,

RESIGNATION OF Mr. C. AHLBERG, TIDESURVEYOR B

My despatch No. 3387, now posted, corroborates what I was writing on 28. ultimo in my S/O No. 159 about Mr. Ahlberg's anxiety for the issue of your pension scheme and the possibility of early retirement, but I must, though, admit I did not expect he would resign so early. In fact I have now pointed out that when the time comes (1. October) the worst of the summer will be passed, and I suggested he should wait for a few more months, but he replied that he particularly dreads the autumn and winter.

He says that some out-door men on resignation were granted one years pay in addition to the regular gratuity, as a kind of make up for the leave to which they would have soon been entitled, and if it is correct I beg leave to recommend him for the same

same privileged treatment.

There now comes the question of replacement. The trial which has now been made for one year of one man acting both as Tidesurveyor and Examiner seems to have been successful, and I take leave to recommend its continuation if you have suitable men. It is an economy for the service, and at a disciplinarian point of view it is better to have a Tidesurveyor busy during Office hours than practically loafing part of the day as was the case before, although Stevens used his spare time to make his map, but Lloyd had very little to do and did not like doing examination work when his Examiner got sick!

Yours respectfully,

[A.—42]

— 4 AUG 1919

INSPECTORATE GENERAL OF CUSTOMS,

S/O

PEKING, 22 JUL 1919.

61

Dear Sir,

I am directed by the Inspector General to inform you that your S/O letter No. 161, dated 8th July, has been duly received.

Yours truly,

W. H. Chappell

Private Secretary.

C. E. Tanant, Esq.,

Wenchow.

CUSTOM HOUSE,

Wenchow, 11th July 1919

62

S/O No. 162.

SIR,

SEIZURE EX I.W.S.N. STEAMER OF OPIUM CONCEALED IN PACKAGES OF TREASURE.

I have to apologise for incorrections in using wrong paper for the copies of Chinese correspondence transmitted in my despatch No. 3388 mailed last night. I had prepared my despatch leisurely and some of the appends, notably the long letter transmitting the Shenpanting's verdict, had also been prepared, and I intended to limit my report there when I received yesterday morning the Superintendent's letter informing me that the Chienchating had reported to the Ministries and that he (Superintendent) had also to report, and I had to hurry up replying and making the Chinese version of my despatch, and it takes a long time for the Writer alone to make all the needed

copies

copies, and besides, the various forms of Chinese paper numbered in foreign figures K.-19 to 21 are rather misleading for a Chinese Writer, hence his errors in using one form for another and owing to the closing of the mail yesterday evening there was no possible delay.

In fact the Superintendent called in the evening and told me that he had just posted his despatch. He seems to side with us against the Court. It remains, however, to see what decision will be taken by the Ministries.

As regards the case itself I have to add that, as may be seen by my letter No. 82 to the Superintendent, I had made my mind on receipt of the Shenpanting's verdict to accept his decision — taking for granted, of course, that the confiscated dollars would be left to us — but now that the case has been referred to the Ministries I beg leave to suggest that you not only insist

insist on confiscating the Chen Chi-mu dollars, but also those of Kuo Ang-yeh, for the Court's verdict in respect to this latter point is rather unsatisfactory.

The Court says Kuo Ang-yeh is a Laodah in Kuo Ch'uang's employ and that he was sent to accompany to Wenchow a certain Tung Chung-fang, the accountant of a Kanmen firm to cash certain cheques one of which in Kuo Ch'uang's name; but it seems rather strange, notwithstanding the Court's finding, that Tung Chung-fang should have handed Kuo Ang-yeh $4,000. to carry and should not have known or noticed that he was also carrying the case containing opium. Tung Chung-fang was himself one of the lot of 10 men arrested (case (b.)) and when I personally, through Mr. Wong Hsiu Geng, at the N.C., asked him what he knew of the package of opium he knew nothing. He had 3 baskets containing some $8,000 and did not lift a finger to say he was connected with Kuo
                                              Ang-yeh

Ang-yeh who was there at the time. My impression is that all this story was arranged between the time of arrest of the men and their trial by the Shenpanting which is easy when one knows the way Chinese jails are kept. Even at the Superintendents those men would not speak. Why then accept those late explanations? Any how Kuo Ang-yeh and particularly Tung Chung-fang should be made to pay for their contempt of the Customs, and a confiscation of $100. out of the $4,100. seems abnormally small.

Yours respectfully,

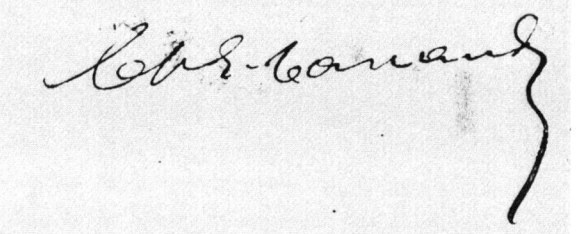

INSPECTORATE GENERAL OF CUSTOMS.

S/O

PEKING, 29th July, 1919.

Dear Mr Tanant,

I have duly received your S/O letter No. 162 of 11th July.

<u>Seizure from I.W.S.N. steamer of opium concealed in packages of treasure: Shen P'an T'ing's verdict: case referred to the Ministries.</u>

As we have the dollars we are in a position to argue the case. I shall hear of it in due course I suppose.

Yours truly,

C. E. Tanant, Esquire,
Wenchow.

S/O No. 163.

CUSTOM HOUSE,
Wenchow, 15, July, 1919.

Sir,

BOYCOTT.

The boycott movement is still strong and is taking a bad turn. This morning word was passed to all the shops to close their doors and they acted accordingly. It appears some days ago the students detected a boat outside harbour limits on its way down river with rice on board which they said was to be smuggled to Formosa. They passed on the case to the Magistrate asking that the owner - the Accountant of the Bank of China - be punished. This man's father was previously Magistrate at Yotsing, a neighbouring town near the sea whence rice is commonly smuggled to Formosa, and he had a Yotsing Huchao for the export of rice to another neighbouring port. He threatened the students to have them arrested, but contrary to his expectations they managed to hand him over to the Magistrate.

After

After two days the Magistrate on the faith of the Huchao released him and his rice, hence the closing of shops which was decided during the night after discussion with the Chamber of Commerce.

Yesterday, 14th July, being the national day of my country, I gave the Officials the usual tiffin which they expected from me, just the same as I had some of the Foreigners in the evening, and everything was going well, when, towards the end, some one came behind me and placed a pamphlet on my plate and also on that of one of my neighbours. I turned round and saw a young man in long white grass cloth coat who evidently expected a subscription towards helping the boycott movement. I got up at once and made him go out, all this without a word, and arrived outside threw him his pamphlet in the face upon which he ran away followed by two youngsters who were waiting for him on the verandah. One might ask why were they allowed to come in? but considering the large retinue of my guests, some with body guards, some with servants, and all with chair bearers, over 50 altogether, I must excuse the gate keeper for he is absolutely powerless to keep a watch on

the

the movements of all those men who come and
go while the masters are having their meal.
The whole place is simply invaded by all this
"valetaille". I returned at once to table,
and while excusing myself for having left them
I told them that privately I had nothing to
say against Chinese national feeling, but that
officially as Commissioner of Customs I could
not tolerate any attempt to the liberty of
trade, and therefore could not encourage the
boycott. The Taoyin expressed his regrets that
those boys should dare to take advantage of
this party to enter the house as they do in
Chinese houses, and I changed at once the
conversation. After tiffin the Sup't told me
the Taoyin was very much annoyed but I told
him as far as I was concerned I would rather
drop the matter and I begged him not to do
anything. I did not know at the time this
rice affair, but nevertheless seeing the daring
of these boycott agitators who seem to run the
whole town, and on the other hand the weakness
of the Officials and Government who tolerate
this agitation, I thought it would be inadvisable of me to make a public complaint which
would turn the people against the Customs.
Some

Some days ago while Matsubara as sending for a barber, one of the boycott boys who was present advised the barber not to go, and also advised Matsubara's messenger, his chair bearer, not to remain in his service, which advice was not followed fortunately.

Yours respectfully,

INSPECTORATE GENERAL OF CUSTOMS.

S/O

PEKING, 29th July, 1919.

Dear Mr Tanant,

I have duly received your S/O letter No. 163 of 15th July.

<u>Anti-Japanese Boycott.</u>

In face of really popular movements our position as a Government administration with a weak Government behind us calls for tact and caution. I think the Customs position is generally recognised and am glad we have had so little trouble so far.

Yours truly,

C. E. Tanant, Esquire,
　　Wenchow.

CUSTOM HOUSE,

S/O No. 164.

Wenchow, 19. July, 1919.

Sir,

RECLAIMING, FILLING UP, AND BUNDING STRIP OF FORESHORE.

In my Summaries of non-urgent Chinese correspondence for December, 1918, February, April, May, and June, 1919, I transmitted copies of correspondence showing that in order to enlarge its College grounds the Methodist Mission had purchased an adjoining property and deviated the road separating it from the College without Customs permission, thus obstructing the access to the Assistant's quarters. The Officials had to agree that my complaint was fair and they built a bridge so as to straighten the road but the question of widening it is still under discussion.

Again in my March and June Summaries I also reported the alienation by the local Office of public works (for $ 12.) of a small strip of land alongside the street leading to the N.C. Office, and the building

of

of a well without railing at the same spot, thus reducing the street to a 5 ft. path. As a consequence of my protest a wall was built to enclose the well and the new owner did not build, but recently he paved the lot in such a way as to give an impression that that portion of the street still belong to him. I again objected, but nothing else has been done.

Now I am told privately - perhaps wrongly, that the same Office of Public works has sold or is on the point of selling our strip of foreshore between the Jetty and the China Merchants S.N.Co's property. In view of these aggressions, and, as explained in my despatch No. 3390, owing to the difficulty to prove our right of ownership, I think that the only way to enforce our right is to reclaim, fill up, and bund that lot at once without asking anybody, and later on put up an Examination shed which is needed, and therefore I hope that you will sanction my request, and to save time I would be obliged if you would wire your decision.

<u>Boycott.</u>

Boycott.

The shops after having been closed for three days re-opened yesterday, the Taoyin having granted most of the students demands. It seems that the affair was very much one of face, for both the man accused of smuggling (who is a friend of the Taoyin) and the students (two of whom were arrested) and finally when things threatened to get worse the Taoyin yelded. The man was fined 10 times the value of the rice, excuses were made to the students and instructions issued to the troops - as well Luchün as Chinpeitui- not to arrest students. The Police only is to arrest them in case of trouble, while their right to search junks is recognised.

I am afraid a lot of this agitation has been caused by the Chief of the Chinpeitui, Mei Tungling, or his friends. Mei Tungling left a few days ago removed from his post here by the Tuchun, no doubt at the Taoyin's demand, and this has highly displeased his supporters, the Hsü clan who have been meddling in all local troubles at least since

since Mr. Bowring's time, as I saw references to it in the S/o Correspondence. Although the attempt to set fire to the Kwangchi last December was a real case of arson yet through Mei Tungling's influence they managed to clear themselves out of difficulties, and of course now that he has gone it will be more difficult and they do all they can against the actual lot of Officials.

Yours respectfully,

C. B. S. Canaul

INSPECTORATE GENERAL OF CUSTOMS,

S/O　　　　　　　　　　PEKING, 29th July, 1919.

Dear Mr Tanant,

I have duly received your S/O letter No. 164 of 19th July 1919.

<u>Commissioner proposes to reclaim, fill up and bund strip of foreshore in order to forestall encroachment of Office of Public Works, and later to erect examination shed.</u>

What will it cost and what is the strip worth?

Yours truly,

C. E. Tanant, Esquire,
　　Wenchow.

CUSTOM HOUSE,

S/O No. 165.　　　　Wenchow, 9th August 1919.

Sir,

RECLAIMING, FILLING UP, AND BUNDING STRIP OF FORESHORE.

The Engineer-in-Chief has sent me copy of his comments to my despatch No. 3390 referred to in my S/O No. 164. He says if there is no hurry he could send an Engineer to survey the intended work in October. I think this is by far preferable so much the more as advantage should be taken to survey and estimate the repairs necessary to my and to the Examiner's houses. In the meantime I could have a small portion of the foreshore filled up so as to confirm our claim before the reported attempt to wrest it from us may materialise.

BOYCOTT.

Things are getting quieter. It is true that no more Japanese goods arrive - not even my own supply of Tansan water for which the

the Companies at Shanghai refuse to issue S/orders - . The man fined for smuggling rice has issued a notification explaining his case and everybody seems satisfied. Nevertheless I understand that the Taoyin warned the chiefs of the movement that further agitation would be punished and it looks like if the agitators had moved inland. In any case at Juian they burned a junk loaded with Formosa coal for use of the launches, while the junk was being detained at the Superintendent's Native Customs pending performance of formalities.

CHANGE OF TARIFF.

A petition has been received complaining of our levy of Inward Transit Dues, on goods imported before 1st August, according to new Tariff. I replied that the Transit rate of duty is one half of the Import Tariff and as the new Tariff is now enforced goods going inland must pay accordingly, since no provision has been made to collect the half duty as per old Tariff.   SEIZURE

SEIZURE EX I. W. S. N. STEAMER OF OPIUM CONCEALED IN PACKAGES OF TREASURE.

The High Court has reversed the Shen pan Ting's verdict as regards Kuo Ang-yeh now **found innocent**. As to Chen Chi-mu he has appealed to Peking. At the same time the Superintendent transmitted me Shui-wu Chu's instructions that the matter of confiscation of the dollars rests entirely with the Commissioner. I am waiting for your further instructions.

MAILS.

Our steam service is disorganised. Of the 3 Ningpo launches, 2 are being repaired, and 1 lost a week on account of typhoons. As to the Shanghai steamers they were also delayed by the weather.

Yours respectfully,

INSPECTORATE GENERAL OF CUSTOMS,

S/O   PEKING, 19th August, 1919.

Dear Mr Tanant,

    I have duly received your S/O letter No. 165 of 9th August.

<u>New Tariff: petition received complaining of levy according to new tariff of Inward Transit Dues on goods imported before 1st August.</u>

    A Circular deals with this. Transit Dues leviable are half <u>Tariff Duties</u> paid.

<u>Opium concealed in packages of treasure: High Court reverses verdict of Shenp'ant'ing in case of one of accused, another appeals to Peking: Commissioner awaiting instructions as to disposal of dollars, etc.</u>

    The dollars won't run away and with all these appeals going on we had better keep the cases unsettled for a bit.

                  Yours truly,

E. Tanant, Esquire,
    Wenchow.

S/O
No. 166

CUSTOM HOUSE,

Wenchow, 15. August, 1919.

Sir,

CHANGE OF TARIFF.

In my S/O No. 165 I reported having received a petition objecting to levy of Transit dues as per 1919 new Tariff on goods having paid Import duty as per 1902 Tariff. I have, since, received your Circular No. 2961 and gave instructions to issue drawbacks for the excess duty collected.

Yours respectfully,

[A.—42]

S/O

INSPECTORATE GENERAL OF CUSTOMS.

PEKING, 26 AUG 1919 19   .

Dear Sir,

I am directed by the Inspector General to inform you that your S/O letter No. 166, dated 13th August, has been duly received.

Yours truly,

W. H. Chapman
Private Secretary.

C. E. Tanant, Esq.,
Wenchow

S/O No. 167.   Wenchow 20. August, 19

Sir,

RECLAIMING, FILLING UP, AND BUNDING STRIP OF FORESHORE. (References : S/O Lrs Nos 164/5.)

I duly received your S/o letter of 29. July enquiring about cost of proposed reclamation and value of the land, and, in reply, I beg to refer you to my despatch No. 5400 which I had to write in reply to yours No. 886/74,419.

SHORT LEAVE.

I have now sent you a telegram asking for two months short leave for September and October. I did not apply sooner for I wanted first to have my desk clear and I think it is now fairly up-to-date. My reasons for asking are that I have not had one day's leave since my return from long leave $3\frac{1}{2}$ years ago, and I would like to have a little rest which would enable me to have my teeth arranged which cannot be done in a hurried visit to a dentist as it means extraction of some old teeth and new plate, and this takes time.

On

On the other hand my wife has been suffering from rhumatisms. I wanted to send her like I did last year to Unzen, but the actual quarantine of 3 full days at the Nagasaki lazaret stops her, and if you will grant me the leave I will first proceed to Yokohama to avoid the quarantine and be attended there for my teeth, and afterwards come back via Unzen. This seems a rather round about way but it is the only possible one to avoid the quarantine, and the extra travelling expenses will be paid by the difference of dentists charges between Japan and Shanghai.

Yours respectfully,

INSPECTORATE GENERAL OF CUSTOMS,

S/O

PEKING, 4th September, 1919.

Dear Mr Tanant,

I have duly received your S/O letter No. 167 of 20th August.

<u>Commissioner asks for 2 months' leave.</u>

This application causes difficulty as I have no one I can send to relieve you. I hardly think Matsubara is senior enough to have charge. If I can arrange it a little later I will do so.

Yours truly,

C. E. Tanant, Esquire,
   Wenchow.

CUSTOM HOUSE,

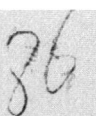

S/O No. 168.   Wenchow, 21st August 19 19

Sir,

CASH DEPOSIT GUARANTEES.

A new steamer, the "Yung Shin", 999 tons, (old Butterfield and Swire "Tungchow"), is now plying between Shanghai-Hsing Hua (Fookien) and -Wenchow under I.W.S.N. Certificate, and again under Maritime Customs Register from Wenchow to Shanghai. She belongs to the Ningshao S.N. Co. but is chartered to a local company Yung Fu Han Yeh Kung Ssu. For the present she takes away only export cargoes but I understand she may in future also call here with import cargo. The only difficulty she has to contend with is the want of a wharf, the other companies not willing to let her use their own wharves and she has to remain in the stream.

The Agent has asked me to accept a guarantee so as to accelerate the ship's movements - i.e. landing under General Discharge Permit and passing cargo in advance, and as a suitable godown has been provided I made no objection. However when it came to to the signature of the usual steamers guarantee I was given as guarantors firms the solvability of which seems to be rather limited. So, seeing that the practice in vogue at some southern outports to accepting cash deposit guarantees is recognised in your Circular No. 2893, I asked the Agent to hand me Shanghai $1,000 to be deposited in the Hongkong and Shanghai Bank which has now been done.

        Yours respectfully,

[A.—42]

INSPECTORATE GENERAL OF CUSTOMS.

S/O

PEKING, 4 – IX – 1919.

Dear Sir,

I am directed by the Inspector General to inform you that your S/O letter No. 168, dated 21st August, has been duly received.

Yours truly,

C. A. Chapman

Private Secretary.

C. E. Tanant, Esq.,
Wenchow

S/O No. 169.   Wenchow   4. September 19

Sir,

MOVEMENTS OF OFFICIALS.

My despatch No. 3403 informed you of the Superintendent's departure on one month's leave. The reason is the funerals of his mother, but I am informed that he is also trying to obtain another post.

Similarly with the Taoyin who left yesterday ostensibly to go to the funerals of the late Tuchün Yang at Hangchow, but who nevertheless took his whole family away including an old mother 80 years old.

I understand both Sup't and Taoyin complain of the unruly spirit of the gentry who constantly defy their authority. As an example, here is a typical one. Some time ago the supporters of the Hsü family, evidently one of the most - if not the most influential clan in this city, wanted to put up a monument in the shape of a stone column, in the main street, in front of the Magistrate's Yamen, to the memory of the

the old Mr. Hsü, a former official who was drowned in the Poochi some 18 months ago. That family's opponents objected. The matter was finally reported to Hangchow to the Governor's decision, but unexpectedly a few nights ago without asking for more the promoters of the scheme had the monument put up by a gang of their supporters, probably the same lot which wanted to set fire to the Kwangchi last December when the old Hsü's son, their leader, was shot dead.

This can give you a fair idea of the repercussion in the provinces of the lack of authority of the Peking Government.

As to the Taoyin who was a friend of the late Tuchün, I presume his removal or retention will be an affair of private arrangement at Hangchow with the new Tuchün.

BOYCOTT.

The boycott affairs, notably those about rice, seem also to have a lot to do with the Taoyin's reported dissatisfaction.

Lately one or two attempts were made to dissuade Matsubara's cook from serving him, but as the man came back after short absences of $\frac{1}{2}$ a day or one day I thought better not to to interfere. Once also he was sending a note to one of the Japanese shops, and it was taken from his messenger and, I understand, carried to the Taoyin who ordered it to be transmitted to destination.

ATTEMPT TO STEAL OUR OWNERSHIP OVER STRIP OF FORESHORE.

My despatch No. 3406 informs you of the sale of the lot by the local Board of Official property, or to say better by the gentry, another instance of these people's daring. I hope you will sanction my request to send the Assistant-Engineer here promptly to report and start work. The only way with these people seems to answer them with their own arguments and render our occupancy effective. A fence and even the Government's decision in our favour will not satisfy them, and if we don't fill up and put up a shed I feel fairly sure they will some day take forcible possession of the lot just as they have put up the monument in front of the Magistrate's yamen.

Yours respectfully,

INSPECTORATE GENERAL OF CUSTOMS,

S/O PEKING, 18th September, 1919.

Dear Mr Tanant,

I have duly received your S/O letter No. 169 of 4th September.

<u>Attempt by local officials to encroach on Customs strip of foreshore: Commissioner hopes Assistant Engineer will be sent to Wenchow to report and start work of bunding and filling in; is putting up fence meanwhile.</u>

We have no Assistant Engineer yet to send. Get on with the fence!

Yours truly,

C. E. Tanant, Esquire,
    Wenchow.

S/O N: 170.   15. September 1919

Sir,

Commissioner's Short leave.

I beg to acknowledge and thank you for your S/O letter of 4th instant <u>re</u> my application for 2 months leave. When I telegraphed for it I was already somewhat under apprehension that it was rather late for my wife for a thermal season, but, as the leave could not be granted then, I am afraid within a month the weather will be too cold and it might even be dangerous to undertake a treatment just at the beginning of the cold season, so I think we must postpone the cure until next summer when the weather will be more favourable.

On the other hand I must have my teeth patched up in the meantime, and in this view I have now wired to ask you to grant me permission to go to Shanghai and stay there the space of time between two

steamers

steamers, which means altogether about eight days in Shanghai anf 4 days journey go and back. Matsubara is evidently rather young, but could, I think, be left in limited charge for that time so much the more as I would have the pay-sheets and other needed documents prepared and signed in advance so as not to occasion delays which one can never forestall.

Pilotage Regulations.

The Ningpo British Consul has informed me of his approval of the intended additions

1o. of the following note at the end of section 1 of Gen. Reg. VIII :" The provision concerning the colour of the Pilot Boat Flag is modified by Local Rule 21"., and

2o. of the following new Rule at the end of the Local Rules :" 21.- Pilot boat flag. The colour of the Pilot Boat Flag has been modified as follows : the upper horizontal half shall be white and the lower red". However his approval is subject to that of his Shanghai colleagues, and although he asked to avoid further delays in the prin to go on with this work, I think it safer to await notification of the general Consular assent to the change before proceeding with the printing as there is always the contingency of some remote objection.

Yours respectfully,

[A.—42]

S/O

INSPECTORATE GENERAL OF CUSTOMS.

PEKING, 30th Sept. 19 19.

Dear Sir,

I am directed by the Inspector General to inform you that your S/O letter No. 170, dated 15th September, 1919, has been duly received.

Yours truly,

W. A Chippen
Private Secretary.

C. E. Tanant, Esquire,

W E N C H O W.

S/O No. 171.   Wenchow   20. September 19

Sir,

Commissioner's short leave.

I beg to thank you for your telegram received last night, authorising me to go to Shanghai. Unfortunately all the trouble is lasted for the present. As you are aware by my S/O No. 168 we have a new Steamer Company, the Yung Fu Han Yeh Kungssu. That Company's object is to oust the China Merchants Co from the Wenchow - Shanghai run but the latter is not willing to submit and the two Companies have started competition by reducing their freight rates. This week, the Yungshin instead of coming here has been chartered to run to Hsing Hua between Foochow and Amoy, and at once the China Merchants also sent there the Kwangchi (our regular Shanghai liner), and accepted return freight for Hingpo, so we may not have another steamer before the 26th

26th and possibly later. Yesterday we had in port the largest of the 3 Ningpo small steamers, and I might have, for want of somrthing better, taken her, but she left after tiffin while your telegram only reached me in the evening. All this is most annoying for departure within a week might postpone my return til the 12th or 15th October, so I have decided to postpone my trip and to wait for my quarterly work and the Assistant Engineer's visit to be over. I only hope nothing untoward will happen in the meantime.

Change of Superintendent.

As hinted in my S/O No. 169 we heard yesterday by the latest Shanghai papers of the exchange of places by the Wenchow and the Soochow Superintendents. Personally I shall regret Mr. Chou Ssu-pei for he was very pleasant to deal with.

Nothing has been heard as yet of the Taoyin's movements.

Everything is fairly quiet here, but business is rather slack.

Yours respectfully,

INSPECTORATE GENERAL OF CUSTOMS,

S/O

PEKING, 30th September, 19 19

Dear Mr. Tanant,

I have duly received your S/O letter No. 171 of 20th September.

<u>Commissioner tenders his thanks for short leave granted but says that, owing to changes in steamer sailings, he has decided to postpone his trip until the quarterly work is over.</u>

    Could you not get " Liuhsing " to call in for you if, and when, she goes to Santuao lights ? I don't know when she makes the trip.

Yours truly,

C. E. Tanant, Esquire,
    Wenchow.

CUSTOM HOUSE,

S/O No. 172.

Wenchow, 6. October, 1919

Sir,

ATTEMPT TO STEAL OUR OWNERSHIP OVER STRIP OF FORESHORE.

Reference : Wenchow despatches Nos. 3406, 3416, and 3420 now posted).

I am not at ease at all the way this case drags on. The Acting Superintendent had told me he would refer the case to the Ministry, having had to deal with a similar case at Chinkiang, and instead of this it now appears he began by referring it to Hangchow. However he now says he relied to the Ministry direct pending reply from the Hangchow board of Official property. In view of all these delays I thought better to inform you by wire, for I think that intervention by you at this stage would if not bring an immediate settlement of the case, anyhow predispose the Ministry in our favour, and punishment of the Official concerned and of the two Hsü would not fail to bring back to the Customs a little of its prestige which has been sapped by the apparent

indifference

indifference we have shown ever since our arrival here forty years ago in all those questions of property.

The TAOYIN has returned, brought back specially by the China Merchants S. S. Haean on her way to Foochow. (Cost to the Company : $50. Pilotage, several tons of coal, and one day's ship upkeep)

The SUPERINTENDENT has not yet returned.

CHOLERA has been very bad at Juian and Pingyang, these two cities in whose neighbourhood the Shanghai firm Slowe & Co wanted to send their agent to purchase hog's lard under Outward Transit Passes. This agent died here a few days ago, also from Cholera. It is still prevailing here, but not so bad as in the neighbourhood.

Yours respectfully,

INSPECTORATE GENERAL OF CUSTOMS,

S/O

PEKING, 15th October, 1919.

Dear Mr Tanant,

I have duly received your S/O letter No. 172 of 6th October.

<u>Attempt to encroach on Customs strip of foreshore: Commissioner wires to I.G. asking him to intervene</u>

I got your telegram but I don't want to intervene at this stage.

Yours truly,

C. E. Tanant, Esquire,
  Wenchow.

CUSTOM HOUSE,

S/O No. 173.　　　　　Wenchow, 18th October 1919

Sir,

COMMISSIONER'S SHORT LEAVE.

I beg to thank you for your S/O letter of 30th September and for so kindly suggesting to get "Liuhsing" to call for me on her return from the Santu Lights. I am, however, informed by Captain Kitcair of the "Pingching" that "Liuhsing" is not due there now, having visited Santu in August so I cannot wait for her.

As I informed you in my telegram of 15th I am leaving to-morrow morning and hope to be back at the end of the month or the beginning of November.

　　　　　　　　　Yours respectfully,

[A.—42]

S/O

INSPECTORATE GENERAL OF CUSTOMS.

PEKING, 29 OCT 1919 19

104

Dear Sir,

I am directed by the Inspector General to inform you that your S/O letter No. 173, dated 18 Oct., has been duly received.

Yours truly,

b. A Dippell

Private Secretary.

C.E. Tanant, Esq.,

Wenchow

CUSTOM HOUSE,

S/O No. 174.

Wenchow, 4. November, 19 19

Sir,

COMMISSIONER'S SHORT LEAVE.

I beg to report, in continuation of my last S/O letter, that I duly returned from Shanghai on the 2nd, and that my Assistants report that nothing unusual occurred during my absence.

INSPECTION OF CUSTOMS BUILDINGS.

The Revenue Cruiser "Pingching" brought up the new Assistant Engineer, Mr. Oswald, before I left for Shanghai and he went all over our property and buildings and agreed with me that repairs to my house and furniture are much needed. The Examiner's house is sound notwithstanding former staff complaints. As to the foreshore lot he took all the necessary data.

OFFICIALS.

The TAOYIN is again leaving for Shanghai tomorrow for two weeks.

The Superintendent, Mr. Chou Ssu-pei, transferred to Soochow, did not return from his month leave in September, and is waiting at

SHANGHAI

Shanghai that Mr. Yang Shih-sheng be ready to vacate his post at Soochow.

The District Magistrate, has been changed.

Yours respectfully,

[A.—42]

S/O

INSPECTORATE GENERAL OF CUSTOMS,

PEKING, 1 NOV 1919   19   .

Dear Sir,

I am directed by the Inspector General to inform you that your S/O letter No. 174 dated 4 Nov , has been duly received.

Yours truly,

W. H. Chapple

Private Secretary.

C. E. Tarrant, Esq.,

Wenchow

CUSTOM HOUSE,

S/O No. 175.

Wenchow, 28. November, 1919.

Sir,

COMMISSIONER'S INCREASE OF PAY.

I beg to acknowledge receipt of your despatch granting me an increase of pay, and to expr express my sincere thanks for it.

STEAMERS MOVEMENTS.

In my S/O No. 168 I reported the formation by local merchants of a new Steamer Company - Yung Fu Nan Yeh Kung-ssu - to run a steamer chartered from the Ning Shao S.N.Co., between Shanghai, Fookien, and Wenchow in opposition to the China Merchants S.N.Co., which has, by its arrangement with B.& S. and J.M.&Co., the big Shipping Companies, a practical monopoly of shipping at this port. The affair has failed lamentably, for The China Merchants Co. first let them establish themselves, charter the ship, rent godowns, and incur various other expenses, and only after two months did it start lowering freights to Fookien as well as to Wenchow; and as the China Merchants steamers call more often than the new Company's solitary steamers call here more often than the new Company's solitary steamer, which took from 10 to 12 days for the round trip, the local supporters dropped the new Company and resumed shipping their goods by the China Merchants Co After 3 months the total loss amounted, it is reported, to $50,000., the business was stopped, and the affair is causing several law suits in Shanghai. The local Manager who had deposited, through this Office, $1,000. with the Hongkong & Shanghai Bank, Shanghai, as Cash Deposit Guarantee, asked me by letter to have his Guarantee cancelled and to return him his $1,000. which was eventually done by the Bank

JAPANESE BOYCOTT.

Students started recently to search the China Merchants steamers on arrival from Shanghai and seized one smuggled basket of glassware which they declared to be of Japanese origin, and smashed it and took it away. The same day a small parcel perfumery addressed to my governess was torn open by the same students on being brought ashore by one of the ships boys. I wrote at once to the Superintendent

to

to the Superintendent to object, and he
replied he would request the Taoyin and
Magistrate to stop the students from searching
No more trouble has since been reported.
OFFICIALS.
The Taoyin and the Superintendent are still
away. The former is waiting for a larger
ship than the Kwangchi to bring him back
from Shanghai, and the Superintendent is
awaiting at Shanghai that the Soochow Sup't
be ready to vacate his post. Mr. Yang, the
Soochow Sup't, is said to be at Peking, and
it looks as if he will stay there until
the appointment of a new Finance Minister.

The Hangchow Postal Commissioner has been
inspecting his Wenchow Office.
FOUNDERING OF A TEA JUNK SEIZED BY THE N.C.
STAFF.

Our N.C. Staff stopped, on information, during
the night of the 23rd, a junk loaded with
65 baskets Unfired Tea, trying to pass Wenchow without reporting. The Junk was heavily
loaded and while anchored to await the tide
to bring it into harbour, it foundered on
account of a very strong wind. The master
and crew bolted subsequently. 26 baskets were
salved

salved by boat people who picked them up floating in the River. I insisted on having them handed over to us, promising a small reward if I could resell them, but I am afraid there won't be any reward, for, the tea put up for auction yesterday did not find any purchasers. I also hear that the junk was subsequently raised by the master, but being in bad condition again foundered.

Yours respectfully,

[A.—42]

INSPECTORATE GENERAL OF CUSTOMS.

S/O

PEKING, 9 DEC 1919 19

Dear Sir,

I am directed by the Inspector General to inform you that your S/O letter No. 175, dated 28 Nov., has been duly received.

Yours truly,

W. H. Chapper
Private Secretary.

C. E. Tanant, Esq.,
Wenchow

CUSTOM HOUSE,

S/O No. 176.

Wenchow, 16. December, 19

Sir,

OUT-DOOR GRIEVANCES.

Your S/o No. 29 was duly handed over to my Foreign Out-door Staff to read when received, in fact before I passed it to my Assistant, and when I called for its return, the same day, I was told by Mr. Ahlberg that they wished to keep it until next day to take a copy of it. I replied it could not be done as the Staff are not allowed to take copies of Circulars.

A few days ago Mr. Ahlberg referred to that S/O Circular and told me they had received a long Circular-memorandum from the O.D. Staff Committee reporting their visit to Peking and stating seriatim all the grievances brought forth at your interview and your replies. He took advantage to bring forth again the argument that most Tidesurveyors

know

know little or nothing about Examination work and that their interference in Examiners' work causes a lot of the ill-feeling which is now openly discussed. In his opinion appraisers should be under the direct orders of the In-door Deputy Commr. I suppose he has particularly in view the Shanghai Office, but this if granted would cause ill-feeling with Assistants as regards relative positions. However I thought better to mention this to you.

SUGGESTION TO ISSUE F. P. CIRCULARS OR STAFF INSTRUCTIONS TO EXAMINERS.

In connection with the above I take leave to refer you to the last part of my despatch No. 339L re Revised Import Tariff, 1/19, in which I suggested to provide Examiners with copies of Factory Products Circulars. Your reply - despatch No. 385/74,411 - only dealt with the Tariff question and did not refer to my suggestion. However I take leave to revert to it and beg to suggest, if F.P. Circulars cannot be distributed to Examiners, that their contents be made known to them in the form of Instructions something like the Postal Instructions. This, I have no doubt

doubt would encourage them to detect substitutions of Factory products which are one of the threatening dangers on account of the practical impossibility to control Shanghai Passes.

REVISED IMPORT TARIFF, 1919.

A new issue of the Revised Import Tariff, 1919, has again been received - the 3rd since last May - but again without the explanations of your Circulars Nos 2948 and 2952, which could advantageously be inserted in interleaves, and I wrote again to suggest it to the Stat. Sec. As I said, this would make the publication homogeneous and facilitate Staff work.

OFFICIALS.

The Question of exchange of the Wenchow-Soochow Superintendents is still unsettled, and my old Sup't continues to wait at Shanghai.

The TAOYIN returned two weeks ago and announced that he would leave by the end of this month. I understand that he is a candidate to the Ningpo Taoyinship which will be vacant in a couple of months.

Yours respectfully,

INSPECTORATE GENERAL OF CUSTOMS,

S/O   PEKING, 30th December, 1919.

Dear Mr Tanant,

I have duly received your S/O letter No. 176 of 16th instant.

<u>Suggestion that Factory Products Circulars should be issued to Examiners.</u>

The examiners should certainly have a copy for reference!

Yours truly,

C. E. Tanant, Esquire,
    Wenchow.

1920 年

CUSTOM HOUSE,

S/O No. 177.

Wenchow, 16th January 1920.

Sir,

STAFF: MATSUBARA SICK.

I intended writing a few days ago but suddenly Mr. Matsubara fell sick and I am rather busy attending to everything. He has been laid up since the 10th with influenza and does not seem to improve.

FIRES.

The end of 1919 was marked by a big fire in the main street at noon on 30th December. There was a blow from the north and the fire soon covered a very large area. In all some 250 houses, or rather rooms, were burnt, with a loss estimated at $150,000.

The same night there were 2 more fires one of which resulting in the death of one baby.

There

There have since been 2 more fires.

The weather has been very dry, and wells and sewers, are practically dry and with the local poor fire appliances nothing stops fires but high walls.

CHINESE FACTORY PRODUCTS.

I take leave to refer you to my despatches Nos. 3443 and 3444.

The Sia Shih Chen Hsing Factory and the Chekiang Tsai Cheng Ting should be properly rebuked, the first one for complaining of our detention of his cargo before it was actually examined by us, and the second for having reported the case to the Ministry of Finance before waiting for the Superintendent's investigations.

As to the Chen Hsing firm they are annoyed at my refusing to recognise their yüntan for parcels sent by post, and they also evidently from perusal of the Hangchow Commissioner's despatch had the same trouble at Shanghai with their packages sent by rail instead

instead of by ordinary ships; but that is no reason why they should complain of detention before the goods arrive at destination. The Sia Shih Tung Chuan Weiyuan probably advises them to complain as he is the first one to blame for issuing the yüntan and he probably heard of my refusing to accept his yüntan for postal parcels.

HARBOUR REGULATIONS.

I received yesterday a letter from the Ningpo British Consul informing me that the Harbour Regulations first approved by you, had been approved by the Diplomatic Body. As I have not yet received your reply to my despatch No. 3433 informing you of the Shui-wu Ch'u's modifications to your text I thought better to wire at once to inform you of the Diplomatic Body's approval so as to enable you to settle the matter with the Shui-wu Ch'u.

CHANGES

CHANGES OF OFFICIALS.

There has been a change of provincial Taoyins by which Mr. Huang Ching-lan, the Wenchow Taoyin, is transferred to Ningpo. The one from Ningpo will replace that of Hangchow who will go to Ching Hua, and the actual Ching Hua Taoyin, Mr. Chao Tseng-fan, will come to Wenchow where he was Taoyin 2 years ago. The whole movement may take several months to be completed. Mr. Huang left on the 10th instant and an Officiating Taoyin, Mr. Yin Chi (殷濟) has come from Peking to act in the meantime.

The Superintendent is still at Shanghai, and I hear he may go to Peking to settle the question of the Soochow Superintendentship.

The Chih Shih who had been appointed 3 months ago has been removed on account of trouble with the students.

A

A new Yang Kwang Chu Weiyuan has also been appointed lately. It is said that he is a mere figure head the Yang Kwang Revenue being farmed to Mr. Yang Chen-hsin local member of the Provincial Assembly (the same Mr. Yang who tried to help me in the purchase of the land adjoining the Commissioner's House, which purchase fell through as already reported).

Yours respectfully,

INSPECTORATE GENERAL OF CUSTOMS,

PEKING, 27th January, 1920.

Dear Mr. Tanant,

I have duly received your S/O letter No. 177 of 16th instant.

<u>Chinese Factory Products: suggesting that Sia Shih Chen Hsing Factory and Chekiang Tsai Cheng T'ing be properly rebuked; the former for complaining that cargo not yet examined by Customs had been detained; the latter for reporting case to Ministry of Finance before waiting for Supt's investigations.</u>

This will right itself I think. If there is any rebuking to be done we can leave others to do it!

<u>Harbour Regulations: approved by the Diplomatic Body; Shui-wu Ch'u's modifications of text.</u>

I am in correspondence with the Ch'u concerning their modifications of the standard text.

Yours truly,

Tanant, Esquire,
Wenchow.

S/O No. 178.   Wenchow 24. January, 20

Sir,

STAFF : Mr. MATSUBARA is better and I hope that he will resume work in a few days. Mr. Ahlberg whose resignation has been accepted from 31st March asked me to issue him when the time comes a copy of his Memo of Service. May I do so or must he apply to you for it ?

CHINESE FACTORY PRODUCTS : ISSUE OF SPECIAL EXEMPTION CERTIFICATES TO GOODS BEARING UNREGISTERED TRADE MARKS.

In my despatches Nos. 3443 and 3444 re Chen Hsing Factory Socks I suggested that Registered Trade Marks should be stated on all S.E.C. or Yuntan and C.C.s. I now have a new case of Nan Yang Brothers Soap and Candles with Trade Marks not stated in Circ. 2613. It seems that a practice has been established to issue S.E.C.s irrespective of
                                                    Trade

Trade marks as long as the goods they cover came out from factories mentioned in Circulars and my refusal to honour such documents as cover goods with unregistered Trade marks may create some slight annoyance for a few days, but if attention is to be paid to the principle established by F. P. Circulars that only registered goods are to be granted the privilege of paying only one duty, then I do not see how we can act otherwise but to pay strict attention to the Trade marks.

But, again, such minute examination will involve more work on the Staff, and perhaps require more personnel. On the other hand, according to actual Circulars, the output of some factories is to be passed at the one duty rate without apparently Trade marks. Will those factories be required to register Trade marks?

For improvement of trade generally the non-enforcement of Trade marks would be most advisable, but as long as we differentiate between factory and other products, and even, as regards factories, between the products of those

registered

registered and of those unregistered, I am afraid it is difficult not to insist on the goods being in accordance with Circular instructions.

Yours respectfully,

[signature]

INSPECTORATE GENERAL OF CUSTOMS,

S/O

PEKING, 3rd February, 1920.

Dear Mr. Tanant,

I have duly received your S/O letter No. 178 of 24th January.

<u>Chinese Factory Products : question of issuing Special Exemption Certificates to goods bearing UNREGISTERED trade marks.</u>

Let me see your correspondence with Shanghai on this subject please !

Yours truly,

E. Tanant, Esquire,
   Wenchow.

S/O. No. 179.

CUSTOM HOUSE,

Wenchow, 7th February 1920.

Sir,

STAFF:

I have again to refer to Mr. Ahlberg's resignation. He has now informed me that he first booked his passage per "Shinyo Maru" leaving Shanghai 4th April, but as I am not willing to relieve him from duty before the end of March (as I do not know when his successor will be appointed and arrive), and also owing to incertitude of Wenchow-Shanghai steamers movements he is unable to book firm and in such circumstance he has written to the Shipping Company to change his departure per S.S. "Korea Maru" leaving Shanghai 6th May. He is therefore willing to stay here on duty until 20/25 April and I told him I would inform you accordingly, as it may facilitate Staff transfers.

BRITISH

BRITISH CONSUL'S VISIT:

    Mr. A. J. Martin, Acting British Consul for Ningpo and Wenchow, paid a visit to Wenchow - arriving on 31st January and leaving on 3rd February - ostensibly for performing the marriage of two of the C.I. missionaries. But I have since heard from the Acting Superintendent that he took up the question of the <u>Yang Kwang Chüan levied on the kerosene oil</u> imported by the Chinese agent <u>of the Asiatic Petroleum Co.</u> It seems that this agent who is a Chinese subject and owner of a large firm here paid the tax heretofore but has refused lately to pay.

    The Superintendent enquired whether the oil imported by this agent was duty paid on importation, or paid duty here and whether it paid on going inland. I replied the oil is always covered by E.C.s which should free it from taxation while in port

as

as the whole of Wenchow is open to foreign residence there being no settlement or concession. As to sending the oil inland I said it is optional to the shipper to pay our Transit Dues or Yang Kwang Chüan on leaving port for inland.

From the conversation it seems that the Superintendent and Taoyin are of opinion that the Yang Kwang Chüan should be collected here on importation because the agent is a Chinese firm, but to t is I said that if such was the argument the foreign firm would turn round by appointing a foreigner, would it be for a couple of months only, to act as the firm's representative. I do not know what decision will be taken.

ROAD OF ACCESS TO HAITANSHAN (ASSISTANT's QUARTERS).

This road was deviated over a year ago as may be seen by reference to various

Summaries

Summaries of non-urgent Chinese correspondence
The principal of the Anglo-Chinese College at the beginning declined to have anything to do with the case as he said his title-deeds were in order. I had therefore to apply to the authorities for recognition of our rights and straightening and enlargement of the new road, but although a small bridge was built in continuation of the new road, the road itself is still too narrow (6 feet) in places, and I informed the Sup't that I could not be satisfied with it. As the British Consul has been kept aware of the question by the College, I thought better to discusss it with him on the spot, and I saw that he backs up the College. However the question is in the hands of the Chinese authorities and if they do not get us a proper road we shall be able to ask for a compensation as regards enlargement of the Assistant's quarters as recorded in my last letter to the Sup't (January non-urgent Chinese correspondence). Mr. MATSUBARA is all right again and returned to duty on the 26th January.

Yours respectfully,

INSPECTORATE GENERAL OF CUSTOMS,

S/O

PEKING, 17th February, 1920.

Dear Mr. Tanant,

I have duly received your S/O letter No. 179 of 7th instant.

<u>Kerosene Oil imported by Chinese Agent of Asiatic Petroleum Co.: British Consul takes up question with Chinese officials of payment of Yang Kwang Chüan on shipments to Interior.</u>

It is of course the old, old question — "What is port and where does inland begin?"

Yours truly,

C. E. Tanant, Esquire,
    Wenchow.

CUSTOM HOUSE,

S/O No. 180.

Wenchow, 11. February, 1920.

Sir,

CARGO CERTIFICATE REFORM : DUPLICATES OF SHANGHAI COASTWISE EXPORT APPLICATIONS NEEDED AS WELL AS THOSE OF RE-EXPORTS.

Matsubara's attack of influenza obliged me to run the whole Office for two good weeks, and though rather too busy at times, I am glad of the opportunity it gave me again to see in detail the working of the General Office which I could not see so effectively when the Assistant attends the Office. As a result I was rather dissatisfied of the way D. P. C. cargo and notably Medicines are lumped in Shanghai Cargo Certificates, a practice which causes waste of time and extra work here without any appreciable saving of work and time at Shanghai, while it facilitates brokers malpractices and notably the indiscriminate use of old passes to cover lots of about the same weight not entitled to them.

This may have existed for some time but had not struck me before. In any case I thought better to call the Shanghai Office attention to these defects and ask that they be corrected. The Shanghai Office, unfortunately is always extremely busy and it is hard to m make its staff accept suggestions from a small port, and seeing the reply I now received from de Luca himself who suggests to check D. P. C. cargo from Shanghai in the same manner as the Shanghai Office checks imports from abroad, I have not the courage to go further in correspondence with that Office on that subject, and this will explain you why I wrote my despatch No. 3450 asking that as duplicates of re-export applications are to be handed in by the public, similarly duplicate applications be required for exports to Coast ports. I hope that with the copies of the various Memos exchanged on the subject with Shanghai, I made myself clear enough and that you will agree that my request is not excessive, and, if granted, will work in the Service interest.

CHINESE FACTORY PRODUCTS : QUESTION OF ISSUING S. E. C. TO GOODS BEARING UNREGISTERED TRADE MARKS

I am mailing this day my despatch No.3451 transmitting copy of the correspondence with Shanghai called for by your S/O Lr. of 3rd inst

The

The main isue of the case is that the Shanghai General Office argues that the single duty treatment is extended to all the products of a factory once the factory concerned is duly registered in Peking, while I maintain that the single duty treatment is only grantable for the present to the goods covered by registered Trade marks. In the mean time I am passing the goods covered by S. E. C. unless they disagree in quality as in the Tsuan case or in quantity as in the Nan Yang Soap case.

REMOVAL OF MARKS OF FOREIGN GOODS.

While on this subject of cargo I have had two rather curious cases recently : one of Cotton Coatings which might be Japanese, English or even Chinese, without any marks or labels, declared as Artificial Silk and covered by a Shanghai E. C. for Artificial Silk ; and another of Yarn-dyed striped brocades wrapped up in David Sassoon's wrappings and packed in an old packing case of W. Little & Co. The Shanghai Office admits substitutions but without being able to indicate the origin of the substituted goods which the two foreign firms consulted

decline

decline to recognize as coming from them, and I am wondering whether they are not Japanese goods unsalable on account of the boycott, whose marks were removed and which were repacked in foreign goods boxes.

MILITARY RICE.

The Military authorities want to export Rice to Amoy for the troops, and an Officer showed me an Official telegram from Hangchow informing him that the Luchün-pu had authorised the exportation, but as I have no telegram he asked me to wire to you, but I declined, advising him to apply to the Sup't. I added that he could export to Amoy on payment of duty at the condition that the Governor would withdraw his prohibition. As I am afraid of private speculation I wrote to the Sup't to inform him of my refusal and I sent him a copy of the 6 rules transmitted in your Circ. No. 2943.

MAILS.   Our last ship before the Chinese New Year will leave on the 17th, and we shall then have no steamers for 10 or 15 days.

SUPERINTENDENT's appointment not settled yet.

     Yours respectfully,

[A.—42]

S/O

INSPECTORATE GENERAL OF CUSTOMS,

PEKING, 2nd March, 1920.

Dear Sir,

I am directed by the Inspector General to inform you that your S/O letter No. 180, dated 11th ultimo, has been duly received.

Yours truly,

W. H Chapman

Private Secretary.

C.E. Tanant, Esquire,

Wenchow.

CUSTOM HOUSE,

S/O No. 181.   Wenchow, 14th Feby. 19 20

Sir,

PENALTY FOR RE-EXPORT UNDER WRONG SHANGHAI PASSES OF FOREIGN PRODUCE UNIDENTIFIABLE.

I am now posting my despatch No. 3454 asking, with reference to foreign Re-exports from Shanghai, to fine one duty instead of cancelling E.C., and collecting again Import duty where marks and numbers of packages do not agree and where there is no intention to defraud, and I hope you will admit of the good reason of my suggestion; we have now a chance to stop, perhaps only partially, the Shanghai trade in old passes, and I think we should not miss it.

FACTORY PRODUCTS CIRCULARS:

In my S/O. No. 176 of 16th December I suggested the advisability to give

Examiners

Examiners a copy of Factory Products Circulars, and in your S/O letter of 30th December you replied that they should certainly have a copy for reference. I therefore wrote to the Statistical Secretary as follows: "I submitted recently to the I.G. the desirability to provide Examiners with F.P Circulars so as to keep them informed of the appearance of new factory products and their treatment, and in his reply the I.G. said: "The Examiners should certainly have a copy for reference".

Such being the case I shall be obliged if you will issue to this Office a complete set of previous Factory Products Circulars with Index and slips, and in future provide us with one extra copy of F.P. Circulars and slips for the Examiner's Office."

I have now received the following reply: "As regards your request that a
complete

complete set of F.P. Circulars, with index, be sent you for the use of your Examiner, I have to say that it has not been Customary for this Department to provide copies of these Circulars for the use of Examiners, that to do so generally would mean a much larger issue than is at present printed, and consequently increased expenditure, and that I must have the direct authority of the Inspector General before introducing the innovation.

Assuming that each of these Circulars is made the subject of a brief Commissioner's order to the effect that such and such products of such and such a factory are placed on the privileged list and will pay a single duty at such and such a rate, it is not clear to me what possible use an Examiner can make of these voluminous pages of print, composed mainly of repetitions of matter which is of no concern
to

to him and is certainly not likely to assist him at all in his primary duty of checking all the items of a merchant's declaration. My own experience has been that the less an Examiner is diverted from this simple duty - i.e. the less he picks and chooses - the more reliable and valuable is his work.

In the very exceptional cases where special marks to distinguish the products of a factory are illustrated in the Circular, extra sheets for the Examiners' use can of course be supplied. I do not know whether this will satisfy your requirements; if not it will be necessary to refer your application to the Inspector General".

I dare say Mr. Unwin objections are right at certain points of view, but nevertheless the constantly recurring appearance of new F.P. Circulars makes the issue of orders in the general order book, to be re-copied re-copied in the O.D. Staff order book, and then again in a special book to be kept by the Examiners Office for the purpose, rather cumbersome. I therefore take leave to revert to my original suggestion that some printed orders or instructions be issued for distribution to the Examiners Offices, and also to each Examiner personally, giving names of Factories and names of products with their registered trade marks, all in English and Chinese, and also names of products exempted <u>pro tem</u> from Maritime or Native Customs duties, with duration of exemption, and generally such like information.

The issue of such lists would be eminently needed if we are to insist on S.E.C. goods bearing their registered trade marks. In fact Mr. Speakman's list of Cotton Socks made in Shanghai, and Mr. Chief Appraiser J. Ferguson's list of Toilet soaps
manufactured

manufactured in Shanghai are a beginning of ~~the~~ lists, as should be printed, issued, and kept au courant by the addition of slips.

Yours respectfully,

INSPECTORATE GENERAL OF CUSTOMS,

S/O PEKING, 2nd March, 1920.

Dear Mr. Tanant,

I have duly received your S/O letter No. 181 of 14th February.

<u>Factory Products Circulars : re extra copy for use of Examiners.</u>

I didn't mean each Examiner should have a complete copy of the issue but all should have ready and easy access to the Circulars !

Yours truly,

[signature]

S.Tanant, Esquire,
　　Wenchow.

S/O No. 182.

CUSTOM HOUSE,

Wenchow, 11. March, 1920.

Sir,

Military Rice.

In my S/O No. 180 I informed you of the request by the Military Authorities to allow them to export Military rice to Amoy under Tuchün Huchao which I refused as no Authority had been received from you. Later on I sent you in my February Summary of non-urgent Chinese correspondence a copy of the letter which I wrote to the Sup't in this connection to warn him against the rescission that would be thus established of the prohibition to export rice, and in which I also sent him a copy of the six rules concerning the exportation of military rice appended to Circular No. 2943.

The Shui-wu Ch'u Authority and yours were duly received subsequently to allow exportation of 5,000 Shih of rice, evidently from Wenchow, and now I transmit in my despatch No. 3460

copy

copy of a Sup't's despatch informing me that one half of the quantity will be exported from Wenchow, while the other half, 2500 bags - no weight stated - have already been ex orted by junk from Pingyang. The Sup't does not seemt t to have raised any objection to this exportati through one of his stations in direct defiance of the rules transmitted in your Circ. No. 2943 In favt he never sent me a copy of those rules while generally I am flooded with copies of unimportant matters, and it remains to know whether the Shui-wu Ch'u transmitted him the rules. Just before receipt of this despatch I had received a petition from local people warning me against smuggling under the guise of Military rice! The case is typical of the Government's want of power over the military chieftains doings, but if it is so could'nt the Gov ernment be told to stop filling up our archives with instructions which itself is powerless or unwilling to enforce ?

The <u>Provincial Camphor Monopoly</u> the establishment of which I now report in despatch
No.

No. 3461 - N.C. No.232 - is another instance of the same Government's weakness. How could such a venture be started without the Cental Government's sanction when we hear of re-afforestation schemes, etc. The whole affair seems started to get hold and dispose of rapidly - within three years - of all the old trees which can only be found nowadays on public lands, around temples, etc., and which local people heretofore were afraid of touching, and the only attempt at replanting seems to be only in cases when it will be specially specified for by the sellers. I have rarely seen such an undisguised attempt to coin money at the public's detriment.

They speak in the correspondence of the <u>Sulphur and Saltpetre provincial Bureau</u>. Well here is an example of that Office doings. We had recently an importation of Sulphur without value stated on the application and on asking for it it was given at $15. per picul, the retail price of the Monopoly. At Shanghai where it is imported from it is valued at Hk.Tls. 3.60 per picul, ~~and this is Hk Ts. 1. more than its value in Japan.~~

Yours respectfully,

INSPECTORATE GENERAL OF CUSTOMS.

S/O

PEKING, 23rd March, 1920

Dear Mr. Tanant,

I have duly received your S/O letter No. 182 of 11th instant.

<u>Rice smuggling by Military : Chinese Government instructions ignored by own officials : cannot Government be told to stop filling up Customs archives with instructions which it is powerless or unwilling to enforce ?</u>

I am afraid not.

Yours truly,

[signature]

D.E.Tanant, Esquire,
    Wenchow.

CUSTOM HOUSE,

S/O No. 183.

Wenchow 15. March, 1920.

Sir,

Your Circulars re Superannuation and retirement schemes have been received and created, I may say, a very favourable feeling and I am sure the whole Staff here will be thankful to you and to Mr. Acheson for the trouble and worry its elaboration must have caused you. There are of course as in every new scheme a few details lacking of "mise au point" and I am now mailing my despatch No. 3462 asking for certain explanations.

There is a point, however, which I want to refer you but which I thought better to keep separate for this letter, and that is the case of Lushih and other employés appointed through the Superintendent. Your grant of a pension to employés and particularly Chinese employés who never dreamed until

a

a few years ago of such a thing as a pension, should make the appointments in the Service still more desirable than before. But Lushih are not entirely our own men. In the beginning they were men detached from the Superintendent's own staff and as such liable on the Sup't's transfer or withdrawal from the Government's service to follow their master. They soon found out it was more advantageous to stick to us, and on the other hand we preferred keeping men accustomed to their work than be obliged to take on new employés anytime a Sup't was moved, and we managed to make their appointment definitive though subject to Sup't's nomination, and that is what I am now objecting to, for I still have in my mind the difficulties the former Sup't, Mr. Mao, surrounded by a gang of rascals as experience has now proved at Chinkiang, tried to raise as regards some N.C. Ssushih (men of about same social standing) whom he wanted me to remove to make room for

for his candidates. And what are those candidates? none of his friends, generally, simply people, possibly friends of his own staff, ready to pay in cash or otherwise for the nomination, and now that the positions which we may give are comparatively so valuable, it is to be feared that when need of new Lushih or N.C. staff will occur we shall, more than before, only have the pick of the men who can be made to pay most, instead of the pick of the most capable men. Such being the case I cannot help taking leave to suggest that you put matter in that line to the Ch'u and ask to be allowed to select your own staff yourself. That in any case would be one less cause of squeeze.

Yours respectfully,

INSPECTORATE GENERAL OF CUSTOMS,

S/O

PEKING, 23rd March, 1920

Dear Mr. Tanant,

  I have duly received your S/O letter No. 183 of 15th instant.

<u>Suggesting that the Shui-wu Ch'u be asked to give I.G. power of appointment of new men to Lushih and N.C. Staff in view of unsatisfactory features of present system.</u>

  I see your point but so long as the Commissioner has power of dismissal we can always get rid of objectionable employès.

  Yours truly,

E. Tanant, Esquire,
 Wenchow.

CUSTOM HOUSE,

No. 184.

Wenchow, 30. March, 1920.

Sir,

SUPERANNUATION SCHEME AND APPOINTMENT OF LUSHIH AND N. C. STAFF.

I beg to acknowledge receipt of your S/O No. 23rd instant replying to my suggestion to have Lushih and N. C. Staff appointed by Commissioners instead of by Superintendent in which you tell me :" so long as the Commissioner has power of dismissal we can always get rid of objectionable employés". Yes, but it is just what the entourage of the Sup't would like, that we sack men by the dozen so as to have a chance to recommend new candidates and thus pocket the fee for each new recommendation or nomination, while it is the very thing I am aiming at stopping. Besides, at a Service point of view, changes of personnel work against Office routine and general efficiency.

MILITARY

Military Rice

I wired on the 22nd inst. to ask how many catties were to be pased for one shih I communicated your reply to the Sup't and the Commissariat Officer came at once and gave me a written promise to obtain an amended Huchao stating that one shih equals 142 catties. 2110 bags = 2500 shih of 120 catties had already been shipped, and the Officer then informed me that he would ship the balance, viz. 390 bags by the next I.W.S.N. steamer as the China Merchants steamer was full up. To-day he came back saying that the season is advanced, and that the rice is beginning to get mouldy, and also that steamer freight is too high, and he finally applied for permission to ship by junk. There being nothing against in the Authority nor in your Circ. No. 2943 whose instructions also apply to Native Customs, and it being an affair only of 390 bags, I allowed it but warned the Officer that in this particular case the rules had been utterly ignored, and that in future I Would insist on fulfilment of all regulations as fixed by the Lu-chiin Pu.

Yours respectfully

[A.—42]

S/O

INSPECTORATE GENERAL OF CUSTOMS.

PEKING, 9th April, 1920.

Dear Sir,

I am directed by the Inspector General to inform you that your S/O letter No. 184, dated 30th March, has been duly received.

Yours truly,

W. H. Chapple(?)
Private Secretary.

C. E. Tanant, Esquire,

Wenchow.

CUSTOM HOUSE,

S/O. No. 4.
National Loans.

Wenchow, 30th March 1920.

Sir,

NATIONAL LOANS STATEMENTS OF COLLECTION AND OF REMITTANCE.

I applied recently to the Statistical Department for the printing of Statements of Collection and Remittance of National Loans Funds as per pro forma appended to your S/O Circular No. 25.

The reply has been "This Department has not received instructions so far to print these forms, so that this part of your requisition cannot be supplied".

Such being the answer I take leave to suggest that you issue to the Statistical Department instructions to print and issue these Statements as Service forms.

Yours respectfully,

[A.—42]

S/O

INSPECTORATE GENERAL OF CUSTOMS,

PEKING, 9th April, 1920

Dear Sir,

I am directed by the Inspector General to inform you that your S/O letter No. 4 (National Loans) dated 30th March, has been duly received.

Yours truly,

W. H. Chap——
Private Secretary.

C.E. Tanant, Esquire,

Wenchow.

CUSTOM HOUSE,

S/O No. 185.

Wenchow 5. April, 1920.

Sir,

BUOYING OF SAND BANK AT MOUTH OF THE RIVER

With reference to my despatch No. 3466 I did not think advisable to discuss in my reply to the Coast Inspector the question of delays, thinking better to take it up in this letter for I can see well enough that the request is only made because the Haean Captain does not like to wait a few hours for the tide before crossing the bar. He wants to come up to the pontoon as quickly as possible anfd finish with his trip and that is all. But I have as well give you here an idea of the way the Company's business is managed.

They received their Shanghai Office telegram of 27th on Sunday 28th that the ship was clearing for Wenchow on 29th, and, as usual, the shippers were informed at once. The ship was delayed one day owing to fog, and

158

In the meantime it was arranged she would ship 4000 packages oranges, but up to 3 p.m. on the 1st (2nd, 3rd, and 4th being holidays) only 1500 had arrived and been passed. The Agent and one of the shippers then quietly came to ask me to pass the other 2500 pkgs in advance - without examination - and allow them to work on special permit on account of the long delay, but I refused and advised immediate clearance or postponement. This state of affairs happens constantly. What gain is there then that the ship comes in a few hours earlier or later ? If the Company is able to stand demurrage of one and two days should we occur such heavy expenditure as that required by an annual survey by a cruiser simply for the Captain's sake ? For it must be borne in mind that once the bar is buoyed it will be necessary to re-survey it at least once a year. When the question of charting the River from Wen-chau Island to the Harbour was raised by Mr. Tyler

Tyler 3 years ago Messrs Acheson and Steve were against it, but the survey was nevertheless undertaken, and a year afterwards I had to request the Coast Inspector to re-survey part of the River. It was certainly done but not to his staff liking!

I have also to add as regards the present demand that no complaint was heretofore received from the Company. The actual one is caused by Captain Wallace's transfer with his ship from the Foochow-Shanghai to the Wenchow-Shanghai run. Captain Wallace objected and was offered the command of the Hsinchi, the ship now on the Foochow-Shanghai run, but as the Company would not allow him to take over with him his steward with whom he has pecuniary arrangements concerning the ship's and passengers food allowances, he has so far refused to quit his ship, and is taking advantage of any chance to complain so as to arrive to his ends. This has been given to me by the Tidesurveyor as the cause of the whole affair.

Yours respectfully,

E. S. Canaval

[A.—42]

S/O

INSPECTORATE GENERAL OF CUSTOMS,

PEKING, April 14th, 19 20.

Dear Sir,

I am directed by the Inspector General to inform you that your S/O letter No. 185, dated 5th instant, has been duly received.

Yours truly,

W. H. Chappere

Private Secretary.

C.E. Tanant, Esquire,

Wenchow.

CUSTOM HOUSE,

S/O No. 186.

Wenchow, 10. April, 1920.

Sir,

DETENTION BY THE YANG KWANG CHŰ OF CAMPHOR OIL PASSED BY MARITIME CUSTOMS FOR EXPORTATION BY STEAMER.

  I have to report the detention by the Yang Kwang Chű of 4 tins camphor oil, out of a lot of 24 tins passed by the Maritime Customs for Foochow, while on the way from the Custom House to the steamer.

  On receipt of the applicant's petition I wrote at once to the Superintendent to ask for the release of the tins. The Superintendent called the next day and said he had got information that the oil belonged to a Chinese firm acting as agents for a Japanese firm, and that, as he is afraid of possible claim for damage, he had asked the Magistrate to whom the Yang Kwang Chű had transmitted the detained

detained oil (He says there are really 6 tins) to release the oil, but that the representative of the Provincial Camphor Bureau had objected and that the oil was being detained while that official was reporting to Hangchow for instructions.

I informed the Superintendent that I had already reported to you the establishment of the Bureau (vide Wenchow despatch No. 3461) and that you had instructed me to recognise its Huchao at the Native Custom (I.G. despatch No. 931/77,607) and only as regards Chinese merchants; but that no mention had been made of Maritime Customs recognition because his own despatch intimating the establishment of the Bureau had not mentioned the Maritime Customs, and besides the Bureau is a monopoly, and by treaty, no monopoly may be established.

I warned him that I took strong objection

objection to the detention of cargo passed at my Maritime Customs, and that if it was not released at once I would not only object on account of the merchant, but that I would complain to you of the high action of the Yang Kwang Chü. He agreed to this and said that when the case is over I should again object and that he would transmit my despatch to the Ts'ai-cheng Pu.

    I am waiting for a few days to see how the case will turn out, before reporting by despatch.

                  Yours respectfully,

[A.—42]

S/O

INSPECTORATE GENERAL OF CUSTOMS.

PEKING, April 20th, 1920.

Dear Sir,

I am directed by the Inspector General to inform you that your S/O letter No. 186, dated 10th instant, has been duly received.

Yours truly,

Private Secretary.

C.E.Tanant, Esquire,

Wenchow.

Inspectorate General of Customs,
Peking, April 14th, 1920.

Confidential.

Dear Mr. **Tanant**,

I enclose for your information a copy of the remarks I recently addressed to the foreign members of the Shanghai Customs Staff, the various departments, and the Inspectorate Staff at Shanghai. As garbled versions of these remarks have appeared in the press I wish you to take an early opportunity of reading to your foreign staff assembled for the purpose this address. The copy is to be filed in your confidential archives and is not to leave your hands.

Yours sincerely,

C.E.Tanant, Esquire,
Wenchow.

I have called you here to-day because I have some information to give you which affects your employment, some advice which I hope will influence your future conduct, and some comment on recent proceedings which have filled me with astonishment. I want you to pay attention to what I say: I do not speak lightly: matters have been proceeding to a point, I won't call it a crisis, but it is essentially a parting of the ways. I am very much in earnest, I speak with the full authority of the Chinese Government, our employers, and you may rely upon it that you are not getting merely a matter of opinion but the bed rock truth about the situation. If any members of the Staff who are not English do not understand what I say I beg that they will stop me by putting up a hand. I shall try to make myself as explicit as possible. Otherwise I wish to have no interruption and I need not say that I am not here to receive views or answer questions but to make statements. My remarks so far as they are of general application apply to all branches of the Service represented here; but, seeing that this assemblage is the result of the proceedings of one section of the foreign Staff, I address myself more particularly to the members of the Revenue Department, Outdoor Staff.

I am going to speak a few words about the nature of our employment and what it means, the relations of the Inspector General to the Government and his position in respect to the Customs Staff. I shall then briefly review the history of the last fifteen months and I shall end by saying a few words on the recent Staff meeting.

Now

Now in the first place this is a Chinese and not a foreign Service. Get that fact into your minds. We speak for purposes of convenience of the Inspectorate and Port organisations: but these are merely administrative divisions. The Foreign Inspectorate is really the whole foreign Staff whether it is stationed in Peking or the ports. The only member of the Service who is directly appointed and who can be dismissed by the Chinese Government is the Inspector General. No one else of the one thousand odd foreign employes and the four thousand Chinese can be directly interfered with in the slightest degree, so far as their employment is concerned, by the Chinese Government. The Inspector General stands between. The Inspector General has been accorded in this respect unlimited authority and he carries a heavy responsibility because you can't ever have things both ways. It is necessary for the protection of the employes from outside interference that the Inspector General should have these powers, on the other hand the Inspector General is personally responsible to the Chinese Government for the behaviour of every employe in the Service and has to answer for it. You may think it strange that in these times such a state of things should be possible, because say what you like the Inspector General is an autocrat - a benevolent one but nevertheless an autocrat. There is no appeal from his decision to the Chinese Government and while of course there is in a sense an appeal to national authority, it is in the last resort merely an appeal to public opinion. An Inspector General who abused or misused his powers could not last three months but so long as he does not abuse his position it is practically one of supreme authority. This is an anomaly, but there is a reason for it. And the reason is of such supreme importance that it far outweighs any

any theoretical considerations. It is nothing less than the continued existence of the Service on present lines. I remember discussing some years ago Service matters and my own position with Sir Edward Grey, as he then was, the British Secretary of State for Foreign Affairs, and what he said was this: "A great many things which theoretically are opposed to modern principles are defensible and even imperatively necessary, given certain conditions".

And now as regards our employment here in China: What does it mean and why are we here at all? It is not because we are intellectually superior in any way to the inhabitants of this country. With the exception of a few technical men, whose number is a mere fraction of the whole personnel, the rest of us from the Inspector General to the latest of our Tidewaiters, so far as mere ability, knowledge, and intellectual capacity are concerned, could be dispensed with to-morrow. We are here simply because we are supposed to act up to a standard of personal integrity as Government employes to which in the mass the Chinese have not yet attained. We are employes then because the interests at stake can apparently best be secured and served by the employment of foreigners who are believed to have collectively a higher standard of personal honesty than the people in whose midst we work: destroy that belief and the Customs Service as we know it ceases to exist, and we are employed only so long as we behave ourselves. The Chinese Government does not invite us or seek us or ask us to wear its uniform. If we are discontented with the terms of our employment or the conditions which it imposes, the Chinese Government does not ask us to stay. There is absolutely no obligation

on

on any one's part to serve the Chinese Government, but so long as we elect to serve we must naturally conform with the wishes and the requirements of our employers. One thing the Chinese Government is determined not to have in the higher departments of its Civil Service, and the entire foreign personnel of the Customs forms such a higher department, is trades unionism in any form. I have full authority to make this statement and I have been asked to make it. It will not be tolerated. Our employment then is dependent, so far as we ourselves are in question, on firstly our personal integrity and secondly our good behaviour. But there are influences which affect our employment which are not in any way under our control. These are from outside. During my tenure of charge the Service has twice been exposed to great danger from without, small beginnings which would have affected the career of every employe in it. I nipped those beginnings in the bud; I stood between the Service and real danger and I staked my career and position on the issue. Even before I assumed charge it was necessary for me to assert my freedom of action for the protection of the personnel. When I was summoned to Peking ten years ago almost to the day, what is known as the "rights recovery" or "China for the Chinese" cry was very insistent. The press of the Capital - inspired I believe - stated in very clear terms what my appointment was intended to effect and what it meant. I was to be the new broom to sweep out the foreigners and to replace them by Chinese; that is putting it rather crudely but there was no doubt about what was meant; the Ministers whom I interviewed left me in no ignorance on the subject. Well I thought it all over and I determined that I could not accept office on such terms or under any misunderstanding. I therefore addressed confidentially an important member of the Government,

a Minister of the Foreign Office and also of our own
Board — the Shui-wu Ch'u — and I put my views on this
question quite candidly before him. I told him that I
had no intention of accepting the leadship of the Customs
unless I was to be considered as the sole authority and
director in this process of evolution — inevitable of
course in the long run. If they were not prepared to let
me take my own line I did not want the position and would
not accept it: I would not come in under false pretences.
The Minister accepted my point of view and asked me to go
on; and I did so. Some of you here in Shanghai have been
unconsciously trying to put on the hands of the clock, or
to change a metaphor to force the pace in this process of
evolution and I am not sure that in this respect you have
not succeeded. Where you have not succeeded, and I want
you to pay particular attention to this, because you have
been making statements to the Service, and also in the
press to the public, which are not true, is in forcing,
by your activities, the pace in the matter of reform or
improvements which have been made. All that I have done
has been in spite of and not because of your activity.
You have not hastened by the fraction of a minute anything
I planned to do or have effected, neither have you delayed
it, although you have wasted a considerable amount of my
time, and made my task more difficult. I told the Service
officially that I would not attempt to inaugurate any
reforms or reorganisations during the war. Now I never
speak lightly and I always mean what I say. The war
ended abruptly when I was out of China. On my way back
to Peking last January I stayed in Shanghai for a few
days, some of you who are here will remember. I was not
officially in charge of the Service and I was not in
position to make any statements or promises. I very soon

found out that there was rent unrest - I anticipated it: you all thought, subconsciously, that the millennium had arrived and you were impatient to see immediate results. I took stock of the position and made my own enquiries: I then returned to Peking and immediately set about an improvement in the pay and prospects of the Outdoor Staff. I did more, I secured within three months the first essential step which made it possible to approach the question of better provision for retirement. But you were impatient, and you did not trust me, who alone can secure anything for you and on whom depends your employment. You set up the Shanghai Committee and entrusted your interests to one of your number whom you made your leader and adviser: he accepted the position: meetings were held, a whole lot of irresponsible talk was indulged in, the ports were canvassed and you discussed the propriety of keeping the Inspector General up to the mark - giving him a time limit and so forth.

Now you will remember that in March last year I issued a warning and reminder: I will read it to you:
"But latterly the movement has gone beyond the bounds originally imposed by the members themselves, and there are indications that further activity on trade union lines is contemplated by the Shanghai Committee. There is danger in this, because such activity, natural and even beneficial in a suitable environment, is quite inappropriate in the circumstances in which foreigners are employed by the Chinese Government. A little reflection will make this plain, and I trust the good sense of the Service to discountenance any further movement on these lines."

That advice was disregarded entirely: the Shanghai Committee knew better, in effect you were told we have the organisation, we can force the pace, let us act together; we have got you an immediate increase of pay and certain promises: the way is then a terrible result - the promises are 'hot air' on the part of the Inspector General: he doesn't mean what he says and we must see he gives effect to them.

The next three months were a period of great activity. The Shanghai Committee was getting into its stride. By July I had made up my mind as to where the movement was heading and I determined to see whether your leader was an intelligent man who would listen to reason or a man who had taken the bit between his teeth. I accordingly wrote a letter to Mr. Chief Examiner Wyatt. I will read it to you:

Dear Mr. Wyatt,

I have seen the circular letter dated 23rd June and addressed by yourself and Messrs. Broderick and Larsen to your brother officers, and I think it well, as you have constituted yourself the leader of a movement which I consider dangerous to the Service, to give you a few friendly words of advice and warning.

So far I have not interfered with your activities in any way and I had no desire to do so because I did not wish to prejudice the question. Although I do not think that departmental associations will have any but a harmful effect on the Service generally, I am not opposed to associations as such. In many directions they may act beneficially and usefully and if they so operate that they do not come officially into contact with me, I have nothing to say but to wish them well. The movement however

which

which you are promoting, so far as I understand it, will sooner or later come into official contact with me, and it is therefore as well that you should understand where you are heading.

The Customs Service is a unique institution and there is nothing like it to be found anywhere else in the world. It has elements of great strength in it but it is also exposed to great dangers. It is a Chinese Service and not a foreign Service and foreign employment in it is conditioned by various factors which neither you nor the majority of the members of the Out-door Staff are in a position to understand. It maintains its equilibrium owing to the play of various forces which tend to reserve equipoise and stability but if this equilibrium is upset the consequences may be very serious and may affect the career of every individual foreign member of it. The Service during the last decade has come creditably through very difficult times, and has increased both in prestige and in the important place it occupies in the Chinese polity. But there are even greater difficulties ahead and anything which tends towards disintegration from within must be carefully avoided. It is my business to steer the Service amid the various shoals of which I alone possess the chart, and I have confidence in my capacity to do so. But when I see a member of the crew, however well meaning and loyal to his comrades he may be, interfering with the navigation, it becomes necessary to warn him. I have no intention of allowing you by misplaced activity to pile up the ship. You are not in a position to foresee the consequences of your

action

action not to understand how exactly it will react in the Service. But I am in a position to do so and I therefore ask you to give it up before you tie yourself and me into a knot which will take some skill in unravelling.

I have a good opinion of your character and capacity as a Customs Officer and I have recently shown this in the Service Movements. I realise that you and many others are reacting to world impulses and I sympathise with you to a great extent. But you have gone far enough. Whatever you may believe, I assure you that you are acting neither in the interests of the Service as a whole nor of your colleagues in the Out-door Staff, and I therefore trust that you will accept these words in the spirit in which they are written and that you will in future do your best to assist and not to embarrass me.

Yours very truly,
(Signed) ....len."

Now no one can say that that was not a letter from a friend, or that it did not convey friendly advice – it also contained a warning, but the warning was a friendly one.

Mr. Wyatt replied to that letter: he assured me that his friends having chosen him as leader he could not withdraw from his position as leader – as he put it "Having assumed the reins securely to the satisfaction of the members I could not, unless utterly devoid of all honour and loyalty to my brother officers, withdraw". Note that expression – "having assumed the reins" please! But

But he ended his letter with the following remark:

"However as we have no desire to embroil the Service or yourself in any political difficulties or in any other manner to embarrass you in the reforms contemplated we will go no further with the formation of a Guild and will exert our influence for loyal co-operation with the Inspectorate General."

I accepted that assurance and I trusted Mr. Wyatt. During the months that elapsed last year I felt uneasy, I was not sure that Mr. Wyatt was acting up to his words. I heard from the ports that a very active propaganda was being carried on; then came the deputations to Peking which you know of: in spite of the expression of loyalty to the Service and myself with which they terminated, the movement I believe still continued.

Then suddenly at a moment when I had secured for the Service a boon - because look at it how you like it is a boon - I saw an announcement in the newspaper that a Guild had been formed. I could not believe it: Mr. Wyatt had assured me that it would not be formed. And yet the Reuter telegram announced that he was Chairman of the meeting which passed the resolution with one dissentient. Surely I thought this must have been done against his very strongest recommendation, and notwithstanding all the efforts of Mr. Wyatt: I awaited the official report of the proceedings and what did I find? a meeting called to discuss the Retirement Scheme and a Saturday half holiday: the occasion taken by Mr. Wyatt to spring on the meeting himself a resolution in favour of forming a Guild. Not a word about any serious Service grievance, not a word about the objects of

11

of the guild - just a guild for defensive purposes for the protection of women and children. Defence against whom? Mr. Wyatt himself stated that the Commissioner was the Staff's best friend: you don't find intelligent people combining for defence against their best friend. No, the objects of the guild could of course not be explained in clear language, because its objects are subversive of discipline and control: Mr. Wyatt had done more than assume the reins, he was now going to drive the coach. The language used was quite unmistakable, the stenographic part of the meeting cannot fail to be understood by anyone with an atom of intelligence.

Now let us see what was to be the first objective of Mr. Wyatt's driving; where was he going to land the coach: the rest of the meeting was taken up with a discussion on the question of a Saturday half holiday. The Customs guild were going to procure this: how? by coercing the shipping firms: the Coast Officers' guild had brought off a successful strike: the shipping firms had had to yield: let the Customs guild go to them with a "punch" behind them and they would soon be brought into a state of submission. Analogies are dangerous things as a guide to action - especially when they are false: there is no parallel between the shipping guild and its action and the proposed action of the Customs guild. Did you attempt anything so foolish and childish the Chinese Government would be requested to dismiss you and even I could not protect you. And why, when he was about it, did not Mr. Wyatt tell you a little more about what was said when the deputation met in Peking? He mentioned my name: he said I was in sympathy with

half holiday: he seems to think that was not worth
wh-- when the "bosses can't get a thing' let the
aff take it into their hands': what he forgot to tell
e meeting was that I had warned the deputation against
y such proceedings: I pulled him up at once when he
 essed, in milder language than he used here, this
 urse of action. I said I would not have it. He should
 ve told you that too.

 M, Mr. Wyatt is not a safe driver: he will upset
 e coach, and in any case I haven't relinquished the
 ins to him. There is not room for him and me on
 e box seat and I mean to drive so long as I hold
  Any one who attempts to wrest the reins out of
  hands will come to grief: I don't mean to have an
 ent.

  And now about the Guild: I can't prevent you forming
 Guild, but any one who joins a departmental Guild the
  ects of which are not entirely of a benevolent nature,
 ll do so on the understanding that his membership of
 e Guild is incompatible with his membership of the
 rvice. This must be so for your own protection. And
 ere must be no more of these irresponsible Staff meetings.
 aff meetings are good and it is right they should be
 ld, but the proceedings must be orderly and decorous.
 aff meetings can only be held on Customs premises and
  the requisition of a number of responsible members
  Staff. Such requisition must be made to the
 mmissioner and his authority to hold the meeting must
  obtained: the subjects for discussion must be stated.
 y one who calls, or who attends, a Customs Staff
 eting for the discussion of Service matters in the
                                                    Palace

...ice Hotel or other public place will be considered to ...e made a formal tender of resignation and his ...signation will be accepted.

And now instead of trying to take matters into your ... hands why not give the other plan a chance: why ...'t you trust me? I have your interests at heart, I ... trying to improve your conditions, I have made it ...sible for you to retire on a competence. Your guild ...ld not have accomplished that. Why do you make me ...amed of you and lose face with the Government when it ... been generous, and why do you meet me when I try ... help you with a 'slap in the face'? It is not ...st, it is not fair dealing. If I can't work with ...u I shall work without you, but the work will go on. ...u will merely succeed in hastening the evolution of the ...rvice and incidentally of depriving yourselves of ...loyment, which in these times is not to be despised. ...k around you, compare your lot with thousands of men ... home of equal education and ability with yourselves, ... have not a quarter of your advantages. If you are ...scontented by all means seek other employment, if you ... ashamed of your uniform no one obliges you to wear ...t for a day longer than you choose. But so long as ...u are in the Service you must work with me and not ...inst me and you must take your time from me. On no ...her terms is employment possible or will it be given.

Before we separate I must say two words about the ...tirement Scheme. There is a good deal of misunderstan-...ing about it. An idea appears to prevail that it is ...en to discussion and acceptance: some men say they will ...t join unless it is given the blessing of the Shanghai
Committee

Committee. I want you to understand and appreciate it, and I shall be glad to answer any questions that are put to me in the course of the next few days. I will receive a deputation or individuals if you will give your names to Mr. Carruthers who is kindly acting as my Private Secretary. But the Scheme is not going to be modified for the present and all that you have to consider is whether you will contribute or not. You are free to do what you please, only weigh it well and look at it from every point of view.

CUSTOM HOUSE,

S/O No. 187.

Wenchow 15. April, 1920

Sir,

NATIVE CUSTOMS : TEA : REDUCTION OF DUTY ON CLAIMED BY PING-YANG MERCHANTS.

While calling to discuss the Camphor Oil case mentioned in my S/O No. 186 the Acting Sup't informed me that the Ping-yang Chamber of Commerce had petitioned the Shui-wu Ch'u for a reduction of the duty on Tea collected by the Native Customs, and that the matter had been referred to him for his opinion. The Ping-yang merchants claim, it seems, that as their Tea is reduced into dust for the manufacture of Tea bricks for Mongolia, and possibly Siberia, they should be granted a reduction of duty. I showed the Sup't the Chinese text of correspondence between yourself and the Ch'u appended to your various Circulars concerning Tea from which it seems that the Ch'u does not wish to change the taxation for internal consumption. I also showed him the

text

text of Circular No. 1438 regulating the dutiability of Tea dust exported from Hankow to Kiukiang or *vice versa* for the making of Brick Tea. The Sup't said that no Tea dust, to speak of, had heretofore been exported, and that his Ping-yang Weiyüan did not favour a reduction of duty as all the tea would then be turned into dust, and while agreeing with him on that point, I pointed out that the Weiyüan was bound to try and keep the duty as high as possible so as to collect as much duty as possible, but that nevertheless the duty on Tea, and notably coarse Tea of that kind, is too high as well at the Maritime Customs as at the Native Customs where the duty is one half of the M.C. duty He finally said that he had not yet made his mind as to the answer he would make to the Shui-wu Ch'u.

SUPERINTENDENT.

The Sup't is still at Shanghai, and it seems that neither himself nor the Soochow Sup't Mr. Yang, with whom he has been ordered to exchange post, are keen on moving the Ch'u to take a decision which requires the Ministry of Finance's assent for they are afraid of of an impending change of Minister, and the next man might discard them and appoint some of his protégés in their places.

STAFF : MESSRS AHLBERG AND CHRISTOPHERSEN.

As reported in my telegram of this day, Mr. Christophersen arrived on the 11th, and as there is no need to keep Mr. Ahlberg here any longer, I suggested, if his despatch has not been mailed yet, to issue him pay here to the end of the month, and let him proceed to Shanghai where his Retiring Allowance could be issued while he settles his affairs, etc.

Mrs Ahlberg left yesterday in advance.

Yours respectfully,

S/O

INSPECTORATE GENERAL OF CUSTOMS.

PEKING, **27th April,** 19 **20**.

Dear Sir,

I am directed by the Inspector General inform you that your S/O letter No. **187**, ated **15th instant**, has been duly ceived.

Yours truly,

Private Secretary.

E.Tanant, Esquire,

Wenchow.

CUSTOM HOUSE,

S/O No. 188.　　　　Wenchow, 24th April 1920.

Sir,

SEIZURE BY YANG KWANG CHÜ OF CAMPHOR OIL PASSED BY MARITIME CUSTOMS FOR EXPORTATION BY STEAMER.

My despatch No. 3473 informed you of the release of the 6 tins. I hear that on receipt of repeated requests from the Superintendent to return the tins, the Magistrate wanted to have them returned to the Tung Mei firm through the Yang Kwang Chü but that the latter refused and finally it was sent back by the Magistrate. As you will see from the enclosure I wrote to the Superintendent asking that the case be reported to the Shui-wu Ch'u and Tsai-cheng Pu and that the Yang Kwang Chü and others be ordered not to interfere with our cargo.

STAFF.

As instructed in your telegram of 20th

20th inst. Mr. Matsubara is leaving by the steamer which carries this letter. I hope his successor will soon arrive as there is too much work for one man alone here. The revenue collected is no doubt insignificant, but that is due to the import duty being collected at Shanghai and all the same work done again - and thoroughly on re-importation here except that we don't collect duty.

       Yours respectfully,

[A.—42]

INSPECTORATE GENERAL OF CUSTOMS,

PEKING, 4th May, 1920.

Dear Sir,

I am directed by the Inspector General to inform you that your S/O letter No. 188, dated 24th ultimo, has been duly received.

Yours truly,

[signature]
Private Secretary.

C.E. Tanant, Esquire,

Wenchow.

CUSTOM HOUSE,

No. 189.

Wenchow, 13. May, 1920.

Sir,

LIGHT : PROPOSED ESTABLISHMENT OF BY MR. YANG HSI-T'UNG.

I am mailing my despatch No 3475 re establishment of a light at the estuary of the Wenchow River. I think, owing to the recent agitation by the China Merchants S. N. Co., and now by this Mr. Yang, that something should be done, b t should it be left to Mr. Yang to establish and keep in order, that is a very doubtful point; besides, the Coast Inspector might wish to select another locality. As to Mr. Yang I must say that he gave me the impression of a clever rogue who wants to impose on everybody, as well junks, guilds, merchants, officials, as Custom In fact it would seem, to judge from the Ningpo Commrs letter as if, on the point of

losing

losing the control of his Taping light (and probably not without some kind of a reward or compensation), he had made plans to continue his levy of light dues at another spot, for that is the clearest of his operations: collection of light dues from junks, etc.

I must also point out that he intends using old lamps which he admits were discarded from the Taping light and I would say that this is another trick to make the Customs pay for them ultimately.

He was much cut up by my refusal to allow him to put up his light even temporarily, and Mr. Ko even tells me he said he would have his materials taken to the Island by some Government boat. The Taoyin told me that on receipt of Mr. Yang's petition he had already instructed the Yü-huan Hsien to report, but that on receipt of my letter through the Sup't he gave new instructions to wait.

I therefore beg that some decision be taken without too much delay as the scheme was well received by the Officials.

Yours respectfully,
C.b.S. Canavan

[A.—42]

INSPECTORATE GENERAL OF CUSTOMS,

PEKING, 21st May, 1920.

Dear Sir,

I am directed by the Inspector General inform you that your S/O letter No. 189, dated 13th instant, has been duly received.

Yours truly,

Private Secretary.

C.E.Tanant, Esquire,

Wenchow.

S/O No. 190.

CUSTOM HOUSE,

Wenchow, 3rd June 1920.

Sir,

KEROSENE OIL: STORING OF IN GODOWN ALONG RIVER FRONT BY TEXAS CO. NOT ALLOWED BY AUTHORITIES.

The Texas Oil Co. opened an agency here recently for the importation and sale of its kerosene oil. No permission was asked for the building of a godown and I heard that the Company was using a godown alongside the river heretofore used by the Asiatic Petroleum Co. I mentioned to the Chinese agent of this Texas Co. that theirs being a new concern and the godown being within Harbour limits they would have to get the Chinese Authorities permission to use it. Unexpectedly on the 15th May, while the Superintendent was sending me a despatch his letter

letter carrier also delivered me a copy of his reply in the form of "pi" to the petition of the Texas Co. informing them that the actual godown could only be used if not surrounded by houses and subject to the District Magistrate's approval. I called at once on the Acting Superintendent to return him his reply and at the same time I explained that the storing of kerosene oil in large quantities within and without the city should be prohibited. I pointed out notably that our Harbour Regulations, now approved by the Diplomatic Body and the Peking Boards, limit the quantities of kerosene oil to be handled by one boat to 50 cases and that not more should be allowed to be stored in any one building by any new firm. We still have along the river within Harbour limits the godwons of the Standard Oil Co. and the Asiatic Petroleum Co. where thousands of cases are stored, and this

this should be stopped as soon as those companies possess re_ular oil installations, for, in their actual locations, they greatly endanger all the neighbourhood and the shipping on the river.

I have now heard privately that the application of the Texas Co. has been refused by the Magistrate.

STANDARD OIL CO'S INSTALLATION.

A few days later a Mr. Harr of the Standard Oil Co., Shanghai, accompanied by their Ningpo agent visited Wenchow in view to obtain from the authorities the right to use their new installation down river. They called on the second day to say that they had at last succeeded in obtaining the so much desired permission and showed me a Superintendent's letter, in his capacity of Foreign Affairs Commissioner, authorising the Co. to use the installation temporarily pending completion of
formalities

formalities for the regularisation of the title deeds. I said I was afraid the document was rather vague as the permission should be definite, and that in any case I would have to receive intimation of the decision from the Authorities. I also informed them of the necessity of abandoning their suburb godown which endangers our N.C. Office. The Superintendent came himself the day after to speak of this affair. I told him what I had heard, seen, and said and I advised him to settle the question of ownership of the land before giving any provisional permission and I also insisted on the Company being instructed to abandon its actual suburb godown. Up to now I have not received any official information that the installation may be used. Before leaving Mr. Harr wrote on behalf of the Company to repeat that he had obtained the authority to use the installation and asked me to
facilitate

facilitate matters, but I did not reply. Meantime I have written to Ningpo and Foochow to enquire of the treatment of such installations.

Yours respectfully,

A.—42]

INSPECTORATE GENERAL OF CUSTOMS,

PEKING, 11th June, 1920.

Dear Sir,

I am directed by the Inspector General to inform you that your S/O letter No. 190, dated 3rd instant, has been duly received.

Yours truly,

Private Secretary.

C. E. Tanant, Esquire,

Wenchow.

/O No. 191.

CUSTOM HOUSE,
Wenchow, 5, June, 1920.

Sir,

My long leave is due next spring and I intended to apply soon for it, but it has become advisable to send my wife and daughter home sooner, if possible, so as to attend to the education of that child better than we can do in China, and in this view I beg to ask whether my leave could be granted this autumn instead of next spring so as to enable me to accompany them.

Yours respectfully,

Ch. Canaut

INSPECTORATE GENERAL OF CUSTOMS.

PEKING. 17th June, 1920.

Dear Mr. Tanant,

I have duly received your S/O letter No. 191 of the 5th instant.

<u>May long leave due next spring be taken this autumn ?</u>

I am afraid that with our present shortage of staff, and the number of men already overdue for leave, ~~that~~ no leave can be ~~presented~~ granted before it is strictly due.

Yours truly,

[signature]

C. Tanant, Esquire,
　Wenchow.

S/O No. 192.

CUSTOM HOUSE,

Wenchow, 19 June, 1920.

Sir,

CHINESE KNOWLEDGE OF ASSISTANTS.

The "China Sun" to which you have suscribed for one month has duly arrived and I handed it to my staff as instructed. However I cannot help pointing out that this very paper reprinted, advertises, and still sells Mr. F. E. Taylor's pamphlet " a plea for reform of the Maritime Customs Service of China".

ASSISTANT.

Mr. Hirano arrived on the 11th accompanied by his wife, and I beg to thank you for his appoinment for I have been too busy since Mr. Matsubara's departure, this being about the busiest time of the port on account of the Tea season.

TEA.

I am mailing my reply to your queries re Unfired Tea. While on this subject I

must

must report the receipt of Shui-wu Ch'u instructions through the Superintendent, authorising Tea (fired) exported to Siberia and Outer Mongolia and shipped by rail from Newchwang, to deposit bonds here and at Newchwang for the duties payable in cases of non exportation, as is done at Hankow. No application has been made yet, and I am waiting for your confirmation of the instructions.

STANDARD OIL CO'S KEROSENE OIL TANK INSTALLATION

With reference to my S/O No. 190, I have so far received no Official communication from the Sup't that the installation may be used. In the meantime, the S. O. Co., argueing of the fact that they have the Sup't's letter allowing them to use their installation temporarily, sent me a Bond License form duly filled in, but I returned it to them saying I had as yet received no Official instructions from the Chinese Authorities.

KEROSENE

KEROSENE OIL TANKS AND OTHER INSTALLATIONS AT HAIMEN.

I must also inform you that I hear that the same S. O. Co have put up a tank installation at Haimen, between Wenchow and Ningpo; that the Asiatic Petroleum Co. have also bought land there for a tank installation; that the Britis -American Tobacco Co. equally put up a house of their own; and finally that the R. C. Mission have built up several houses in view of the development of that port, and when time comes to open it it will perhaps be too late for the Customs to obtain sites and make reservations concerning those oil tanks and the danger they create. The recent explosion of gasolene at Kobe is more than sufficient proof of danger.

    Yours respectfully,

INSPECTORATE GENERAL OF CUSTOMS

S/O

PEKING, 30th June, 19 20.

Dear Mr. Tanant,

I have duly received your S/O letter No. 192 of 19th instant.

Reporting that the "China Sun", subscribed to for foreign assistants studying Chinese, still advertises and sells Mr. F.E.Taylor's pamphlet.

The attention of the paper has been called to this and the advertisement is to be withdrawn.

S.O.Co.'s tank installation at Haimen; other foreign firms buying land there; reporting.

Can this information be reliable? I have heard nothing of the opening of this place and cannot understand how foreign firms can be purchasing land there, unless it is done in the name of Chinese.

Yours truly,

.Tanant, Esquire,
Wenchow.

CUSTOM HOUSE,

S/O No. 193.   Wenchow, 8th July 1920.

Sir,

FORESHORE RECLAMATION: DIFFICULTY WITH CHINA MERCHANTS S. N. CO. (Reference to I.G. despatch No. 941/78,689 and Wenchow despatches Nos. 3482 and 3484).

  The Act. Sup't called this morning, and amongst other subjects told me that the local Agent of the Company - Mr. T. C. Szee - had returned from Shanghai, and had shown him more title deeds for the purchase of 2 more cesspools located on the other side of the street and which the Company had bought and removed. The Sup't. added that all that was not denied, but that the purchase of cesspools established on "Kuan Ti" meant simply the purchase of the cesspools as holes for the dumping of garbage, etc. but could not be regarded as an alienation of
           official

official property, and he said he told Mr. Szee that this new proof of purchase of cesspool was not bettering the Company's case and that he could not write again to the Ch'u.

I thanked him for what he said and pointed out that the whole affair had been caused by the Company's equivocal and evasive replies to my first queries. Had they then in January openly claimed the foreshore I would have had to refer the matter to you before doing anything, but their want of sincerity caused the matter to become official and they made it worth by applying to Admiral Tsai direct. The Sup't. agreed to all this.

Mr. T. C. Szee, the Agent, is either a brother or a cousin of Mr. Alfred Sze

the

the Chinese Minister to London and of the Lung Hai Railway Director, and I told the Sup't. I was glad all the correspondence on this case had taken place by order of the Company's directors, as I had no wish to be in bad terms with Mr. Szee with whom and his family we have, my family and myself, the best friendly intercourse.

Yours respectfully,

INSPECTORATE GENERAL OF CUSTOMS.

S/O

PEKING. 23rd July, 1920.

Dear Mr. Tanant,

I have duly received your S/O letter No. 193 of 8th instant.

Foreshore Reclamation.

The matter has been put before the Ch'u who, I suppose, will come to some decision or other. The case seems to me a difficult one as I gather that neither party holds title-deeds to the ground in dispute.

Yours truly,

E. Tanant, Esquire,
Wenchow.

CUSTOM HOUSE,

S/O No.194.　　　　　　Wenchow, 8. July, 1920.

Sir,

Application for Short leave.

I beg to thank you for your S/O Letter of 17th June informing mre that Long leave cannot be granted before it is due.

In the meantime could I get 6 or 8 weeks short leave ? I came back from home leave in April, 1916, and my only short leave since has been 8 days spent in Shanghai last autumn in the Doctor and Dentist's hands. As it was the dentist had told me to return to him 2 or 3 months afterwards, and I always postponed, but this cannot go on for I require a a new plate which will take some time to fix properly and try. Besides I would like a change of air, ideas, and people, and I think there is nothing excessive in such a demand after $3\frac{1}{2}$ years of such a small hole where one learns to know too well the few people one has to meet everyday. Please do not take

this

this for an application for transfer. Far from it! I am just as well here as anywhere else. If you can grant me this short leave could I get it from the middle of August, and must I send an official application?

Yours respectfully,

S/O No. 195.

CUSTOM HOUSE,

Wenchow, 10. July, 1920.

Sir,

Incorrect issue of Government Stores Certificates by Ningpo Superintendent.

I take leave to call your attention to my despatch No. 3486 now mailed. In so doing I must ask you to make abstraction of that divergence of opinion with my Ningpo colleague as it is only accessory to the case. What I particularly had in mind in bringing it to your notice was the action of the Ningpo Sup't who seems bent on ignoring us, Customs.

As far as I am concerned I may quote as precedents the establishment by this Official of the "Fen-yün-tan" system (Wenchow despatches Nos. 3189 and 3209, and I.G. desp. Nos. 702, 711, 715, and 725), allowing transhipment at Haimen of Native Customs steamers goods, a very serious procedure which, if known, understood, and introduced at other places along the Coast, might jeopardize our Maritime Customs Coast Trade Duty which the impecunious actual Government does not seem ready to to abolish. This Fen-yün-tan system was planned and put into operation simply to protect the trade of Ningpo small Inland steamers of which this Sup't, according to Officials' practice to invest their money in all local enterprises, might be a shareholder, and as such bound to see that their trade be prosperous, and that anything be done to foster it without caring how the result affects other districts or institutions or even the Government.

We have had again difficulties with the same Ningpo Sup't over squeezes, to put it plain, from timber rafts by his Tsumen Weiyüan (Vide February to June 1920 Summaries of non-urgent Ch. correspondence), and also on account of Wheat smuggling allowed by the same Weiyüan (Wenchow despatch No. 3339).

As regards Ningpo He seems to act very much as he likes to judge of the case of Ningpo N. C. Weights and scales of which I was informed by a despatch of the Ningpo Commr transmitting copy of his desp. No. 4565 to you. Now comes this irregular issue of Govt. Stores Certificates. And what is the concern in whose favour he shows

so

so much liberality and issues his Govt. Stores Certificates ? the Hwa Hsin Military Uniforms Co. 華新軍服公司 This simple name gives at once the suspicion of one of those concerns officially promoted for the purpose of providing to the needs of the Army, but which only serve to fill up the pockets of the promoters or managers I should add that this is the first we happened to see the products of that company, the Wenchow Police and that of neighbouring districts being still provided with uniforms made locally.

All this is again a small affair, but it only adds to the cases of disregard of the foreign Customs by this man who, in my opinion, reflects the desire of the Peking cliques to place Commissioners under Superintendents. He is the brother of Mr. Sun Pao Chi and as such is bent to be an exponent of his politic, only, possibly, overdoing it.

To sum up, as the Ningpo Commr. dares not object to this practice of irregular issue of Govt. Stores Certificates by his Sup't, it seems that the matter might possibly be taken up officially as the result of the checking of Govt. Stores Returns.

<u>Timber for furniture for former Taoyin.</u>   A

A few days ago the Acting Sup't sent me the N.C. Weiydan to show me a letter from the former Wenchow Taoyin, Mr. Huang Ching Lan, now Ningpo Taoyin since the last five months, asking to pass free some timber sent from Inland by a district Magistrate to Mr. Huang to make private book cases! I replied that Mr. Huang had all possible opportunities to take his timber with him when transferred, but that now we should not pass such timber free for if we did it we would establish a precedent unheard of. I saw the Sup't a few days afterwards and he did not refer to this case.

    Yours respectfully,

S/O No. 196.

CUSTOM HOUSE,

Wenchow, 10. July, 1920

Sir,

HAIMEN : Kerosene Oil tanks and other foreign installations.

I have just received your S/O Letter of 30th June, asking with reference to the last paragraph of my S/O Letter No.192, whether my information can be reliable, and, in reply, I must say that chronologically it may not be, but in fact, though I have not verified it personally, I feel fairly sure of what I wrote.

Chronologically, I think the R. C. Mission was first on the field and began to put up houses for rent already a few years ago. It is represented at Haimen by a father under the Ningpo Mission (Lazarists).

The B. A. Tobacco Co. then followed, represented by its Wenchow Agent, Mr. C. Cance, a Eurasian,

Eurasian, who speaks Shanghai, Ningpo, and Wenchow dialects all fluently, and since last year made very frequent and long stays at Haimen. He openly said he had been arranging and fixing a foreign house and office for his firm.

The S. O. Co. came afterwards. Last year I heard a few words in conversation between Mr. Cance and the foreigner then in charge of the Wenchow Agency of the S.O.Co. and shortly after the Haimen R.C.Missionary visited his Wenchow confrères, but I have suspicions that the visit was to make arrangements with the S. O. Co. This foreign agent is not here any longer having been replaced by a Chinese Agent brought up and trained by the Company.

A month ago when the Shanghai representative and the Ningpo Agent of the Company came here about the Wenchow installation (my S/O No.190) they left for Haimen and mentioned they had to visit their agency there. Now, yesterday, the Assistant of the Ningpo agent

agent who was passing through Wenchow called on me, and as I wanted to know about their doings I questioned him straight about their Haimen installation and the reply was " We have had very bad luck, we put up the tank on reclaimed foreshore and it co lapsed and now we must begin again." That was quite enough for my requirements and I changed the conversation for Haimen is within the Ningpo district, and that i only because we hear so much of Haimen here that I took leave to mention to you what I had heard.

About the Asiatic Petroleum Co. I only heard very vague reports.

If you want more information I might send one of my Clerks there. He would pass unnoticed, while if any foreigner was going it would cause queries and comments.

Yours respectfully,

.—42]

INSPECTORATE GENERAL OF CUSTOMS,

PEKING, 23rd July, 19 20

Dear Sir,

I am directed by the Inspector General to inform you that your S/O letters No. 8, 195 & 196, dated 10th instant, has been duly received.

Yours truly,

Private Secretary.

C.E.Tanant, Esquire,

Wenchow.

CUSTOM HOUSE,

S/O No. 197.   Wenchow 13. July, 1920

Sir,

HAIMEN : QUASI OPENING OF.

With reference to my S/O Letters Nos.192 and 196 re Haimen : Kerosene oil tanks and other foreign installations, I thought advisable to change the heading of that paragraph as it seems there exists there a state of affairs about similar to the half opening of Yunnanfu. When writing my letter No. 196 I had in mind some information furnished to my predecessor by Mr. E. Stevens, Chief Tidesurveyor, who then inspected Haimen on a trip to Ningpo, but I could not remember where I had seen that report. I have now found it and beg to refer you to Mr. Acheson's despatch No. 3077 of 1915. The most important point of the information is the establishment of a Harbour light by the local authorities, and the building of three wharves for the accommodation of steamers.

While

While on this subject I extract the following from the Shanghai Mercury of 6. July, Page 8, column 1 : " A branch Hospital in connection with the C. I. M. hospital Taichowfu, is now being built at Haimen, where for many years a branch dispensary work has been carried on."

GOVERNMENT STORES REGULATIONS.

With reference to my despatch No. 3488 re transmission of Postal stores and Customs stationery, it might perhaps be pertinent to point out that while full charges for telegrams sent and mail matter posted are paid by the Customs, the two Telegraph and Postal Administrations enjoy exemption of Customs duties. Such being the case it seems that either the Customs should, if not enjoying franchise, at least be favoured by a reduction of tariff from those Administrations, or else that their materials and stores should pay full duty.

Typhoon.

Typhoon.

19. July, 1920.

We have just been a whole week without outside mail on account of a severe typhoon which must have been particularly bad between this and Haimen. It caused a small flood locally, the water gauge recording $22\frac{1}{2}$ ft, an unprecedented level ever since we opened this Office over 43 years ago. A lot of small damage is reported all round. A Japanese Steamer on her way from Singapore to Kobe is said to have taken refuge at Shihpu, between Haimen and Ningpo, rather battered by the seas.

The NEW TAOYIN arrived this morning, six days on his way from Ningpo.

Yours respectfully,

[-42]

INSPECTORATE GENERAL OF CUSTOMS,

PEKING, **30th July,** 19 **20**

ar Sir,

I am directed by the Inspector General
form you that your S/O letter No. **197**,
13th July, has been duly
ed.

Yours truly,

Private Secretary.

E. Tanant, Esquire,

Wenchow.

INSPECTORATE GENERAL OF CUSTOMS,

PEKING, 15th July 1920.

Dear Mr. Tannant,

I am directed by the I.G. to forward to you the enclosed letter (with translation attached) accusing Mr. Matsubara, formerly in the Wenchow Customs, of connivance in the smuggling of rice to Japan and to request you to investigate and report on the matter semi-officially.

Yours sincerely

Lde Luca

Private Secretary.

C. E. Tannant, Esquire,
    Wenchow

敬告者宏我甑天時欠旱不雨值兹來臻新桂正值

食民飢苦之時我有排外用人風潮查其庫用皆由於

人承辦漏米出境之故該用人勢力廣大官所不予嚴此以

致明目張膽從由漏米出境兹查去年七月間有日商

三夫（姓名不起）來澀与甑海關包辦日人松原又日商盧贊

堂藤末鹹一合办漏米共有數次去歲十一月間迄今春

三月已敘十一號地船查獲一次計有二百傑袋目下時有

出境不知其敍止日清連二事又一

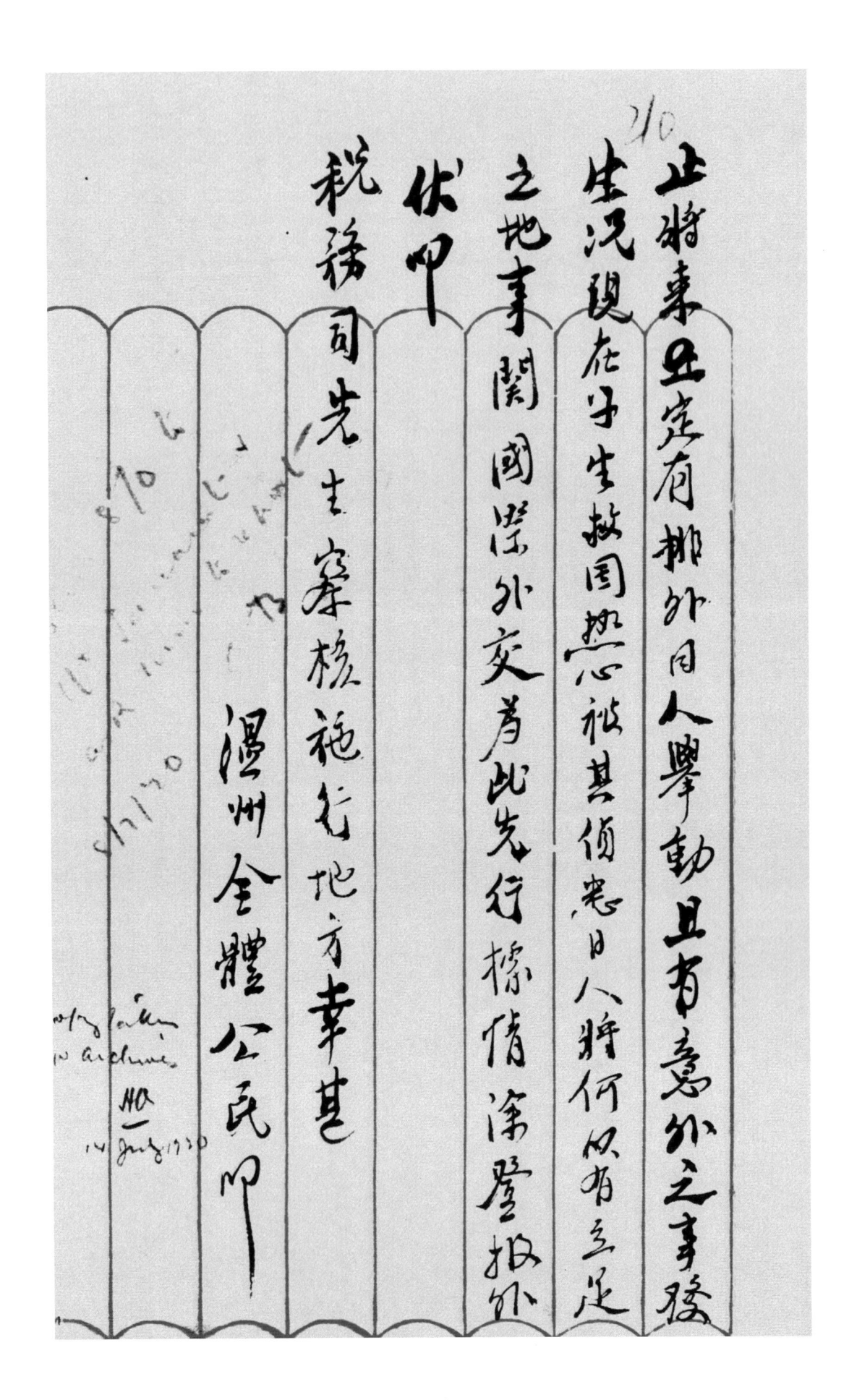

此将来必定有排外日人举动且有意外之事发生况现在于生敌国热心被其侦悉日人将何以有立足之地事关国际外交为此先行据情呈禀报祈

伏乞

税务司先生察核饬令地方幸甚

瓯州全体公民叩

Translation of Letter from Wenchow citizens to the I. G.

Wenchow has had dry weather for a long time and there has been a great dearth of rice and fuel. During this time when people are bemoaning their hard luck, an anti-Japanese movement has nearly broken out, owing to the smuggling abroad of rice by the Japanese. The Japanese concerned are influencial and, as the local officials are merely winking at them, they become very bold and are given a free hand in the smuggling of rice. In July last year, three Japanese merchants (names unknown) came to Wenchow and associated themselves with Mr. Matsubara, Assistant of the Wenchow Customs, and 廣體堂籐末誠一 as accomplices in smuggling rice. They have smuggled several times already during the period from November 1919 to March 1920 and they were discovered only once, by patrol boat No.11, which made a seizure of 200 odd bags. Smuggling is still going on but the quantity is not known. Unless the Japanese Consul be requested to put a stop to this, it is feared that an anti-Japanese movement will be inevitable and that accidents will occur. It is hard to know how the Japanese will stand in case they are found out by the students who are now so ardent in their attempt to save the country. As this matter concerns diplomatic relations, we beg to report the facts for your consideration, besides publishing them in the newspapers.

True Translation:
4th Asst. A.

No. 198.

CUSTOM HOUSE,
Wenchow, 26. July, 1920.

Sir,

SHORT LEAVE : COMMISSIONER'S.

I beg to thank you for your telegram of 23rd received yesterday, allowing me to take six weeks leave from 16th August if Hirano fit to assume charge. I considered the question very carefully and I regret to say that I felt bound to send you the following reply : " your telegram of 23rd July I cannot advise placing in charge actual assistant ".

I have nothing against this man, and in fact though socially I preferred Matsubara I think he is a better Office man, but beyond knowledge of General Office he has none of other work. At a Service point of view I would even say that until the boycott has subsided and the actual political crisis ~~khxxnushatued~~ be settled I think it would be preferable not to place a Japanese Assistant in charge so much the more as we have here a very able Assistant in charge of the Native Customs, Mr. Wong Hsiu Geng, and

the

the Chinese would complain of unfairness were we to place the younger Assistant in charge.

If no other arrangement can be made then I must drop my demand for leave, and I hope this will be taken into consideration when I apply for home leave for next spring.

Yours respectfully,

INSPECTORATE GENERAL OF CUSTOMS,

PEKING, 6th August 19 20.

Dear Mr. Tanant,

I have duly received your S/O No. 198 of 26th July.

<u>Request for short leave dropped.</u> I am sorry you had to forego your leave, but in the circumstances there seems no help for it.

Yours truly,

Tanant, Esquire,
    Wenchow.

CUSTOM HOUSE,

S/O No. 199.   Wenchow 2. August, 1920

Sir,

FORESHORE RECLAMATION.

I have just received your S/O letter of 23rd July, and I am glad to see that you and Staff are all in safety.

You tell me you put the foreshore reclamation case before the Ch'u for decision. May I take leave to suggest that you push up the case? The Acting Sup't assures me that he sides with us, and that he told the China Merchants S. N. Co's agent that although they bought two or three cesspools that land was "Kuan ti" and could not be sold by the people tolerated to squat on it or dig holes on it, while there was no objection whatever when the land was given to us. The Company's claim only dates really since the last few months since they put the Hsean on the Shanghai-Wenchow run. My idea is, if you wish to keep that fore-

shore

shore to take advantage of the good dispositions of the actual Acting Sup't and push on the case.

LIGHT ON LITTLE SANPWAN.

I do not know whether you have already replied to my despatch No. 3489. In any case I take leave to suggest that something be done by us even to light junks passages, rather than all this Mr. Yang to establish his light. He has been clever enough to work up his way amongs Officials and gentry and if we do not do something he will insist on being allowed to put up his light, and when it is established we are sure to have new claims from steamers I would rather suggest to put up a gas buoy like those below Woosung.

TYPHOON. HAIMEN.

The Acting Taoyin, Mr. Yin Chi, has left The new Taoyin, Mr. Tuan Wu-tai, arrived nearly two weeks ago delayed en route by the typhoon at Haimen. He witnessed the tidal wave which caused the partial destruction of the town, and his

his first thing on arrival was to get the gentry to send the 240 pichls of rice passed free for flood relief as reported in my despatch No. 3490.

In the North China Herald of 24th July there is a long account of the destruction of Haimen: 700 lives and $1,000,000 lost.

Yours respectfully,

INSPECTORATE GENERAL OF CUSTOMS,

PEKING, 13th August 19 20.

Dear Sir,

I am directed by the Inspector General to inform you that your S/O letter No. 199, dated 2nd August, has been duly received.

Yours truly,

Assistant *Private Secretary.*

A. Tanant, Esquire,

Wenchow.

CUSTOM HOUSE,

No. 200.

Wenchow, 8, August, 1920.

Sir,

ANONYMOUS ACCUSATION AGAINST Mr. MATSUBARA OF CONNIVANCE IN SMUGGLING OF RICE TO JAPAN.

I duly received your S/O Letter of 15 July enclosing a letter, with translation attached accusing my former Assistant, Mr. Matsubara, of connivance in the smuggling of rice to Japan, and instructing me to investigate and report on the matter semi-officially : and, in reply, to say that I do not believe that the accusation, if smuggling really took place, is worth of credence.

There are two Japanese shops here : TOYODO (東洋堂) and KOKANDO (廣貫堂), quite distinct firms, according to my Assistants, though dealing both in sundry Japanese products. Each shop is managed by the owner and his wife, Japanese citizens, occasionally one Japanese assistant, and several Chinese, and the presence of those Chinese would render smuggling rather difficult. I have had since my arrival here in 1916 only Japanese Assistants, Messrs Kaneko,

Kaneko, Matsubara, and now Hirano, and I never heard anything wrong on their part. Having no other countrymen to associate with, and the foreign community (Missionaries and the representatives of the B. A. Tobacco Co, and Standard Oil Co.,) showing them a cold shoulder generally, the missionaries because they dont listen to their fads, and the others because they are Asiatics, it must be clear that the position of my Japanese Assistants is not very enviable here. I see them as often as they care to come and see us, but there is in all this such official obsequiousness that it would seem it is for them more a duty than a pleasure to come round. Mr. Matsubara, I should say, was in that respect rather an exception and we saw him more intimately, and I think he appreciated it towards the end of his stay here. So, on the whole, having nobody or practically very few persons to associate with it should not be found strange if they occasionally seek company with their own nationals though of a lower social standing. The ladies have been

been the same, and Mrs Kaneko took a great deal of pain in looking after the Toyodo man's wife during an illness. So much more the reason for Mr. Matsubara, alone, to see these people. But as to associate with them for smuggling I still doubt it.

Coming to the accusation I must first say that I heard nothing locally, not even about Toyodo or Kokando being concerned in rice smuggling.

But admitting smuggling took place, how could Mr. Matsubara be mixed with it ? Surely not on account of his position at the Maritime Custom House. If smuggling took place it must have been in junks which all are under the control of the Native Customs. How then could Mr. Matsubara facilitate it ? By issuing documents which he has not got, as they all are issued by the Native Customs Assistant, Mr. Wong Haiu Geng, who has been in good terms, but nothing else, with my Japanese Assistants? It is all very well to mix Mr. Matsubara's name in an accusation, but this accusation must be substantiated.

To

To arrive as quickly as possible to the truth I mentioned to the Superintendent that I had been apprised by an anonymous letter of misdeeds of Mr. Matsubara in associating with his countrymen for smuggling and I asked whether any Japanese had been caught mixed up in it. The reply was NO. In fact the Superintendent does not believe in the accusation particularly as regards Mr. Matsubara. He did not seem to know or remember the case of the No. 11 Police boat mentioned in the letter; he finally mentioned that a Japanese giving himself as a seller of some kind of armours or coats of mail had recently reported to him that he visited Wenchow some months ago and was enticed by Mr. Matsubara to lend money to Kokando and that the money was not returned to him notwithstanding repeated demands. He mixed in his affairs a Pingyan Chinese who seems to be a rice dealer, but the Superintendent does not see how Mr. Matsubara can be mixed up in the case.

From

From all this and from the wording of the letter I would rather believe that it emanates from the same man who may have been swindled by his countryman Kokando and who, to give weight to his accusation, thought best to mix up in it Mr. Matsubara's name because he may have met him at the other's house.

This is all I am able to find and I hope you will remove from your mind the bad impression such an anonymous accusation has no doubt created. This would in one way support my suggestions not to leave young foreign Assistants, and particularly bachelors, too long in small ports.

Yours respectfully,

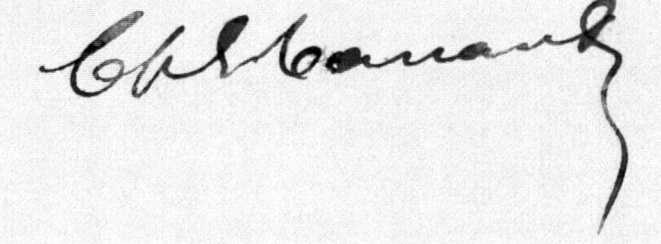

INSPECTORATE GENERAL OF CUSTOMS,

PEKING, 20th August, 19 20

ar Sir,

I am directed by the Inspector General form you that your S/O letter No. 200, 8th instant, has been duly ved.

Yours truly,

Private Secretary.

C.E.Tavant, Esquire,

Wenchow.

CUSTOM HOUSE,

S/O No. 201.   Wenchow, 11th August 1920.

Sir,

SHIP'S PAPERS: QUERIES RE FEES CHARGED FOR ISSUE OF I.W.S.N. CERTIFICATE (CIRCULAR NO. 3040).

I have now mailing my despatch No. 3495 written a few days ago and I notice that in §4. re effect of the levy of fees upon inland waters trading, I attributed the initial levy of a fix fee of Tls. 10. for all ships uniformly to the possible fact that it might have been thought that small steamers, ably by their reduced size and dimensions to proceed further inland, would thus derive as much advantage as the larger steamers unable to proceed so far. This is a theory which may be argued on; but I should perhaps have added this other explanation: Circular No. 927 was written in 1899 not long after the I.W. Regulations had been

framed

framed and the idea at that time was that Inland Waters Navigation should be restricted to a port's inland waters, and by this fact would only allow of the use of small steamers generally, and it must have then been thought that a uniform Tls. 10. fee would meet all requirements, and this seems corroborated by the establishment of the other schedule of fees for costing steamers (Circular 927. 2º).

But the Mackay Treaty extended the meaning of "Inland Waters" and gradually no restriction was placed on the size of the ships navigating inland waters, but in the mean time the initial fee remained unchanged. It seems therefore that this could be taken as an argument for the proposed change of I.W.S.N. Certificate fee from a fix to a sliding one.

Yours respectfully,

CUSTOM HOUSE,

S/O No. 202.   Wenchow, 14th August 1920

Sir,

FORESHORE RECLAMATION.

I take leave to refer you to my despatch No. 3496 informing you that the Superintendent has at last reported to the Shui-wu Ch'u. In the Hsü Ti-chiu case, the man being a local man of no importance and his case being a glaring one of land grabbing the Superintendent had no difficulty in having the sale cancelled by the Ministry of Finance, but in the actual case it is somewhat difficult for the Superintendent to fight against the China Merchants S. N. Co. backed up by all the high Officials who are its share-holders - possibly the Superintendent himself -, so we need not be astonished to see him pass on the case for decision to the Shui-wu Ch'u. But, as he acknowledges that the land was given to us, that the sale to Hsü Ti-chiu was cancelled at his request, and as he does not find

fault

fault with my arguments and even admits that the building of an extra examination shed would be advantageous I think you could argue from this with the Ch'u and show that he admits our claim. One point must be particularly emphasised and that is the want of good faith of the Company in putting me off three times with evasive answers from the beginning instead of putting clearly its claim.

Yours respectfully,

[－42]

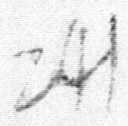

INSPECTORATE GENERAL OF CUSTOMS,

PEKING, **24th August,** 19 **20**.

ar Sir,

I am directed by the Inspector General

orm you that your S/O letter No. **202**

14th instant, has been duly

ed.

Yours truly,

Private Secretary.

.Tanant,Esquire,

Wenchow.

CUSTOM HOUSE,

/O No. 203.

Wenchow, 24. August, 1920.

Sir,

COMMISSIONER'S ABSENCE.

I am taking my family to Shanghai to send them home by the mail steamer leaving 3rd September, and at the same time to have a new plate made by the dentist, and I hope to be back about the 6th September. Following last year precedent I am leaving Mr. Hirano in temporary charge.

I am now sending you the following telegram "Custos Peking Leaving for Shanghai returning about 6 September placing in charge Hirano temporarily letter follows Tanant &

Yours respectfully,

INSPECTORATE GENERAL OF CUSTOMS,

PEKING, 31st August, 1920.

S/O

Dear Mr. Tanant,

I have duly received your S/O letter No. 203 of 24th instant.

<u>Commr's absence from port notifying.</u>

I gather from this that you have changed your opinion as to Mr. Hirano's competency to take charge during your absence. I daresay your second thoughts were correct after all. Men have a wonderful way of rising to meet responsibility when it is suddenly thrust upon them.

Yours truly,

E.Tanant, Esquire,
   Wenchow.

CUSTOM HOUSE,

Shanghai, 27. August 1920.

Sir,

On arrival here yesterday I found that the "Andre' Lebon"s departure - the ship that takes my family home - has been postponed from 3rd to 10th September, and I beg to ask whether you would be so kind as to allow me to stay here the space of another trip of the Wenchow steamer thus returning to Wenchow on the 14th instead of the 6th as per schedule time. As I left a fairly clean desk I don't think there could be much difficulty; the only trouble is that I left Mr. Hirano in temporary charge with instructions not to sign despatches, his being only a Commissioner's appointment, and this would delay the transmission of Monthly Revenue and Staff Reports another week; but this could be avoided by my instructing Mr. Hirano to transmit the Reports by signing them " for Commissioner".

I shall be thankful if you will wire me your decision through the Shanghai Commissioner.

Yours respectfully,

本局號數 JOURNAL NO. 24472

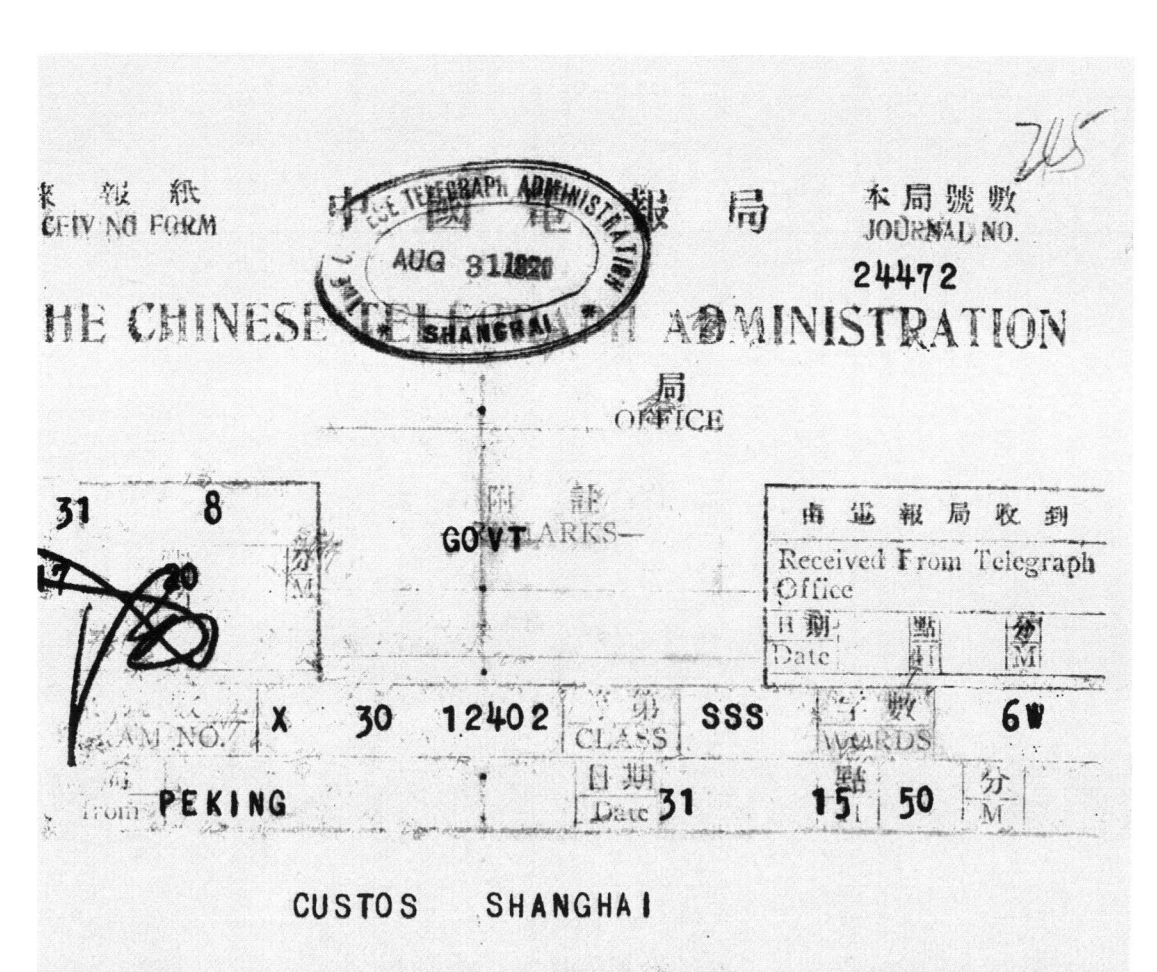

THE CHINESE TELEGRAPH ADMINISTRATION

AUG 31 1920 SHANGHAI

GOVT

From PEKING Date 31 15 50

CUSTOS   SHANGHAI

IQYHOKXY   IQNAUWHEEN   LUOBAPUFSU   INYFEXZYZY

For Tanant — may extend leave as required = Bowra.

CUSTOM HOUSE,

S/O No. 204.

Wenchow, 29. September, 1920.

Sir,

FORESHORE RECLAMATION.

I duly received your telegram of 24th intimating the offer of the China Merchants S.N. Co., through the Shui-wu Ch'u to forego their claim on condition that the Customs allow their steamers to overlap their actual wharf frontage if or when necessary.

This offer, as I see it, grants us nothing, as the Company refuses to sell us its small house; on the contrary it takes away of our disputed rights as we should thus lose the 7½ ft. frontage of the small house. I should add that when in Shanghai I called on my Superintendent, who has now resided there for about ten months, and he then mentioned this new offer of the Company. I replied I thought this offer came rather late, just the same as the production of proofs of ownership for the land occupied by by t e small house (vide my S/O No. 199), and that the matter having been reported by the Company to the Shui-wu Ch'u, investigated, and reported on, the best was to await the Ch'u's decision.

Now, as the Ch'u who seems to be the master in this affair has transmitted you this offer I could not help noticing that the validity of our claim if not entirely sustained, anyhow has been recognised, and if that is so then I think we should be entitled to more concessions on the part of the Company in exchange for the right to overlap over our frontage. Hence the 3 conditions I stated in my reply : 1o. <u>sale of the small house by the Company to the Customs</u>. Without it we would have a very annoying corner protruding into our building when we build ; besides it might lead to further litigation, for if we build we shall have to obliterate the light which the small house receives through the

the window on the North (the window is shown in the photo appended to my despatch). 2o. underlining that the overlapping does not exceed the frontage of the small house, i.e. 8 feet (really 7½) east of the actual boundary wall. If that is not clearly stated the Company might in years to come claim that the overlapping extends to the frontage of the whole lot up to the public jetty. 3o. the Company's pontoon not to be enlarged or changed from its actual position. I asked this because even in allowing steamers moored at the actual pontoon to overlap 3 feet there is just sufficient room between the bow of the steamer, the pontoon, and the bundwall for a small launch to go alongside the bund, and as we shall some day or the other require a launch or motor boat of some sort this would be a very good place to moor her. Were the Company allowed to enlarge or moor its pontoon up to its actual boundary line

the

the space left would be very much reduced and be hardly of any use.

COMMISSIONER'S RETURN FROM SHANGHAI.

I am very thankful for the extension of leave transmitted through the Shanghai Commr. There being no direct steamer for Wenchow after the mail's departure, all the time tables having been disorganised on account of the typhoon, I left via Ningpo so as not to wait another 5 or 6 days at Shanghai, and from Ningpo took the small coasting steamer calling at inland places en route, a very pretty trip only marred by the absence of comfort and the promiscuity of pasengers as is the ryule on board all those boats. After stranding on a sand bank off Haimen and a consequent loss of one day the ship nevertheless reached Wenchow 4 days before the regular weekly steamer. I shall write later on what I saw at Haimen.

Yours respectfully,

INSPECTORATE GENERAL OF CUSTOMS,

PEKING, 9th October, 1920.

S/O

Dear Mr. Tanant,

I have duly received your S/O letter No. 204 of 29th ultimo.

Foreshore reclamation.

Your counter-proposals have been sent in to the Shui-wu Ch'u and I am awaiting their answer.

Yours truly,

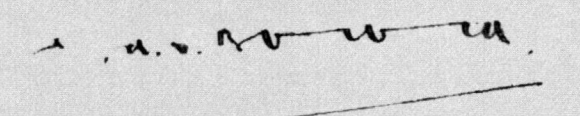

E. Tanant, Esquire,
    Wenchow.

CUSTOM HOUSE,

S/O No. 205.

Wenchow, 15th October 1920.

Sir,

TYPHOON OF 3RD SEPTEMBER.

I have to report that while I was away on leave, Wenchow was badly struck by a typhoon which blew from the 3rd to the 7th September doing enormous damage as well in the city as in the country. Some 1,200 people are reported drowned or killed mostly in the Nanchi River valley (occasionally called here North River) which joins the Wenchow (Ou) River opposite Wenchow. It would seem that some water spout must have struck that unfortunate region thus taking whole villages unaware and not only killing people but devastating the whole country.

In other parts of the plains surrounding Wenchow, rain water flooded the whole country and the rice crop is reported

as

as damaged by one half. In town the damage is equally enormous for there is hardly one house, in which part of a wall did not subside. The outlets of the canals in the River being dammed so as to prevent the ingress of sea water, and keep a constant level in the canals, the extra quantity of rain water which poured in from all neighbouring mountains could not find a sufficiently quick exit in the river and flooded part of the city thus adding to the damage by rain and wind. In fact the damage has been so great that a public subscription for relief was started locally, a case of extremely rare occurrence here.

As regards Customs the entrance hall of the Native Customs, an old and rickety building, was nearly flattened to the ground and had to be pulled down, and is being re-erected, at a cost of about $200. The N.C.
house

house boat (a covered sampan) which was under repairs at the time was smashed up by floating beams and is a complete wreck (new one $130). In the Assistant's Quarters part of the compound wall, chimneys, etc. were blown down (over $50.). Even at the Custom House, well and strongly built 20 years ago, rain water percolated all the surface of the wall facing east.

DUTY COLLECTED ON DEPOSIT ON A LOT OF MILITARY UNIFORMS COVERED BY LUCHUN PU HUCHAO BUT NOT ACCOMPANIED BY GOVERNMENT STORES CERTIFICATE.

  I have got now a very interesting case going on, all verbally so far. A lot of 1,307 (30 packages) suits of Military Uniforms arrived on 25th September, said to have come from Shanghai and to have been transhipped at Haimen to the Ningpo-Wenchow Inland Waters Steamer "Yungning". A Luchun Pu small Huchao was the only document presented to cover the lot but no Government

Stores

Stores Certificate. The Huchao was not countersigned by either the Shanghai Maritime Customs nor the Shanghai Native Customs, and I claimed payment of full and half duty pending receipt of a Government Stores Certificate to be issued by the Shanghai Superintendent. The duties were deposited by the steamer company as agent. Yesterday the Acting Superintendent called and said the matter had been referred to him by the Military Authorities and asked what to do. I explained him that it was a case where the Officer in charge of transport was most probably pocketing the cost of transport but that without caring for that I could not free the lot from duty without a Government Stores Certificate. I added that in ordinary circumstances I would have accepted a Government Stores Certificate issued by him (Wenchow Superintendent) but in this case some sanction seemed necessary as the Huchao plainly stated

the

the goods were from Shanghai and therefore not only should a G.S.C. have been issued by the Shanghai Superintendent but also both Huchao and G.S.C. should have been presented to the Shanghai N.C. for countersignature. He said he would transmit those explainations to the Officer concerned. In this connection I take leave to call your attention to the fact that some similar lots of the same quantity of Military Uniforms and even smaller are not only covered by Luchun Pu small Huchao but also by your and Shui-wu Ch'u Authorities. Why was this lot thus not covered by regular Authorities? Perhaps the result of the recent war in Chihli, and consequent changes in the Ministry?

       Yours respectfully,

INSPECTORATE GENERAL OF CUSTOMS,

PEKING, 26th October, 1920

Dear Sir,

I am directed by the Inspector General to inform you that your S/O letter No. 205, dated 15th instant, has been duly received.

Yours truly,

[signature]
Private Secretary.

E. Tanant, Esquire,

Wenchow.

CUSTOM HOUSE,

S/O No. 206.

Wenchow, 29th October, 1920.

Sir,

FORESHORE RECLAMATION.

The Superintendent was the first to intimate the Ch'u's decision. After confirmation by your despatch No. 967/80,719 I called on the Superintendent and discussed the matter. He agreed with me that the small house belongs to the C.M.S.N.Co, while its foreshore is ours. I then said: they want to moor their ships in front of it, this we are ready to admit; but in exchange they must give us something tangible, and I ask them to sell me the small house which is of very little use to them while it would make our property square. I also mentioned that I could not allow the dolphins of the actual pontoon to be remoored in front of our foreshore as they would be in the way of a small launch or motor boat which we shall have to moor alongside the projected

reclamation

reclamation some day.

The Superintendent said the agent on receipt of the Ch'u's instructions had already written to Shanghai to ask for further instructions, and gave me to understand that not only the Company wants to overlap 8 feet but that it even wants to overlap further in front of the undisputed foreshore. This, I said, I did not think I could allow. In fact it would interfere with our mooring of a launch.

The matter stands there and I want to ask your instructions for further discussion. My opinion is that we should refuse to discuss this last proposal to allow them to overlap our own foreshore over which there is no possible discussion and which was not mentioned when they transmitted their complaints to the Ch'u. I would also point out that there is private land to the west of the
             Company's

Company's property which they could buy and bund, but of course that will be expensive and it would be cheaper to let the Customs bund their foreshore and have the advantage of it by overlapping. This I should say we must strongly resist, and my idea is that we should plainly tell it and finish with it if they do not sell us the small house in exchange for the right to overlap 8 feet. Beyond that nothing, and if you have any opportunity to refer the matter to the Ch'u by writing or verbally I take leave to suggest that you point out the Company's greediness at our expense for I can not harm it otherwise.

NINGPO CARGO IMPORTED BY I.W.S.N. STEAMERS.

The change of practice in obliging Ningpo cargo to be reported to the Maritime instead of the Native Customs, reported in my despatches Nos. 3513 and 3514, begins to show a result, but not the one expected, viz., increase of revenue. Part of that cargo which

which used to pay N.C. duty at Ningpo and was passed free here on arrival, is now covered by Maritime Customs M.C.s which would tend to show that there is at Ningpo like at Shanghai too much laxity over the checking of cargo on importation or re-exportation. It seems inadmissible that merchants for the sake of a few Customs formalities would have paid N.C. duties, which means extra payment at intermediate N.C. Offices, when knowing that their goods could reach Wenchow free of duty if reported at the Maritime Customs.

I am going to try to fathom the matter by correspondance with Ningpo.

SEIZURES FROM LORCHAS.

Mr. Christophersen while out sailing down river on Sunday made a smart seizure of a sampan which he caught being loaded from a lorcha with packages of sundries some 5 miles below Harbour Limits. He further had the same lorcha searched on arrival in port and again a big lot of cargo was

seized

seized which probably could not be landed outside Harbour Limits. I confiscated the cargo and fined the ship for landing cargo inland and for false manifest. Another lorcha which arrived the same day was equally seached and found to carry some 160 packages not manifested. She was fined for false manifest and the cargo was confiscated.

  Yours respectfully,

INSPECTORATE GENERAL OF CUSTOMS,

S/O

PEKING, 5th November, 1920.

Dear Mr. Tanant,

I have duly received your S/O letter No. 206 of 29th ultimo.

Foreshore Reclamation.

I do not think the Ch'u want to handle the matter further. Their idea is that you should come to an understanding locally and I hope you will be able to do so.

Yours truly,

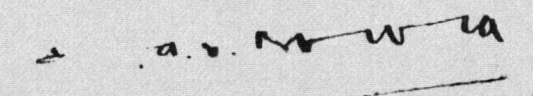

---nant, Esquire,
---enchow.

CUSTOM HOUSE,

Wenchow, 29, October, 1920.

No. 207.

Sir,

STAFF : Mr. K. HIRANO.

The wife of Mr. K. Hirano expects a baby, I should say in a couple of months. I asked the Customs Doctor whether he had been consulted and he said yes, once, and I asked further whether she would be delivered here, but he does not know, and he added he would prefer if it did not take place here.

On the other hand Mrs Hirano only speaks Japanese which makes it more difficult for the Doctor, and such being the case I beg to ask whether it would not be advisable to transfer Mr. Hirano to Shanghai. If you think so I would recommend it be done at once so as to save her fatigue in packing, etc., and also the discomfort inherent to a transfer in winter.

I did not mention this matter to Mr. Hirano.

Yours respectfully,

INSPECTORATE GENERAL OF CUSTOMS,

S/O   PEKING, 5th November, 1920.

Dear Mr. Tanant,

I have duly received your S/O letter No. 207 of 29th ultimo.

Re Mrs. K. Hirano.

This is a purely private affair in which I should be very reluctant to intervene, and transfer at Customs expense and at Service inconvenience could not be granted in such a case. There is no reason why Mrs. Hirano should not go to Shanghai for her confinement if she sees fit to do so.

Yours truly,

Tanant, Esquire,
Wenchow.

CUSTOM HOUSE,

S/O No. 208.

Wenchow 11. November, 19 20.

Sir,

H. B. M. Consular Residence offered for sale.

I am now mailing my report on the British Divisional Architect's offer to sell us the British Consulate. I wonder what started them all of a sudden to write to you direct? However I may say this, and it is, I believe that they are tired of this property. The Standard Oil Co. used to rent the Constable's house, but owing mostly to a feud between Mrs Ahlberg, wife of the former Tidesurveyor, and Mrs Kurt, wife of the foreign representative of the S. O. Co., the latter abandoned the Island to live in the S. O. Co's new installation last year, and Mrs Ahlberg remained the Queen of the deserted Island. But the clearest result was that the British Crown lost a tenant for the Constable's house at $ 30. a month, and this the Divisional Architect's Department which seems very business like, does not cherish. Already before when the Consulate was rented to the Tidesurveyors privately, there happened to be a gap between either

Captain

Captain Palmer's or Mr. Tonkin's and Mr. Stevens occupancy, and a loss of 6 months rent, and that was the real cause why the Customs were asked to take over the lease officially. Now they see that we have taken to the house, and as they have lost the rent of the Constable's house my ideas is that they are trying to sell us the Consul's house so as to get rid of it at a good price.

There is, besides, another reason. The Constable house is now rented to some American 7th Day Adventists Missionaries with whom the other Protestant Missionaries wont have anything to do. This is gossip, but all the same amusing. When these Adventists arrived the C.I.M. and Methodists came round discreetly asking whether we had met them and what sorts of people they were, etc. In fact, Mrs Kurt of the S. O. Co., herself the daughter of an American Missionary of Nanking, invited all the foreign ladies over to the Island to meet Mrs Wilkinson, a meek young lady of about 25, the wife of the new Adventist Missionary. They all went there, sat round the room, listened to the Victrola, had tea and cakes, but not a word was said to Mrs Wilkinson. - It may be they had ice cream too! - Later on I heard indirectly

indirectly that they (Wilkinson) were accused of stealing the others' christians!

To revert to the Constable's house it remained vacant for several months after the Kurt's departure and was finally, reluctantly - I heard it from Mr. Wilkinson - rented to them, and I now wonder whether no indirect complaint has not been sent to Legation Quarters against this renting of British Government property to foreign unwanted competitors.

Besides, again, the typhoon of 15th July did some damage to the Bund wall of the Consular property which was already requiring minor repairs. I reported on it to the Divisional Architect, and I heard afterwards Mr. Wilkinson also, and this sudden call for expenditure coupled with the fact that the Consulate and Constable's house have hard been kept in regular repairs ever since rented to us instead of being attended to every three years as is the Board of works rule, may have made them fear to have to spend a lot of money in maintanance of the property in proper repairs, which to be well done, should be made under foreign supervision, a very expensive business when steamer fares for the Clerk of works and his staff, their salaries, hotel accomodation, etc., are taken into consideration.

I

I estimate that if we had to put the Consul's House in the same good state of repairs as it should be it would cost us over $1,000 if we did the work together with other repairs to other properties while to the British Board of Works obliged to send its Staff specially it would probably come to $1,500.

Yours respectfully,

[.—42]

INSPECTORATE GENERAL OF CUSTOMS.

PEKING, **23rd Nov.,** 19 20.

ear Sir,

I am directed by the Inspector General
form you that your S/O letter No. **208**,
11th instant, has been duly
ved.

Yours truly,

Private Secretary.

.E.Tanant, Esquire,

Wenchow.

CUSTOM HOUSE,

S/O No. 209.

Wenchow, 24th Nov. 1920.

Sir,

MR. K'O YU-P'ING'S SENIORITY TOWARDS RETIREMENT:

With reference to my despatch No. 3527 reporting the purchase of the Chin and Wang properties through Mr. K'o Yu-p'ing's assistance I beg leave to call your attention to his Service career.

When the issue of Retiring Allowance to the Native Customs Staff was settled by Circular No. 2590, Mr. K'o Yu-p'ing, now 3rd Clerk A, who previous to his transfer to the Maritime Customs had served 7 years, (from November 1903 till October 1910) in the Native Customs at Foochow, applied - Wenchow despatch No. 3176 - for issue of a Retiring Allowance for the period 1903 to 1915,

covering

covering his first Duodecennial period of Service, so as to find himself on about the same footing in that respect as other candidates who joined the Customs or Post Office together with him but were assigned to the Maritime Customs or the Postal Service.

  I.G. despatch No. 697/63,908 in reply regretted that the I.G. was unable to make an exception in the case of Mr. K'o to the rules regarding issue of Retiring Allowances to the N.C. Staff; though, I think in one way, that his passing the Customs examination,— the same for Maritime Customs, Native Customs, and Postal Clerkships, I understand, might have been a reason sufficient to stretch the rule in his favour; his case not being the same as that of purely Native Customs employés.

  Later on when Circulars Nos. 2006, 2011, 2013, re Superannuation and Retirement Scheme, were issued, I submitted in Wenchow despatch No. 3462, $10, amongst various

       queries,

queries, Mr. K'o's case, asking whether his years of Service in the N.C. would count towards his 40 years Service necessary to obtain the full benefit of the new scheme, but no reply has ever been received, and in view of Mr. K'o's excellent work not only in procuring for the Service the two Chin and ang properties above referred to, but also at the Office generally, I beg to ask that his case be taken up and that he be granted the small favour asked for, the grant of which would only place him as regards retirement on the level of the other men who joined the Service with him, and some of whom already rank as 2nd Clerks C while others who joined in 1904 are 2nd Clerks C and D.

PROPERTY: ENLARGEMENT OF COMMISSIONER'S RESIDENCE.

  I am glad to be able to report the purchase of the Chin and Wang lots for now the Works Department may plan to improve the house as suggested in my former despatch. I hope if we know how to wait a little longer that

that we shall be able to get the remaining property within honest figures. Everybody knows we are after it and they all want to make money from us and can not imagine that I be so cantankerous as to save Customs money and bargain! The last I heard about this lot is through a visit of Mr. Heywood the head of the Methddist Mission who came to say that one of the teachers of their college had heard I wanted to buy and offered himself as go between. I replied I did not require more meddlers, that I knew the actual owner had paid $285. and if he would not be satisfied with say double, he would have to wait, for having bought land enough to enlarge my house the garden could wait. This is typical mission assistance - the Chinese rightly term it interference - but everything is well that promotes the interests of one's adepts. In one way all those difficulties in purchase of that land are the result of the former Sup rintendent, Mr. Mao Kwang Sheng's work in asking the local

Member

Member of the Provincial Assembly Mr. Yang Chen-hsin to help me. This man was willing and did his best but employed brokers who were going to make a good business of this affair and I have reasons to believe that the actual owner's demands have been prompted by them. It is an affair to know how long he will wait before coming down.

COMMISSIONER'S HOME LEAVE.

I beg to thank you for granting my home leave. I should say that all this bargaining is quite enough to make one sick and certainly did not improve my general state.

Yours respectfully,

INSPECTORATE GENERAL OF CUSTOMS,

PEKING, 3rd December 19 20

Dear Mr. Tanant,

I have duly received you S/O letter No. 209 of 24th November.

Mr. K'o Yu-p'ing's seniority for purposes of the Superannuation and Retirement Scheme may date from 19th November 1903.

Yours truly,

Tanant, Esquire,
    Wenchow.

CUSTOM HOUSE,

Wenchow, 4. December, 1920.

No. 210.

Sir, _unofficial light._

In my despatch No.3529 I brought to your notice the fact that the establishment of an unofficial light on Middle Island, Sampwan group, estuary of the Wenchow River, was giving rise to claims from various parties for the collection and private use of fees to be collected under the pretext of maintenance of the light, and I suggested that instead of remaining indifferent we should try to take in hand the collection and attend to the light. I think the authorities would be willing and it would be a beginning towards the collection of Tonnage Dues from Native shipping which was denied to the Commissioner by the Taotai when handing over the control of the 50 li radius N. C. Offices.

Maritime Fisheries Office.

I now send another despatch, No. 3530, informing you of a difficulty which has risen between a newly created Maritime Fisheries Office and the Maritime Police over the collection of Registration Fees of fishing Junks which is

nothing

nothing but part of the N. C. Fees collected formerly by the Taotai but the collection of which was also denied to the Commissioner when he assumed control. Both cases might perhaps give you an opportunity to claim the reversion of the payment of those Dues to the Commissioner. That would be one way, in any case, to solve all those local scrambles for positions leading to squeezes.

ASIATIC PETROLEUM CO'S PROJECTED INSTALLATION.
I have to report the visit of Mr. H.D. Wilding, a Civil Engineer, in the employ of the Asiatic Petroleum Co. He informed me he had come to survey some land bought or to be bought by that Company, close to the Standard Oil Co's installation in view to putting up their own installation. He asked in this connection information *re* height of tides, etc., I took advantage of his visit to explain to him that so far I had not been informed by the Chinese Authorities of any permission being granted to his Company to erect this installation, and that I could not take any official recognition of their intended works until informed officially. In the conversation we spoke of contactors and cost of materials, and he said that they would probably contract with a Shanghai contractor under certain guarantees, for from what they had seen

by

by experience at other ports they were of opinion that work done under foreign supervision of Clerks of works assisted in most cases by Shanghai contractors, the initial cost of any building was raised by one half, due to inflation of prices under pretext of obtaining the best procurable materials. He particularly laid stress on prices paid for Customs works at either Chinkiang or Nanking which were cause of of a general increase in the cost of foreign buildings at that place. I do not know the kind of works he referred to, but I thought as well to mention it because when a Clerk of works came to Yochow to inspect the Commr's House and estimate cost of repairs, he informed me that the work would most likely be given to a Shanghai contractor who was then building for the Customs at Changsha. This is all very good but cannot fail to increase the cost of works for this contractor not only has to live, but not being a Native has most likely to pay more for his materials and labourers than a native contractor whom finally he is probably obliged to employ, and who, again, takes his

percentage

percentage on all contract prices. Hence too many cooks.

TAOYIN.

I hear from the Acting Superitendent that our Taoyin, Mr. Tuan Wu-tai, who arrived in August, has resigned.

      Yours respectfully,

INSPECTORATE GENERAL OF CUSTOMS,

S/O   PEKING, 14th December, 1920.

Dear Mr. Tanant,

I have duly received your S/O letter No. 210 of 4th instant.

Unofficial Light on Middle Island.

It would perhaps be best for us to take over the light. A similar question has already arisen elsewhere and the matter needs study. We have no authority yet to collect Light Dues from junks.

Maritime Fisheries Office : establishment of : is collecting fees which rightly should be controlled by N.C. : suggesting that claim be made to have payment of Registration Fees and Tonnage Dues of Native Shipping revert to Native Customs.

Such action raises delicate questions just now when we already control so large a part of the Government's available resources. I doubt whether the result would be worth the trouble such a claim would cause!

Yours truly,

[signature]

t, Esquire,
chow.

No. 211.

CUSTOM HOUSE,

Wenchow, 9. December, 1920.

Sir,

APPOINTMENT OF PILOT.

I am now mailing my despatch No. 3526 asking for instructions concerning the appointment of a successor to Habour Master Tingchai Lin Yin-chiu in his capacity as acting Pilot, and from its perusal you will see that the question is very complex. I earnestly deprecate the continuance of the practice to allow the No. 1 boatman to act as pilot. This is wrong at all points of view and particularly that of safety of the ships. That kind of men only care to make dollars by any means. The No. 1 swears he knows the river and is able to pilot, but this is very doubtful as he never goes out sailing. In fact how could he as he never gets leave to go? His only chance to pilot successfully would be to go and question junks and trust luck. If he succeeds he will pocket his dollars, if not, maskee, he he will not lose by it, but if by bad luck the ship was stranded everybody would fall on us for recommending a useless man and my arguments would be appropriately turned against us. If he wants the job let him pass the examination and resign. The trouble is that the Tidesurveyor, like all his predecessors, is practically in the hands of the number 1 without whose assistance he is nowhere as none of the other boatmen speak pidgin, and even should the Tidesurveyor speak Mandarin or Cantonese it is not understood fbym the natives who only speak their abominable Wenchow dialect.

I only see two ways to solve the question: either hold an examination as best as we can, or if no proper candidate can be appointed, inform the Companies accordingly and let them provide their own pilots. After all the trouble I gave in having the Pilotage Regulations re-arranged as desired by Captain Tyler that might look abnormal to say the least, but it is the only advisable course to follow.

Yours respectfully,

INSPECTORATE GENERAL OF CUSTOMS,

S/O

PEKING, 23rd December, 1920

Dear Mr. Tanant,

I have duly received your S/O letter No. 211 of 9th instant.

Appointment of pilot.

If as you say there is money in the business there should be candidates and they should be examined. If there is no money there will be no candidates. I quite recognise the objection to our men being employed as pilots.

Yours truly,

Tanant, Esquire,
    Wenchow.

CUSTOM HOUSE,

No. 212.

Wenchow   24. December 1920.

Sir,

DIFFICULTIES CREATED BY QUESTION OF REPAIRS TO COMMISSIONER'S HOUSE.

I received yesterday your despatch No. 981 / 81857 informing me that repairs to the Commissioner's House had been decided upon, which information I had already received by the Clerk of Works, Mr. Sheridan, who arrived three days ago bearer of a despatch to that effect from the Engineer-in-Chief. My successor will no doubt be very thankful to you, but may I take leave to say that I am not in this particular regard. I am not any longer young, and I think more of my bones and health than of anything else, and as this is the coldest weather of the year for us here, I cannot hide that I am rather afraid at the idea of moving to temporary quarters just when it is the appointed time to keep in a cosy corner.

On

On the other hand I must also point out that I cannot find vacant quarters for rent. The Engineer-in-Chief in his despatch No. 2008 / 2874 to you lightly stated that I could, if necessary, stay in my house. This, as shown in my despatch in reply, No. 3512, is a rather preposterous proposal when repairs of such magnitude are undertaken, and the best is that the Clerk of Works who is anxious to be quartered close to the house does not intend to stay in it. In fact he has now reported that the beams supporting the first floor will have to be replaced, and also the ground-floor wooden flooring, not to speak of the other repairs and ameliorations such as the necessary bath rooms at the back. I am therefore very much concerned with the question of quarters, and I only see the following solutions :

1º Take two rooms in the Tidesurveyor's house in the Island, which may not suit him, and is rather inadvisable at many points of view for the Commissioner, or

2º move away the Tidewaiter from his quarters over the Post Office at the Custom House, take his

his two rooms, and the room rented as Office to the Post master, thus making three rooms but lacking very much of privacy as the groundfloor is open to the public who goes in and out of the Post Office on either side of the stairs. The Tidewaiter would be moved to the Island in the semi-detached Examiner's House, one half of which is now occupied by the other Tidewaiter. As to the Clerk of Work he would have to be quartered in the two rooms in the Tidesurveyor's house, thus far from his work.

I am not at all keen on all this, and I beg to ask whether I could not be spared all this inconvenience. You have plenty of young men who would be only too keen on being placed here in charge and who could devote their energy perhaps more advantageously than I can do to Office work and superintendence of the repairs. In fact the Works Dept. made it clear in their despatch that if the works cannot be finished early the last part of it
will

will have to be superintended by the actual Wenchow staff. If it is so it seems that it would be so much the better to appoint here a man who could take the matter in hand, push it, and finish it if necessary. If not too old, he would perhaps not mind living in the Island with the Tidesurveyor or anyhow in the same house, possibly messing separately, or else take the Tidewaiter's quarters as explained above.

To show you another aspect of the trouble this change of quarters would put me to I would also ask you to kindly consider the question of packing and see how inconvenient it would be for me to pack now for removal to temporary quarters and again pack up in a few months when my leave is due in April, and as it is only an affair of three months I would be willing, if you can see your way to grant my request, to take my leave at once at the risk of waiting at my own expense for steamer accommodation. I do not think I

would

would experience much difficulty in having my passage changed from April to January or the beginning of February as there are then fewer passengers than in the spring.

I had been hoping all the time those repairs would be undertaken in the spring or summer when the question of weather inclemencies and also that of more suitability for this kind of work would have been resolved without the slightest difficulty. However time presses, and as the Clerk of works is keen on beginning at once I shall be thankful if you will be so kind as to let me have your decision by wire.

Yours respectfully,

1921 年

CUSTOM HOUSE,

S/O NO. 213.   Wenchow, 21st January 1921.

Sir,

SEIZURE OF OPIUM.

Mr. H. Gaylard, 2nd Class Tidewaiter, has just made a seizure of 64 catties of raw opium on board the I.W.S.N. Steamer "Kienkong" a small steamer, 148 tons, net, with a crew of 30 men all told, running between Chuanchow, Amoy, Wenchow, and Ningpo. Already in June last we had seized 195 one tael tins of prepared opium from the Régie de l'Indochine, and 2 catties raw native opium on board the same ship, but there was no proof that the crew were implicated in the case, and I simply confiscated the opium warning the Compradore. This time the opium was seized under coal in the cook's coal box on deck. The Compradore swears his staff is innocent, which I doubt; but which one or ones of the staff are the culprits? I cannot find and on the doubt I told the

Compradore

Comprador that I made the ship responsible and would fine Tls. 500. (maximum penalty for false manifest) and that recurrence would mean the whole or part of the crew being sent to the Authorities and possibly other difficulties for his ship such as cancellation of I.W.S.N. Certificate. The man says that they take all possible precautions and that at Chüanchow some passengers refused to remain on board on being searched. He further points out that opium is openly cultivated and sold in Chüanchow, which may be possible but is not nevertheless allowed by the Central government. If you think my fine is too heavy it may be reduced but if you want to stop the traffic I do not think it too heavy, and I would even ask whether I could inflict heavier fines if necessary. I do not see what Treaty rule to invoke for infliction of heavier penalties, and the only remedy seems to arrest the smugglers and pass them on to the judicial authorities, but to judge by the few cases I have had settled by them here I am very averse to send anybody to the Courts as it

means

means small official fines while it gives ample time and opportunities to all the official leaches to bleed the patients, to no good result to us, not even to the State.

The <u>Superintendent</u> who called this morning to say good bye <u>on a trip to Shanghai</u>, did not seem to have any objection to my decision. I showed him the text of Shui-wu Ch'u's despatch No. 42 appended to your Circular No. 2218 and pointed out that since its issue the government though impecunious had bought and destroyed the stock of foreign opium and thus showed its determination to stamp out the smoking.

In view to checking smuggling by crews of ships I think it would be advisable that each port informs the ports of call of a given steamer when seizures of opium are made so as to help to mitigate or possibly increase penalties of other seizures are made on the same ship during the same run.

PURCHASE OF ADDITIONAL LAND FOR COMMISSIONER'S RESIDENCE.

I am reporting in despatch No.3547 the

the acquisition of the Yeh Yü-chieh tombs property overlooking the eastern side of the Commissioner's residence. Mr. K'o Yu-p'ing has again been instrumental in all the bargaining and I take leave to request that Mr. Bowra's promise (S/O letter of 3rd December) that Mr. K'o's seniority for purposes of the Superannuation and Retirement Scheme will date from 19th November 1903, be sanctioned by despatch for inclusion in his Memo. of Service and Office Records.

STAFF.

After receipt of your telegram of 5th I removed the Commissioner's House furniture to the Island, to the Office, and to the Tidewaiters' quarters whence I moved Mr. West and Mr. Sheridan (Clerk of Works) to the Island. Mr West has been sick with rheumatism for about a fortnight nut is better now, and the Clerk of Works Mr. Sheridan also suffered from rheumatism these last few days. Yesterday he passed through the verandah's flooring, but fortunately didn't kill himself.

Yours respectfully,

INSPECTORATE GENERAL OF CUSTOMS,

S/O

PEKING, 28th January 1921.

Dear Mr. Tanant,

I have duly received your S/O letter No. 213 of the 21st instant.

<u>Seizure of Opium : Commr. requests I. G.'s views as to penalty inflicted :</u>

I don't know what the value of the opium is and cannot therefore offer an opinion as to the penalty. What is it worth ?

Yours truly,

Tanant, Esquire,
Wenchow.

CUSTOM HOUSE,

S/O NO. 214.

Wenchow, 5th February 1921

Sir,

I beg to acknowledge receipt of your S/O Letter of 28th January:

<u>Seizure of opium referred by Commissioner for I.G.'s views as to penalty inflicted.</u>

in which you ask the value of the opium, and, in reply, to say that it is practically impossible to reply to such a query. Importation has been prohibited here for years and the trade, if existing, is clandestine, and being such there cannot be any fixed market value. My Tidesurveyor thinks from vague hear says that the opium (Native raw opium) is worth $2. a Tael, therefore 64 catties = 1,024 Taels would be worth $2,048.

A letter has now been received from the compradore addressed to Mr. H. Gaylard, the Tidewaiter who made the seizure, reading

"Foochow 25th January 1921.

Dear

Dear Mr. Gaylard

Dear Sir,

I beg to inform you that on the 22nd instant the S/S "Kienkong" arrived Foochow and the manager of our company asked all the peoples of S/S "Kienkong" to discuss the opium question in his Office.

Finally the manager found out the fire man had hiding the opium in the coal box, then the fire man was sent to the Chinese official for punishment.

But it is very surprise to me that the fire man and the Engineer of our ship told our manager that I am the partnership on this business. Now the sum on of Chinese official is necessary, and I will report to the Chinese official to prove that I am not the partnership as follow+ I am the partnership why I had informed to the Customs Officer Mr. Gaylard of this business when the S/S "Kienkong" dued(?)at Wenchow, and I had advised Mr. Gaylard to search the opium more carefully.

I

I will be much obliged if you confirm or report if necessary that I the compralor had advise you as above before the searching, then this case will be cleared up that I have no fault upon this question.

Many thanks in anticipation and to remain,

Dear Sir,

Yours faithfully,

(Signed) Tang Hauk Han."

I instructed Mr. Gaylard to reply he could not furnish any information and that if the court wants any it must apply to me officially.

It would seem from this that my fine has had some effect as 1 of the culprits at least has been arrested, but it seems strange that the compradore could not say anything here.

APPOINTMENT OF PILOTS.

I duly received your S/O Letter of 23rd December in which you said: "If there is money in the business there should be candidates

candidates and they should be examined. If there is no money there will be no candidates. I quite recognise the objection to our men being employed as pilots". Accordingly I told the Tidesurveyor we would have later on to hold an Examination and that the head boatman could compete if he cares but that if appointed he would have to resign from his Customs position. Now I have received your despatch No. 969/82,413 in which you say: "The Harbour Master should train some one to take over and carry on when Lin can no longer do the work". Does this "some one" means one of our boatmen to act conjointly as pilot, or an outsider?

  Further, how can the Harbour Master go and teach a pilot to know the river when he (Tidesurveyor) most probably does not know it. The bar, off Rocky point, where the pilot is particularly needed by ships, is about twenty miles from Wenchow and with shifting sand banks the Harbour Master would have to live on the spot to be able to know his way about. Short manned as is this Office Staff

Staff I am afraid it is impossible to ask him to go up and down river. Besides, to go there and return means 1½ days at least and we have no house boat. The only available crafts are fishing junks or sampan and the Harbour Master deserves some kind of consideration which we are not in position to afford him. Why not then simply hold an ordinary examination and appoint the most suitable of the candidates. If the China Merchant S.N. Co does not care for the man thus appointed I would let the company find its own pilot.

STAFF.

All all right now. I gave 2 weeks leave to Mr. Wong Haiu Geng to go and meet his brother during the New Year Holidays, at Shanghai. Mrs. Hirano has just given birth to a son.

Yours respectfully,

INSPECTORATE GENERAL OF CUSTOMS,

S/O.

PEKING, 17th February 1921.

Dear Mr. Tanant,

I have duly received your S/O letter No. 214 of the 5th instant.

<u>Pilot : Commr. suggests holding an examination and appointing most suitable candidate</u> :

I gathered from your despatch that Lin gave satisfaction and could go on for some time and that the other man mentioned showed promise of being able to step into Lin's shoes. If you can get a <u>competent</u> man by examination that, of course, is the best way ! But can you ?

Yours truly,

Tanant, Esquire,
Wenchow.

CUSTOM HOUSE,

S/O No. 215.   Wenchow, 28th February, 21.

Sir,

OLD CHINESE NEW YEAR.

The old Chinese New Year has been celebrated with, it seems, more pleasure than these last few years and though for lack of money festivities were not so apparent as before, yet business took longer to be resumed. We were just two weeks without steamer.

RICE FOR DISTRESS RELIEF.

A lot of rice has been imported recently from Shanghai for distress relief. Amongst it was some Nomi rice used mostly to make alcohol I referred the matter to the Shanghai Customs who replied all this rice is duty paid either from Anhwei or Hunan and we need not bother about its quality though local authorities should see that in time of scarcity none of the rice should be diverted from food purposes. As the

the Shanghai Customs were satisfied I did not think worth while raising any question locally. However a lot of 13,600 bags rice has now been imported from Wuhu passed free there for famine relief and amongst them we found, on information, 140 bags of superior quality rice and 138 nomi rice which should certainly not be passed free of duty for distress relief. I submitted samples to the Superintendent for the local authorities decision and if they agree I will confiscate.

REPAIRS TO COMMISSIONER'S HOUSE.

Work is progressing but it will be a costly affair, for of the old house only the 4 walls and the stairs have not been rebuilt, all the rest is new including galv. iron roof. There have been two petty thefts of timber but the thieves have been caught and sent to the police for punishment. The wall round the property is also being erected and I am bargaining for the purchase of the small Lu lot in front of Yeh's tombs. The Lu owner came round and offered to give us

his

his small lot free and after being pressed for his exchange requirements, admitted he would be satisfied with a Customs job. I advised him to put his expectations in dollars as that would be the only thing I could offer him.
STAFF.

 Mr. Wong Hsiu Geng duly returned from leave. The Staff are all well.

      Yours respectfully,

INSPECTORATE GENERAL OF CUSTOMS,

S/O PEKING, 9th March 1921.

Dear Mr. Tanant,

I have duly received your S/O letter No. 215 of the 28th ultimo.

Rice for distress relief passed free at Wuhu:

Rice passed at Wuhu for Famine relief ought not to turn up at Wenchow; it should be confiscated.

Purchase of Lu lot: Commr. will only bargain in money:

Quite right!

Yours truly,

Tanant, Esquire,
Wenchow.

S/O No. 216.

CUSTOM HOUSE,

Wenchow, 4th March 1921.

Sir,

APPOINTMENT OF ASSISTANT EXAMINER S.R. AMBROSE.

On receipt of your despatch No. 997/82,752 appointing Mr. S.R. Ambrose to this port I had no other alternative but to wire and point out that we have no spare quarters whatever now while my house is being repaired, and I am afraid the repairs will take another month and more. Besides, the Tidewaiters quarters at the Custom House, where I now live, require a thorough overhauling which should be done before the Quarters are returned to the Tidewaiters, and I think all this must cause at least two months delay in Mr. Ambrose's transfer.

PILOT.

I duly received your S/O of 17th February I am only too anxious to keep Lin and in this view I beg that you instruct your Pensions Chief Accountant not to include him

him amongst employés whose Retirement is to be started from 1st April.

As to examination of possible candidates it has not been attempted so far for want of definite ruling about the kind of advertisement that should be circulated amongst seagoing people. Your S/O letters and despatch left that point unanswered. But on the whole I must warn you of the responsibility the service assumes in recommending to ship captains who call for a pilot, a man who is not a licensed pilot, for, although he carries a letter of introduction stating his true standing, yet if there was a bad accident, all the moral blame would fall on the Customs for recommending an unsuitable man and as the No.1 Boatman is but an ordinary coolie who wishes to take to piloting only because he sees the 50 or 60 dollars which each up and down pilotage trip brings him, I simply say "beware". As Lin can serve for a few more months I shall leave the matter of finding suitable substitutes for my successor. The Tidesurveyor

says

says there are none, but really no attempt has been made to get candidates.

Yours respectfully,

Ch.E. Carrall

INSPECTORATE GENERAL OF CUSTOMS,

S/O   PEKING, 15th March 1921.

Dear Mr. Tanant,

I have duly received your S/O letter No. 216 of the 4th instant.

Appointment of Assistant Examiner S. R. Ambrose:

Ambrose has been temporarily appointed to Shanghai. Please request your successor to inform me as soon as quarters are ready for Ambrose to be transferred to your port.

Yours truly,

[signature]

E. Tanant, Esquire,
    Wenchow.

CUSTOM HOUSE,

S/O NO. 217.

Wenchow, 11th March 1921.

Sir,

PROPERTY PURCHASE: LU CHING-TSAO'S SMALL PARCEL IN FRONT OF YEH YU-CHIEH TOMBS.

This has at last been bought after a lot of trouble to make the man understand that we do not want to promise a job to his son, which promise we would not or might not keep. Mr. K'o Yu-p'ing has again been instrumental in all the bargaining. We are still trying to obtain the last lot (before Yeh's property now Lin's) which I want to add to the Commissioner's residence.

COLLECTION OF JUNK DUES BY NATIVE CUSTOMS.

I must call your attention to the memorandum by Mr. Wong Haiu Geng appended to my despatch No. 3561 mailed with this letter reporting the abolition of the Hu Shang Chü, and suggesting collection by the Native Customs of Tonnage Dues from junks as is done

at

at other ports. The matter, if we want
to be successful, should be taken up at
once, for other greedy administrations will
probably take advantage of the abolition of
the Hu Shang Chü to try either to incorporate the collection of those Junk Dues to
their own revenue, or have the use of the
building which we should claim not so much
for actual requirements as for possible rebuilding of the N.C. Office later on.

FAMINE RELIEF

The Government much advertised
"drive" is being carried on. A meeting of
officials and notable merchants was convened
recently and foreigners requested to attend.
The officials were bound to foster the
scheme but the Chinese merchants objected to
sending away the money which is badly needed
locally. The Taoyin was elected Chairman and
I vice Chairman but as I do not understand
a word of the local dialects I declined the
honour and finally the Acting Superintendent
was elected. At subsequent meetings of the
Committee it was decided to wire to the
Central

Central Distress Relief Committee the plight of this place, and the reply was "send us your subscriptions and when apportioning the funds derived from the national drive we shall allot you a percentage". As a matter of fact this place and neighbouring districts were badly hit by two typhoons on 15th July and 5th September which destroyed the two rice crops, and part of the oranges crop. Besides, owing to prolonged rains, sweet potatoes rotted, and as a tangible proof 168,458 piculs of rice, equal to about 120,000 bags of 140 catties, representing, at Tls.3.50 per picul, close to $900,000, were imported from November 1920 up to the 5th instant and about 60,000 more bags will have to be imported. These figures only refer to rice, so you may imagine not only the loss by want of production from the soil, but the drain on all economies and money reserves. The position may not be absolutely so bad as in some northern districts, but on the whole it is not brighter, and if you have

any

any opportunity I sincerely hope you may mention it for heretofore this local distress has passed unnoticed.

Yours respectfully,

CUSTOM HOUSE,

Wenchow 16. March, 1920

S/O No. 218.

Sir,

REPAIRS TO COMMRS HOUSE : INADVISABILITY TO WITHDRAW CLERK OF WORKS AS LONG AS REPAIRS ARE NOT COMPLETED.

In my despatch No. 3555 I asked for authority to begin the reclamation of the foreshore lot which had to be postponed on account of the difficulty with the China Merchants S.N.Co. finally settled in our favour by the Shui-wu Ch'u. A copy was duly sent to the Engineer-in-Chief, and I have now received his comments dated 10th March in which he mentions *inter alia* that Mr. Sheridan, Clerk of works, will not be available for the supervision of the bunding as his withdrawal from Wenchow towards the beginning of April had been foreshadowed in his comments on Wenchow despatches Nos 3512 and 3527 and his own despatch No. 2008.

This may be so, but I cannot help pointing out that the withdrawal of the Clerk of works

works at this juncture is practically impossible. If Mr. Sheridan must be recalled then another competent man must be sent here to take his place for the repairs to the Commrs House are far from being completed. I visit the house nearly every day, and to-day in view to leaving no doubts on the sayings of the contractor I took my Secretary along, and from the various replies to my questions the work inside the house will be completed in about a fortnight, the work on the bathrooms (a kind of new verandah added to the back of the house) is likely to be begun to-morr and will take a fortnight; and the new servants quarters have not yet been contracted for, and there will elapse at least three weeks and probably more until the building is completed. Nothing was said about painting and varnishing.

  In these conditions I beg to ask, if Mr. Sheridan is to be withdrawn now, that a successor be sent to take his place, and that

that he be instructed to stay here until the bunding and reclamation work be well in hand and out of the water, as the laying of the piles and foundations is a most serious work and should be done under the supervision of a competent man if you do not want to have the wall collapse some day like the one of the China Merchants Co. last year.

I am posting a copy of this letter to the Engineer - in - Chief.

Yours respectfully,

Ch. S. Canaval

P.S. Rice for distress relief is now retailed at 9½ cents a catty — about 14 catties for one dollar.

Engineer-in-Chief's comments on Wenchow Semi-official letter No.218/I.G. dated 16th March, 1921.

Mr Sheridan's services will be required for Lungkow whenever the work there is started. However as far as can be foreseen at present Mr Sheridan will not need to be withdrawn from Wenchow until the end of April. He will, therefore, be able to complete the repairs, etc. to the Commissioner's House. I see no likelihood of having a Clerk of Works to replace him and in order to find one for Kiungchow we shall probably have to withdraw Mr Vail from Wuhu before the work at that Port is completed.

A period of from three to five months will probably be required to complete the bunding at Wenchow.

Engineer - in - Chief.

THE MARITIME CUSTOMS,
Works Department,
Shanghai, 21st March, 1921.

INSPECTORATE GENERAL OF CUSTOMS,

S/O

PEKING, 29th March 1921.

Dear Mr. Tanant,

I have duly received your S/O letter No. 218 of the 16th instant.

Repairs to Commr.'s house : Inadvisability to withdraw Clerk of Works as long as repairs are not completed :

I am afraid I cannot make it possible for a man to be in two places at once. I hope the Engineer-in-Chief will be able to arrange for completion of the work in hand under supervision.

Yours truly,

E. Tanant, Esquire,
Wenchow.

CUSTOM HOUSE,

S/O. No. 219.   Wenchow, 23rd March 1921

Sir,

REPAIRS TO COMMISSIONER'S HOUSE: CLERK OF WORKS STILL NEEDED FOR AT LEAST ANOTHER MONTH.

  The contract for new servants quarters was only signed on the 10th and the contractor said he could not get his bricks and materials before 3 weeks so this will show you that I was far from exaggerating in saying there would elapse at least three weeks and probably more until the building be completed. A clerk of works is absolutely necessary to see the completion of all work. Painting in the Commissioner's House itself has not yet been begun and now rainy weather very much needed for the country seems to have set in, and this will no doubt occasion more delays.

  You may ask why were these servants

quarters

quarters were not settled and contracted for before? I will simply say because the Works Department did not plan anything and sent its man here to do for the best, which he has done certainly to the best of his abilities, but when nothing is planned in advance execution of works is bound to be delayed. The house with the exception of three walls has practically been rebuilt and it would not have been more costly to plan and put up a new building.

COMMISSIONER'S LEAVE – PREMATURE DEPARTURE POSSIBLY NECESSARY ON ACCOUNT OF STEAMERS ADVANCED DEPARTURE.

On receipt, in November of your despatch granting me long leave I wrote to various Shipping Companyies for a passage and met generally with the reply that all passage were booked until July. I finally fell on the Messageries Maritimes which booked me for the S.S. "Chili", to leave within "the second part of April". Recently I wrote again to ask for a precise date and the

reply

reply was that I would be informed of the departure after the ship's arrival from home (on 19th inst.) I then asked to be informed by telegram. As no telegram came I wired on the 21st and was informed in reply that the "Chili" would leave on 11th April. This is rather annoying as it changes all office arrangements, for if I had to go it would mean leaving here on the 3rd or 4th so as to have time to complete all formalities and necessary purchases for the travel at Shanghai. In such conditions I wired yesterday to ask to change my passage to the next ship, i.e. a fortnight, possibly three weeks, later. If it is granted I hope I will be able to await Mr. Alabaster's arrival. If not I will have to wire to inform you and ask you to make arrangements for my relief. I am very annoyed of all this which has been absolutely independent of my will, for it looks like if I wanted to shirk the quarters work, not to mention all the trouble such affairs cause you.

Yours respectfully,

INSPECTORATE GENERAL OF CUSTOMS,

S/O

PEKING, 6th April 1921.

Dear Mr. Tanant,

I have duly received your S/O letter No. 219 of the 23rd ultimo.

<u>Commr.'s departure on leave: alteration in date of departure of steamer may make him appear as shirking the quarter's work:</u>

You need not worry: you were never a shirker!

Yours truly,

E. Tanant, Esquire,
Wenchow.

CUSTOM HOUSE,

S/O No. 220.   Wenchow, 24th March 1921.

Sir,

COMMISSIONER'S DEPARTURE POSTPONED.

I am glad to say that I received yesterday after my letter had been posted a telegram informing me that my passage for the 11th April was cancelled and that I could get one by the next steamer. This will facilitate office arrangements.

STAFF.

MR. HIRANO has been sick with fever these last two days. I hope the Easter holidays will give him a chance to recover.

DISTRESS.

Our importation of rice amounts up to date to 180,000 piculs = about 125,000 big bags.

Yours respectfully,

[1.—42]

INSPECTORATE GENERAL OF CUSTOMS,

PEKING, 6 April 19 21.

Dear Sir,

I am directed by the Inspector General inform you that your S/O letter No. 220, d 24th March, has been duly ived.

Yours truly,

Private Secretary.

Tanant, Esquire,

Wenchow.

CUSTOM HOUSE,

S/O No. 221.   Wenchow, 1st April 1921.

Sir,

ARREST OF N.C. WEIGHER LIN YIN-LI BY JUDICIAL AUTHORITIES ON CHARGE, NOW PROVED FALSE, OF OPIUM SMOKING.

Weigher Lin Yin-li, detached to the Native Customs, was arrested, without intimation to me, on the 26th, by warrant of the Procurator on a charge of opium smoking by a certain Wang, and sent me on the 28th a petition through Mr. Wong Haiu Geng, Assistant in charge of the N.C. Office, protesting against his arrest and the charge of smoking opium. I wrote at once to the Superintendent transmitting copy of the petition and asking, as the man denied that he was ~~not~~ a smoker, that he be liberated at once. This letter was sent in the forenoon. In the evening, I received a letter from the Superintendent intimating that he had been informed of the arrest of the Weigher by by the Procurator. This letter seems therefore to have crossed mine and there is nothing to say. It would in one way explain the arrest without reference to me.

Then, on the 31st, I received the Superintendent's reply to my letter of 28th, telling me the Weigher had been arrested on being charged with smoking, and that his detention pending his test examination could not be avoided. As we cannot shield any man smoking opium, and should not say anything if the man is really found guilty, I could not say anything. I am glad, however, to report that the man has at last been liberated and reported for duty this morning, complaining of his arrest and asking me to obtain for him redress of this arbitrary arrest. I advised him to first make out a written statement and I am now waiting to see what the Superintendent is going to write to explain Lin's liberation. I shall then report by despatch for something must be done to prevent recurrence of such unfounded accusations.

Mr.

Mr. Hirano returned to duty after Easter.

Yours respectfully,

[signature]

[4.—42]

INSPECTORATE GENERAL OF CUSTOMS,

PEKING, 8 April 1921.

Dear Sir,

I am directed by the Inspector General to inform you that your S/O letter No. 221, dated 1st April, has been duly received.

Yours truly,

Private Secretary.

E. Tanant, Esquire,

Wenchow.

CUSTOM HOUSE,

S/O No. 222.

Wenchow, 6th April 1921.

Sir,

ARREST OF WEIGHER LIN YIN-LI ON FALSE CHARGE OF OPIUM SMOKING.

I am glad to report that after one week's test which proved that he did not smoke, Lin Yin-li was released on the 31st March.

No letter, nothing in the way of apology was received, and I am writing to complain of this illegal arrest as the informant should be punished and also the Official who sanctioned the arrest without first enquiring in the veracity of the accusation. Lin says that the man who denounced him makes a living of it by accusing people as he gets a reward when he strikes on a smoker.

MR. CHEN HUA, 2nd Clerk D, is being operated for piles.

Yours respectfully,

[1.—42]

INSPECTORATE GENERAL OF CUSTOMS,

PEKING, 12 April 19 21

Dear Sir,

I am directed by the Inspector General to inform you that your S/O letter No. 222, dated 6th April, has been duly received.

Yours truly,

Private Secretary.

Tanant, Esquire,

Wenchow.

CUSTOM HOUSE,

S/O No. 223.   Wenchow, 9th April 1921.

Sir,

WEIGHER LIN YIN-LI FALSELY ACCUSED OF SMOKING OPIUM.

My S/O letters Nos. 221 and 222 have told you of the arrest and ultimate release of Weigher Lin Yin-li. As a week passed after his release without receipt of any official information about his case, I wrote to the Superintendent to point out how astonished I was of the whole affair which not only affected Lin personally, but was a regular slight of the Customs by the Chien-chia Ting, and I asked for the court's explanations. No reply has come but the Acting Superintendent called yesterday and said he had discussed the matter with the Chien-chia Ting who had replied that if Lin feeled aggrieved he could bring an action against the man who falsely accused him, and that

that as regards Customs he didn't want to ignore us but felt justified in enforcing the law as it should be, and if there was any doubt on this last point the matter could be referred to higher authorities for settlement, and the Superintendent suggested a settlement in that line. I said no, Lin was innocent, and in ordering his arrest without a preliminary private inquest, and therefore reference to me, his chief, the judge acted absolutely on presumptions which gives a very bad idea of his justice, and moreover on Lin being found innocent the accuser should have been arrested immediately and sentenced by the same Chien-chia Ting for false testimony as is done in foreign tribunals for false testimony in criminal cases.

As to ignorance of the Customs I added that literally the judge might perhaps be excused, but when everything is taken into consideration - as it should be in all judicial cases - and particularly in view of the special position of the Customs, recognition should be taken of all our effort to
to

to help the government in the suppression of opium smoking, and there again I thought the judge at fault. I then quoted the case of one of our Watchers accused anonymously of having been punished by the Chih-shih for opium smoking, and who on reference to the Chih-shih (through the Superintendent) was found innocent. The Superintendent then told me: why then did you not report to Peking at once? To which I said no: How could I report a man and accuse him of lack of justice before hearing his explanations? He then said the Chien-chia Ting was of opinion he need not reply, to which I again said I strongly objected and I asked him (Superintendent) to obtain a reply of some sort and that I would then report to you for action with the Shui-wu Ch'u and Ministry. The matter stands there.
STAFF.

    Mr. Hirano sick, since the last 2 days, fever and possibly influenza, so he says.
    Mr. Chen Hua, 2nd Clerk D, sick operated not for piles but for fistuta.

    Yours respectfully,

INSPECTORATE GENERAL OF CUSTOMS,

S/O PEKING, 20th April 19 21.

Dear Mr. Tanant,

I have duly received your S/O letter No. 223 of the 9th instant.

<u>Weigher Lin Yin-Li falsely accused of smoking opium : Commr. unable to obtain satisfaction from authorities :</u>

My experience is that very little satisfaction is got from tilting at the Law authorities. I would drop the matter if I were you.

Yours truly,

E. Tanant, Esquire,
    Wenchow.

CUSTOM HOUSE,

S/O No. 224.   Wenchow, 26th April 1921.

Sir,

MR. ALABASTER'S ARRIVAL, MR. TANANT'S DEPARTURE.

Mr. Alabaster arrived on the 24th after an unusual long delay of two days over the bar on account of heavy fog. We spent the day visiting the properties. The Commissioner's House unfortunately is not finished not completely painted and the parts of walls that were filled up, patched up and rebuilt are not dry. The Servants quarters are not even finished. I am afraid he may not be able to go into those quarters until at least a month until all workmen have left and then even it is a personal matter to decide whether he cares to go into a house so freshly done up for it may not be healthy. So, he thought of taking the Tidesurveyor's quarters in the Island which of course the Tidesurveyor will not like on account of the trouble to pack up up and remove his own furniture, etc., and to find quarters in a stinking neighbourhood. So, before deciding anything Mr. Alabaster wired to you.

I have now handed him over my office and propose leaving after to-morrow and as we have the Hsinchi leaving for Foochow I decided to take her and proceed to Hongkong from Foochow, thus having a chance to see Foochow and Amoy which I hardly know, and I will join my mail steamer at Hongkong on the 9th or 10th inst.

Yours respectfully,

[.—42]

INSPECTORATE GENERAL OF CUSTOMS,

PEKING, 11th May 1921.

Dear Sir,

I am directed by the Inspector General to inform you that your S/O letter No. 224, dated 26th April 1921, has been duly received.

Yours truly,

B. Phillips Durham
Private Secretary.

P. Alabaster Esquire
Wenchow

CUSTOM HOUSE,

S/O No. 225.

Wenchow, 11th May 1921.

Dear Sir Francis,

cials: calls on.
    I have made my round on the local officials, - of whom I had met the Taoyin before at Hangchow, - and received their return visits.

erty: Commissioner's e:
    The Commissioner's House is gradually progressing, but is not yet completely painted externally, the Servants Quarters are not yet plastered, and other details - such as tiles for the hearths and proper glass for the front door - remain to be completed. By the close of the month, work should be at an end, and in a further month or six weeks and after a sufficient airing, the house should be in a fairly habitable state.

The

FRANCIS A AGLEN K. B. E.,
Inspector General of Customs,
   PEKING.

The grounds are being arranged in a suitable manner. The constant deluge which this place has undergone - and is still undergoing - these past few weeks has not contributed to a rapid conclusion. Meanwhile my wife - who will have to leave this place for an environment more suitable for a white lady - and I are occupying the Tidesurveyor's House on the island, and for the first week after our arrival lived in the unspeakable quarters in which Mr. Tanant resided. The Tidesurveyor has taken rooms in the Examiner's House on the island (next door to us) sharing it with the Tidewaiters.

Customs.
I see little reason why, with closer supervision, some readjustments, and attention to detail, the Revenue should not be ~~being~~ sensibly increased.

Unofficial Light House.
The Harbour Master reports to me that the unofficial light on one of the Sanpwan Islands - referred to in previous official and semi-official correspondence - is now regularly exhibited. I have instructed him to watch his chance and try

and

and visit the spot and collect a few details as to exact position, kind of light, etc.

Mr. Hirano has recovered from his fever: and Mr. Chen, Chinese Clerk, is convalescing after his operation.

Yours truly,

INSPECTORATE GENERAL OF CUSTOMS,

S/O.   PEKING, 18th May 1921.

Dear Mr. Alabaster,

I have duly received your S/O letter No. 225 of the 11th May.

Commissioner's house under repairs and not ready for occupation.

I am very sorry that the repairs could not be finished in time for your arrival, and that you and Mrs. Alabaster have been put to so much inconvenience. But I supposed that you would have found out how the land lay before proceeding and would have made arrangements for Mrs. Alabaster until she could join you!

Yours truly,

E. Alabaster, Esquire,
    WENCHOW.

CUSTOM HOUSE,

S/O No. 226.   Wenchow, 27th May 1921.

Property: Commissioner's
House; Bunding; Examin-
er's House.

Dear Sir Francis,

The rainy weather has retarded matters a good deal: but about ten days more should see repairs to the Commissioner's House practically completed. As regards the bunding nearly all the piles have been driven in, and the concrete base has been made. This would form later on a very good site for the Examination Shed with quarters for an Examiner over: but building will not be possible on this plot for another 3 years. As regards the Examiner's House (on the Island) the small, absolutely essential repairs, are now in hand. I intend to vacate the Tidesurveyor's House at the earliest possible moment

as

FRANCIS A AGLEN K. B. E.,
Inspector General of Customs,
PEKING.

Standard Oil Company's
Kerosene Oil Tank
Installation.

as I do not feel justified in keeping him out of it too long.

On the 24th I received a visit from Messrs Corbett, Kimes and Chu, (the two former from Shanghai) relative to their Oil Installation here. They asked me for temporary permission to work, pending adjustment of their case: but I replied that this was impossible. As they appeared to have an underlying feeling that the Customs was making difficulties, I thought it as well to inform them that, so far as we were concerned anything that made for trade activity here was welcome, but that it was for them, first of all, to regularise their holding and come to an amicable arrangement if possible, with the territorial officials. The Company wishes to bring here their former agent, the man who got the land for them and now in Shanghai not in their employ: while the man, feeling that he is "wanted" by the officials here, is fighting shy of Wenchow.

A

mine Relief.   A gift of $10,000 having been received from Shanghai for local famine relief, a Committee of officials, missionaries and merchants with myself as Chairman, has been formed to administer relief.

aff.   Mr. Christophersen, Acting Tidesurveyor, left for the round journey to Shanghai the last trip of the "Haean" to visit an oculist. Mr. Chen Hua, Chinese Clerk, is now on duty again: but Mr. Chang King-shuen, another Clerk, is off duty with a mysterious complaint which the doctor classifies as neurities, but is now making a further diagnosis of.

pping.   An unusual number of steamers (for this port) visited here lately with rice for famine relief - among them a vessel under the British flag, which has not been seen at Wenchow for a long time past.

Yours truly,

INSPECTORATE GENERAL OF CUSTOMS,

S/O.   PEKING,   14th June   1921.

Dear Mr. Alabaster,

I have duly received your S/O letter No. 226 of the 27th May.

<u>Standard Oil Co's Kerosene Oil Tank Installation - Commissioner refuses permission to work before position is regularised with territorial officials.</u>

That is the correct attitude: keep the cart behind the horse!

Yours truly,

E. Alabaster, Esquire.,
    Wenchow.

CUSTOM HOUSE,

S/O No. 227.   Wenchow 12th June 1921.

reshore reclamation.
spatch 967/80, 719
m and 3555 to I.G.)

perty: Commissioner's
se: Bunding:
miner's House.

pping.

Dear Sir Francis,

I have adjusted this case with Superintendent and C.M.S.N. Co. and am reporting officially.

I moved into the Commissioner's House yesterday. The outbuildings are not yet fully completed. There has been rain practically every day for the past six or seven weeks and in every way work has been impeded, while it is practically impossible to get the distemper to dry satisfactorily. The bad weather has also been unfavourable to our bunding operations which, nevertheless, are progressing. The Examiner's House on the Island is now being put shipshape. Work on it will take about six weeks.

The C.M.S.N. s.s. "Kungping" with
relief

SIR FRANCIS A AGLEN K.B.E.,
    Inspector General of Customs,
        PEKING.

2.

relief rice, said to be the largest steamer in the China coast trade, visited the Port last week; she came up without difficulty, lying alongside the C.M.S.N. Co.'s wharf. With this vessel, and likewise the "Haean" and "Kwangchi" plus the Ningpo steamer, and one from Amoy in simultaneously, this port presented a scene of unwonted activity.

Mr. and Mrs. Manico Gull were here ten days ago, coming from Mokanshan, overland via the Chientong River and Chuchow. They returned to Shanghai via Ningpo coasting steamer.

Clerk Chang is still off duty, otherwise we are all well. The weather has been depressing and relaxing.

Yours truly,

INSPECTORATE GENERAL OF CUSTOMS,

S/O.　　　　　　　　　PEKING, 24th June 1921.

Dear Mr. Alabaster,

I have duly received your S/O letter No. 227 of the 12th June.

<u>Increase of shipping - five steamers in Port at **one time**.</u>

I hope you will study the question of pilotage!

Yours truly,

E. Alabaster, Esquire,
　　Wenchow.

CUSTOM HOUSE,

S/O NO. 228.   Wenchow, 28th June 1921.

pperty: bunding;
aminers House;
mmissioner's House;
aff Housing.

Dear Sir Francis,

About three feet more, and three weeks' work, will see our bunding completed. About a month more will be needed to put the Examiner's House (Island) to rights. The Commissioner's House has still workmen in it, fixing the mosquito proofing satisfactorily and painting, etc.: while the grounds are in process of arrangement. Mr. Sheridan, Clerk of Works here, will be free to go, so far as we are concerned, in about a fortnight's time. The weather, though lately improved, has upon the whole been abominable for working purposes - or indeed any other. I have been giving consideration to the question of Staff Housing, and I will submit something later on. Of one thing I am sure: and that

is

SIR FRANCIS A AGLEN K. B. E.,
    Inspector General of Customs,
        PEKING.

is that I side with Mr. James Acheson in considering the Island as a most suitable place - strategically, and from other points of view - for the Out-door Staff; *one man, however, being housed over here.*

ndard Oil Company's tallation.

The Company has lately tried bluffing. The local agent (Chinese) showed me, a few days since, a telegram from his divisional manager at Ningpo instructing him that he was shipping some oil for the Installation here, and to notify me. I, of course, turned down the local agent. The Ningpo Divisional manager (American) also saw me twice a little later, on the same lines. I turned him down also, with a few added words of advice.

ne Relief.

The condition here is very serious, and probably were it not that the area affected in North China is so vast by comparison, these parts would have received more attention. The Roman Catholic Missionaries tell me that the people are living on roots, even eating earth. Meanwhile the Central Committe in Shanghai (Chinese and Foreign Famine Relief Committee) has

has given another $10,000 to our Committee here and the local officials have also assigned us $2,000 from their own local "Drive" funds. Meetings have been held at the Methodist College (as I had no house) but are now being held from time to time at my house. However this sort of relief is but a drop in the bucket: we can only relieve cases of extreme necessity in certain districts specially affected, and then each case relieved will have rice only sufficient - carefully used - to last about twelve days. A better kind of relief would be for the unemployed to be employed on road making and widening as far as possible existing roads, say a road suitable for motor and vehicular traffic linking Wenchow, Chuchow, Chinhua, Lanchi, Yenchou, Tunglu, Hangchow.

With rice steamers arriving from north and south our tonnage figures are swelling to an unprecedented size. We had a direct entry (nearly unheard of here), also, the other day - not rice cargo, but sandalwood - in the shape of a Japanese

motor

4.

motor craft. It took ten days to reach here from Hongkong. Altogether more steamers are comming here than there is suitable accommodation for. There are now in port; three large and two small sea going steamers and two more of the larger kind are due.

|cials.

I have seen a good deal of the officials lately: the Acting Superintendent (a very obliging and hard working official) in connexion with the foreshore matter, and all the others at various banquets. There were two feasts: one by the Superintendent for me at the C.M.S.N.Co.: and the other, to which the Taoyin kindly invited me, at a semi-foreign house on the town's outskirts, belonging to that Mr. Yang who endeavoured to assist us with his kind offices in obtaining our additional land. There sat opposite me here the brother of Mr. Chou Tzu-ch'i former Financial Minister. Seemingly a Consular luminary formerly, and now director of the Chekiang Revenue Stamp Bureau at Hangchow. He comes here to investigate the sale of Revenue Stamps: is a a Columbia graduate: and Chinan native.

The Roman Catholic Missionaries tell me Bolshevist agents are at work even in this Sleepy Hollow: even recruiting from amongst the destitute for service in Russia.

Clerk Chang has returned to duty, but is still shaky. There is a good deal of malaria about: and the weather has been exceedingly hot.

Yours truly,

INSPECTORATE GENERAL OF CUSTOMS,

S/O.   PEKING, 16th July 1921.

Dear Mr. Alabaster,

I have duly received your S/O letter No. 228 of the 28th June.

Famine Relief - Commissioner says condition at Wenchow is very serious and suggests that the unemployed should be employed on road making and widening.

Could you not get a move on in this direction while the famine is acute!

Yours truly,

E. Alabaster, Esquire,
    Wenchow.

CUSTOM HOUSE,

S/O NO. 229.　　　　　Wenchow, 14th July, 1921.

Dear Sir Francis,

liang t'ou ch'ien.　　　I trust that we shall be able to arrange a simply worked and feasible Tariff which will contribute materially to our very moderate collection. I have to find out, first of all, and from the old employés we have, exactly how the former Tariff operated and we shall have to follow that, I suppose, any way to begin with. But if we can introduce something simple, and which is a better revenue producer, it may be advisable to introduce such from the start: instead of chopping and changing later. It is precisely there that investigation is needed. Ningpo (with which this Customs has historical affinity) has kindly supplied me with their procedure: I will address Foochow also.

An opportunity seems to be now afforded of establishing a system uniform as far as possible for the Checking and Native ports, at least, in this connexion.

SIR FRANCIS A AGLEN K.B.E.,
　　Inspector General of Customs,
　　　　PEKING.

Maritime Customs revenue decrease. June.

This showed a heavy drop compared with June of last year: total (with Surtax) Hk.Tls. 4,102.125 this June: Hk.Tls. 8,021.858 June 1920 (no Surtax). Nor are the figures for this month, so far, any improvement. It is due to a decreased export of unfired tea, and green tea, and of pigs lard to Shanghai. The market for tea is poor: and as for the lard, farm produce has suffered in common with ordinary agriculture, as a result of last year's typhoon.

(I.G. S/O 4th June).

I have already, and for some time, been giving attention to this: but one thing and another called my attention off it, though my intention has been to report ultimately - indeed I had a despatch in hand. I hope to submit my views shortly. It is a knotty problem, I admit: but not, I think, insoluble. To a certain extent, of course, it is an abstraction in view of established facts, but its bearings are important; and, in most ways, I agree with Mr. Tanant.

In

erty: acquisition
ill crest and of
s site.

In my opinion we should lose no time in securing a moderate sized site on the crest of our hill — which crest lies about 25 feet above our boundary wall — with a small connecting neck of land, avoiding two big graves, linking such crest site with our present property. The Adventists are already after this particular site. Without it, there can be little or no privacy in the present Commissioner's House; and it is on that crest site that, one day, the Commissioner's House should be built — the present house being assigned to the foreign assistant, a senior, perhaps, in charge of the Native Customs. I think also that if the owner will sell at a moderate price it may cause Lin to come down in his demand for his small lot, a place equally essential to us. But of this I am not very hopeful. I am making enquiries, and will report.

a: Mr. Gaylard,
b lass Tidewaiter,
a e of name to
od.

I have had to give a few days leave to Mr. Gaylard, 1st Class Tidewaiter, to visit Ningpo and see his Consul (British). It appears the name under which he was born is is Garwood: and the Tidesurveyor tells me that when he (Garwood) ran away to sea as a boyish freak he changed his name to Gaylard. I will report the circumstance in due course. He is a very good officer. The matter came up as a result of your Circular No. 3113 regarding superannuation. I hear that Mr. Gaylard (or Garwood) proposes to marry the Macanese girl with whom he is living. As to this I will report when I have further details.

There is not much of an independent spirit in the air here, I judge, whether among the officials or the people generally. The state of the rice crop (good, they say) is the main interest.

I have read and initialled - passing on the principal, in translation, to the Superintendent for the information of territorial officials - 38 storm warnings in the past month. So far nothing has struck here, but it is about due. It has been excessively hot: but one expects it during the <u>fu t'ien</u>, of course. Most of the missionaries are in their hill bungalows.

Yours truly,

INSPECTORATE GENERAL OF CUSTOMS,

S/O.   PEKING, 29th July 1921.

Dear Mr. Alabaster,

I have duly received your S/O letter No. 229 of the 14th July.

N.C. liang t'ou chüan - Commissioner gives procedure for arranging a simply-worked and feasible Tariff.

You are going in the right lines in trying to establish uniformity.

Staff - Mr. Gaylard wishes to change his name to Garwood as that was his original surname.

We have had many such cases revealed by the Pension scheme!

Yours truly,

E. Alabaster, Esquire,
    Wenchow.

CUSTOM HOUSE,

S/O NO. 230.   Wenchow, 31st July, 1921.

Dear Sir Francis,

endence movement: I attach copies of two Notifications issued by the Chief of the Military Staff here setting forth, the first, that on account of distress caused by lack of rice and consequent apprehended trouble, Wenchow is placed under martial law for the time being. This stopped the general Elections. The second notification stated that the Chief of Staff had received petitions from some twenty odd persons expressing fear of trouble on account of rice famine and asking that the municipal elections be postponed two months.* It is to be noted that the aim - to stop the elections is not specified in the first proclamation.

Both

FRANCIS A AGLEN K. B. E.,
Inspector General of Customs,
    PEKING.

*Martial law is still in force, loosely operating in a sense: censorship at the Post and Telegraph Offices exists however.

Both use the distress as an excuse. The specific reason for the military desiring election stoppage is to involve the Civil Governor in trouble with the Central Government. In fact not only do the local civil officials not appear anxious for the success of the movement, but they are opposed to it: and the people generally are unconcerned. The military hirelings of the martial swashbuckler at Hangchow, acting under orders, are of course responsible. I hear that when the first notification was issued, the General wrote to the taoyin and magistrate asking them to wire to the Civil Governor and stop the elections. This the taoyin refused to do: the magistrate did so, after consulting with the taoyin. The repercussion of the events in Kwangsi is, of course, likely to have its effect in this province: though the Chekiang tuchün wishes to play a very first fiddle — especially after a bottle of champagne — and not to be merely one of a number of leaders: although the prospect of stopping his Peking Remittances and utilising all

sources

3.

sources of Chekiang Revenue must be very alluring. Nine of ten of the local people are apathetic as to their country's fortunes and are thinking in terms of rice, the first crop of which was a success, but the young shoots of the second appear likely to be burnt dry by the drought and fiery heat which this place has lately been suffering from.

There is an increase of about 25% this July compared with last: but it is more apparent than real, as July 1920 was the bad typhoon month.

I did speak to the officials: and notices are now to be seen posted everywhere on the subject of road making in this province. But I do not think these facts have any connexion. I sincerely wish the officials would get a move on: but the existing official machinery is regrettably rotten. This requirement could only be met by an effective audit of the territorial works departments finance. Impossible in present conditions,— ~~now~~: for while many of the

the civil officials are excellent they are of course impotent in face of their military masters. What I think may possibly be stimulating the officials at present in a mild way is the establishment of non-official road making committees in various provinces. But the soldiers won't do a stroke of work if they can avoid it: and honest civilian work is blocked while they exist.

Piracies are not seldom reported by the Chinese lorchas plying between this Port and Shanghai. I have drawn the attention of the local officials to this from time to time: and they, in turn, have reported to the <u>tuchün</u>. The tuchün appears anxious to oblige: but these Provincial Maritime Police launches are of little use. A Chinese naval patrol - if there are available vessels - might be of service: but if the *Government's* naval forces patrol the Chekiang coast just now it may, I imagine, *be* for reasons other that piracies. If our Revenue Cruisers were to show the flag occasionally

occasionally in such waters it might serve as a deterrent. On the other hand I don't see why we should be placed to expense in this connexion, which is certainly an affair of the Maritime Police.

df.

We have all been fairly well: though I have had, I regret to say, an unpleasantly acute attack of dysentery which did not keep me from work at all, and only one day from the office. Our lame duck is Clerk Chang King Shuen, as to whom I made a proposal in our Staff Return. Hard work would be the best medicine for him, I fancy: and to be removed from this Port where he has too many friends and relations.

perty: Examiner's me.

I have inspected this and it appears to be in a satisfactory state, clean, and neat. There are one or two details however, such as repairs to stove needing attention. I hear Mr Ambrose has applied for leave: we need an additional man, however, so as to release a tidewaiter for N.C.

cut: Newspaper.

I attach cutting from the local newspaper of the 20th instant which is amusing. It is the first I have heard about it, but I suppose the paper must

live

live.

Cutting from local vernacular newspaper of 20th July attached.

Yours truly,

E. Hubash C.

6.

Wenchow S/o No 230

Append.

浙江温處戒嚴正司令部佈告第七號

照得溫處各屬承去秋災歉之餘民食不繼迨至今年夏令青黃不接之候屢次釀成聚眾鬧米風潮匪徒即從中煽動甚至即發生搶劫財物及搗毀官署等種種軼執行為迭據所屬呈報來部並審查得現在海防不靖盜匪出沒無常意圖乘隙擾事殊為可慮溫處各屬原為警備地域防範不得不嚴本司令官察酌近情為預防非常事變起見業經呈報督軍請予重申戒嚴之宣告藉以維持地方安寧秩序頃奉電令內開現在戒嚴期內既稱海防不靖准由該司令官查照戒嚴法重申宣告以維治安等因奉此查戒嚴條文前經佈告遵行在案茲應時機之必要由本司令按照戒嚴法第十四條一二三四各款暨浙江戒嚴施行條例第二十五條及二十六條所規定之範圍內訂定規則十二

係續行佈告仰軍民人等一体遵照勿違切切此佈

規則列左

一傳止集會結社之認為與時機有妨碍者

一新聞告白傳單等認為與時機有妨碍者禁止印發

一造謠生事者嚴拿究辦

一郵電各局得派員隨時檢查出入信件

一查出用密碼通信之件得沒收之

一旅館飯店小客棧等夜間得由軍警隨時檢查

一軍警行政各機關每日自晚八點鐘起至次早五點鐘止各派軍警偵探等輪流梭巡遇有事故發生即行報告司令部

一在晚間八點鐘以後禁止燃放爆竹

一、各商船到埠時由軍警嚴密檢查但不得故意留難

一、夜間街市上十二點鐘以後行人非攜帶燈火者不准行走

一、海洋面飭由水警加意巡查

一、本規則自佈告日起實行

中華民國十年七月二十一日

正司令官王國楨

浙江溫處戒嚴正司令部第八號

案據溫屬公民代表葉佩璈湯于光等二十八人呈稱溫屬饑饉薦至伏荞潛滋適逢省選紛擾當此山荒告警之時饑民匪徒勢必乘機而起擾及閻閭人心皇皇若臨大禍環請准予將三屆初複選一律展緩兩個月宣告大眾以安人心等情前來據此查此次永嘉會昌鎮聚眾鬧米一案本

10.

部迭接飭海道尹永嘉知事警察局長暨地方人民等報告幾民匪徒附和肆刦請兵維持節經飭派軍警彈壓並嚴拿匪類各在案茲據該公民代表等呈稱各節委係實在情形現值申令戒嚴期內本司令官對於地方治安事宜責無旁貸自應竭力維持業已照准通飭所屬將本屆初複選一律暫行停止用副人民公意而防事變發生除據情呈報督軍並咨飭海道尹轉呈

省長外合亟佈告仰公民等一體知悉凡遇有盜匪滋擾地方情事即行協拿解部按法嚴辦以靖地方決不姑縱切切此佈

中華民國十年七月二十六日

正司令官 王國楨

INSPECTORATE GENERAL OF CUSTOMS,

S/O. PEKING, 18th August 1921.

Dear Mr. Alabaster,

I have duly received your S/O letter No. 230 of the 31st July.

Independence movement - endeavour to stop municipal elections by the Chief of the Military Staff, etc.

The day of the Tuchuns is I think perceptibly drawing to a close!

Piracies - Commissioner thinks that if Revenue Cruisers were seen more, between Wenchow and Shanghai, they might act as a deterrent, although it is really the work of the Maritime Police. Quite so: it is the business of the Navy, but I fear it will never be properly done!

Yours truly,

E. Alabaster, Esquire,
    Wenchow.

CUSTOM HOUSE,

S/O No. 231.   Wenchow, 15th August 1921

Dear Sir Francis,

tical: departure
taoyin: *provincial government.*

The taoyin left this port somewhat hurriedly two days ago for Shanghai and Ch'angchow (Kiangsu). His position had become intolerable, being virtually that of a prisoner in his own Office, under military guard. It remains to be seen what will happen, with the tuchün subject to the sway of a party of agitating politicians, whose desire is to stop the regular elections pending the drawing up of a Provincial self-government constitution (有自治憲法), and to purge the Province of the more especially pro-central-government civil elements. The success at the moment of the extreme Democratic Party in South China will no doubt tend to stabilise the tuchün - rival jealousies permitting -

FRANCIS A AGLEN K. B. E.,
Inspector General of Customs,
    PEKING.

2.

permitting - in his political programme, aided by the residents of the more fairly disciplined troops under his orders. The censorship continues at the Post and Telegraph Offices.

What appears to be a bad case has today been represented to me (in writing and verbally) wherein a lorcha (Chinese flag) - formerly trading to Wenchow, and the owner of which is resident here - cleared from Shanghai for Ningpo 27th July, has not yet arrived at the latter port and, on the report of an escaped member of the crew, has been pirated and is now held to ransom (for $2,000, the owner says). The lorcha owner, when I saw him, told me that these evil-doers are Taichow people, and on my asking now it was that the deed occurred at a spot distant from Taichow and on a route frequented by steamers, he replied that the route of the lorchas is other than that of the steamers and that the Taichow representation in question was placed in the way of being on the track by the Marine Police -

in

3.

in fact were passed the tip. The Marine Police have of course an evil reputation: and as it is ridiculous to appeal to the Central Government, in the circumstances, the main prospect of solution appears to lie in the fact of the pirates overstepping their caution, and attacking a foreign flagged craft; which, so far, has been carefully avoided. The case now cited is of the more orthodox and conventional kind, but the offenders are, usually, of the sort which combines honest courses with dishonest lapses - seemingly impeccable fisher folk. There appears to be, however, a more general tendency to greater boldness, a natural result of the present slump in administration, whether central or provincial. Thus the lorcha trade in these parts, under the Chinese flag at all events, is likely to be seriously affected. I am, of course, notifying the provincial officials of the circumstances as reported to me: and also the Ningpo and Shanghai Customs.

  We experienced the "tail-end" of a typhoon

4.

typhoon four days since, which served as a dress rehearsal for the fuller display we have been witnessing the past couple of days: - the centre of the disturbance being in our neighbourhood. The S.S. "Kwangchi", which left two days ago for Shanghai, had to put back here after a perilous time, being driven out towards the Formosan coast line. I am glad to say, as regards Customs property, I have no damage to report. There appear still to be various typhoons in the vicinity.

Mr. Sheridan, Clerk of Works, is down with diarrhœa: otherwise we have all been fairly well.

Yours truly,

P.S. A still further lorcha piracy - in this case of cargo from Shanghai to this port - has been reported to me when on the point of closing this letter.

INSPECTORATE GENERAL OF CUSTOMS,

S/O.   PEKING, 3rd September 1921.

Dear Mr. Alabaster,

I have duly received your S/O letter No. 231 of the 15th August.

<u>Political Situation - departure of Taoyin - party of agitating politicians drawing up a Provincial self-government constitution.</u>

I hope the self government agitators will keep their attention off the Revenue. Let me know if there is any tendency to encroach. Is your collection fairly secure?

Yours truly,

E. Alabaster, Esquire,
    Wenchow.

S/O No. 232.

CUSTOM HOUSE,

Wenchow, 25th August 1921

tical.

Dear Sir Francis,

The taoyin will shortly be returning here, I understand: as the local storm, in sympathy with matters at Hangchow, is blowing over. Lu tuchün, they say, is no longer opposing the usual Central Government elections. Nevertheless the fact remains that the military censorship continues at the Post and Telegraph Offices here, though possibly in rather a perfunctory way. Intrigues and jealousies appear to have been too much for Lu tuchün: his own 4th Division Commander Ch'ên Lo-shan (陳樂山) - who himself is credited with aspiring to the tuchünship - has withdrawn his support from his chief. The Shanghai Defence Commissioner is

FRANCIS A AGLEN K. B. E.,
Inspector General of Customs,
PEKING.

2.

is also anti-Lu. The Commanders of the two Chekiang Divisions also support the Civil Governor: so that Lu's own following is somewhat split at the moment. Everybody here goes about their business just as usual: and, as far as permitted, leaves politics to the politicians and intrigues to the intriguers.

munication.

What with the prevalence of typhoons, and the fact that our regular steamer, the "Haean", has been laid up for the usual summer docking, our communication with the outer world has been extremely poor of late: something like one mail a fortnight.

With the exception of Mr. Sheridan, Clerk of Works, and Mr. Chang King-shuen, who has just gone sick again, we have all been well. Mr. Sheridan, who is now fit, will be leaving for Shanghai by the first suitable steamer, his work here being at an end. As regards Mr. Chang, I await a Certificate from the Medical Officer. Mr. Chang's

Chang's last Medical Certificate described his case as neuritis. My own opinion is that, though doing no good here, he would probably show improvement elsewhere.

Yours truly,

E. Habate

CUSTOM HOUSE,

S/O No. 233.

Wenchow, 12th Sep. 1921.

(reply to I.G.
Circular No.35)

Dear Sir Francis,

In reply to your S/O Circular No.35, I can only say that I am in favour of your proposal. The amounts issued to informers should, I consider, be materially reduced: the amounts issued to seizing officers perhaps increased - though in view of the anomalous state prevailing outside our jurisdiction I am in favour of a general and material reduction of all opium seizure rewards issued by the Chinese Central Government. I am decidedly in favour of the division you propose monthly <u>pro rata</u> port by port: and agree that the amounts issuable to individual officers actually making seizures should be larger in proportion

SIR FRANCIS A AGLEN K.B.E.,
    Inspector General of Customs,
        PEKING.

proportion than the share of the port seizure rewards enjoyed by those not actively concerned. I think that provision might be allowed for any special ingenuity shows, and that on special report to the I.G. from the Commissioner concerned, a still higher proportion should be issued as reward, subject to the circumstances of the particular case. No doubt relegalisation of the trade, and the natural play of public opinion would appear to offer the only real solution: but of course it would be a step quick to be taken advantage of by every anti-Central-Government political organisation in the country, and none but the very strongest of Central Governments could, I imagine, hazard the attempt.

Locally, there is a good deal of opium illicitly consumed: though this is not a port where the drug bulks large. There was a fracas only the other day, however, between the local police on opium search and certain Fukien house owners, who badly knocked the police about the latter then giving orders for

for the arrest of Fukien people on the slightest excuse. This led to a meeting of the Fukien Guild which passed a motion of protest and telegraphed proceedings to the Civil Governor.

ical situation
anking of Revenue
to query in
/O of 3rd
mber).

In reply to your query, the collection is as secure as possible. The Banking is done by the Bank of China on our premises here, and only small balances are allowed to remain in the banker's hands; the rest being remitted to the Hongkong and Shanghai Bank. I will apprise you in good time of any attempted encroachment. There is a general public desire for the taoyin to return, and he is being urged in that sense. I understand the tuchün has succeeded in patching up an opportunistic understanding with the Civil Governor, who probably finds it advisable to move with the strongest currents of the moment. This won't please Lu's own rivals however, unless they are also included in the arrangement and, can "share the sway." However, a characteristic attempt has anyway been

4.

been made to save everybody's face, including the <u>tuchün's</u>. This idea of creating a safety valve for provincial aspiration by devolution of authority provincially, resulting from Central Government weakness, beautiful in theory, reasonable in conception (if not modern in idea) is, of course, a further playing with fire unless managed by those who have no axe to grind!

I ~~append copy~~ *enclose original* of a petition regarding piracy of lorchas, which has been handed to me by the head of the lorcha guild here. This same head handed me further copies for presentation to yourself, Superintendent, and others to be presented, through the Superintendent, to the Chiao-t'ung Pu, <u>tuchün</u>, and Civil Governor. The petition, as you see, recapitulates ten cases of piracy which have occurred to date since November 1920. The criticism is rather destructive than constructive: the complaints are, of course, numerous; and the petitions concerning the individual cases and the various

complaints

petition. copy myst here

5.

complaints have already been forwarded on by this Office as the cases arose, through the Superintendent to the tuchün. I told the petitioner that - while I would of course forward on his petitions if he really desired it - as far as I could see nothing was to be gained by his proposed action, as he merely recapitulated what had already been represented. That, in place of sending on his petitions now - and it was of course open to him to petition at any time - I could take the opportunity given me of the case of the "Chin Yung Fu" lorcha, - petition just to hand and about to be reported to the Provincial Authorities through Superintendent - to mention that this made the tenth case notified to the Customs since November 1920, adding certain suggestions as to the employment of the Maritime Police and remarks calculated to act as a special stimulus to the Provincial Authorities. With this he seemed very content, and took back his petitions. I told him, further, that the conduct of the
lorcha

6.

lorcha crews in giving in without a struggle was of course likewise instrumental in encouraging piracy. Copy of my letter to the Superintendent referred to above re "Chin "Yung Fu", will be included in the Non-Urgent Correspondence for this month: it suffices to say that in it, inter alia - referring to the numerous piratical cases which, with that reported now, number ten since November 1920, and to the dissatisfaction among lorcha people - the necessity is urged of the Maritime Police launches actually and constantly patrolling the specific beats to which they are assigned of renewed and general vigilance, while the temptation of the lorchas to change their flag is referred to, and also the possibility of emboldened pirates attacking foreign craft. Actual results in the circumstances are problematical no doubt - there is the serious question, for example, of expenditure on coal. The lorcha representatives rightly refer to us regarding vessels carrying our Papers, though in the
present

7.

present mixed administrative state, piracy forms a practical question not so easy of solution. The original idea at the back of the petitioner's head was, I think, to gain his end by way of playing off the Central Government against the Provincial Authorities, using ourselves as a convenient channel. This would but lead to bad blood, without any compensating advantage. I may add that the Head of the Lorcha Guild was himself once in the Navy and is up to all the various tricks. He is therefore a useful man to keep in touch with.

Our August decrease was chiefly due to the Export falling off - export duties giving Hk.Tls. 3,050 in August last year, and only Hk.Tls. 2,004 this August: for this, typhoons were the cause, by restricting shipping movements to this. I wish Wenchow made a better showing in the Revenue List.

The Harbour Master is about very much, endeavouring to keep pace with the almost daily changes in channels.

I have seen a certain amount of the
Superintendent

nery (Circular
34).

Superintendent lately, and gave him a lunch the other day.

I suppose local purchase of Chinese stationery - paper, pens, ink, etc. - has been found preferable to purchase through a **depot** in Shanghai - the best and cheapest producer of good Chinese stationery in China. It is a matter which must already have been before you, and been well sifted: but much, which I will not take up space and your time by mentioning - can be said in favour of the depot system, certainly from the small port's point of view.

Yours truly,

P. A. Caburel.

Append

具禀甌海夾板船商代表陳百川等同投商船蓋章列后

為浙洋多盜水警廢弛叙具歷次擄劫各案並容貨停裝船隻辭歇情形僉懇

恩賜電達 總稅務司並函請 監督轉呈 督軍 省長暨 交通部嚴令水警巡船實行駐守防地常川派遣兵艦督緝勦滅盜氛一面勒限救回被擄人船破獲駐盜衛商旅而維稅政事竊商等航行海上所恃者水警之保護所憚者海盜之劫掠証料近來台州海盜蜂起常川出沒窺伺為害商旅擄刦傷命之案屢見迭出他種商船之被害者姑置弗論茲就溫州一口所有夾板船二十艘而言自去冬十月迄今閱時僅及半載被刦被擄連出十案節畧呈 電（繕備節畧六份內一份

贵关存案一份转　总税务司四份转　监督分呈）至节署内所叙被劫被掳十案

均经禀报

贵关函请　监督拍电弈由各该船主呈请饬缉何如该管水警事前既疎於

防范事後又不能破获一赃一盗警政废弛已达极点伏查浙江外海水上警察设有

厅长一员驻节镇海统辖全省外海警务所部第一第二第三等区弈有超武

兵轮暨新宝顺兵轮听其指挥督巡其第一区区长（係厅长兼任）驾坐永定小

兵轮一艘（常泊镇海港内）所部第一第二第三队长三员分队巡船二十一号

管船辖洋面北自大羊山起南至东西衖止第二区区长驻紮海门驾坐永安小

兵轮一艘（常泊海门内埠）所部第四第五第六第七第八等队队长五员除第八队专巡台州内港外应有外海分队巡船三十一号管辖洋面北自东西柱起南至石塘止第三区区长驻紮温州驾坐小兵轮一艘（该轮常泊双门外渔棚廟前為 贵税務司日日所目覩）所部第九第十第十一队长三员分队巡船二十一号管辖洋面北自石塘起南至镇下关止按浙江外海水程自南迄北七百餘里以七十三号之水警巡船按段分驻猶陸地巡警之岗位相距十里之水程首尾应各有巡船一艘驻守加之以兵轮五艘往来督察稽巡果能實行則巡船星羅棊布防務周密各商船循照航綫行駛豈虞盗刼奈今之水警廳长暨区

长队长率皆安居陆地养尊处优亚无驾坐兵轮出洋督巡之事所设兵舰巡船非停歇内埠即偷泊僻港亚不实施驻守巡护而月报表上所列某巡船驻守某段如何勤务悉属纸上谈兵毫无事实致令海盗猖獗任意游弋如入无人之境常川在洋劫掳各商船畏盗如虎视航路若畏途近时温州夹板船额二十艘被刼被掳竟至十案之多且掳去黄万兴船影三人尚未救回又有金承多全船被掳生命财产悬于盗手故各船现役水手珍重生命纷纷辞歇南货广货豆麦各商号虑及盗险相率停装长此以往不仅商等航业受害即税政前途亦大有障碍为此万急联名禀恳

稅務司鑒閱懇迅呈達

總稅務司並函請

監督分呈

交通部

督軍嚴令水警巡船實行駐守防地常川派遣兵艦督巡勤減海氛一面勒限

省長

上緊救回被擄人船破獲駐盜衛商旅而維稅政大德謹稟 全役各船蓋章於后 民國十年八月 日

金瑞祥章 金同發章 金源豐章 金永潤章

黃萬興章 金源發章 金源利章 金飛鯨章

金永利章 金瑞康章 金瑞豐章 金瑞利章 金恒興章

新寶順章 金德興章 金華興章 金永孚章 金同華聯名木蓋章

謹將甌海夾板船近時被盜擄劫十案遇盜情形暨損失贓額并被擄難民人數開列節略呈

閱

今開

第一案

新寶順船去年十月在銅沙洋面被台州海盜劫掠船上所有銀錢雜物暨洋油等貨損失贓額計一千餘金

第二案

金瑞康船同月在台州臨床洋面遇盜劫掠損失贓額四百餘金

第三案

金同發船本年正月間在銅沙洋面被盜擄劫將船牽至箆絲門洋面停泊三日所裝公米被盜掠賣六百包之多並鹹魚等貨損失贓額五千餘金查該船被盜牽捉至五晝夜之久始行放回當停泊第二區第七隊管轄之箆絲門時訛盜招集小船多隻公然駁運公然銷賣該管水警毫無聞見足證該處隣近之第六隊南北澤泰第七隊之牛頭門白淡門防地空虛並無巡船駐守並劫去部頒船牌等件

第四案

金瑞利船二月間在銅沙洋面遇盜擄劫至石浦洋面時逾四日始行放回損失三百餘金

第五案

金永孚船三月間在磨盤洋面被盜擄劫牽至普陀山洋面逾五日將船放還損失贓額一千餘元

第六案

金華興船四月間在石浦口洋面被盜劫掠船上所有銀錢雜物及各夥衣物舖蓋共計贓額損失五百餘金當時被擄船夥周阿贊侯沛寬二人勒洋一千六百元取贖旋周阿贊擄至徒跳逃回

候沛寬被禁旋盃匪窩中四天後逃回得悉葭沚之趙美才蔣晥盃之老七相均有通盜嫌疑由事主黃國治將盜首萬德龍所繕字條呈送第二區核辦已否查拿迄無消息

第七案

金同華船同月在台州吊硼洋面遇盜搬掠銀錢衣物等件損失四百餘金

第八案

金源發船六月間在台州三門洋面遇盜刼掠洋銀衣物損失三百餘金並刦去部頒船牌等件

第九案

黄萬興船六月二十三日在大戢（大羊山）洋面遇盜擄掠擎至距離海門甚近之蔣兜浜（一潮可達）閱時半月歷程數百里並無兵艦巡船前來取締追該船在洋遭風損壞檣具不堪駕駛盜魁李榮昌即白眼小李遂攜去船夥南阿珍明法阿南嚴介四人（內嚴介一人現已逃回）勒贖千金令該船停在石浦候修估計客貨船家損失約共四千餘金

第十案

金永孚船陰歷七月二十一日（即八月十八號）在石浦口洋面遇

盗人船貨物統被擄去船上水手諸人生死未卜該船成造價值一萬餘金所裝板炭客貨約值一萬餘元

CUSTOM HOUSE,

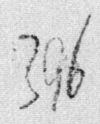

S/O NO. 234.

Wenchow, 4th October 1921.

Dues protests:
being locally
sted.

Dear Sir Francis,

I am sorry that you have been troubled with this matter, quite unnecessarily I have seen the various petitioners, who had referred to Ts'ai Cheng Pu and Shui-wu Ch'u before having seen me, and the petitioners told me that they regretted they had acted hastily, and did so under misapprehension. I am telling them that the Regulations have been carefully thought out and drawn up and being provisional in character can be revised at any time, that during the current three months the results of working will be carefully noted, and that thereafter any necessary changes* here and

FRANCIS A AGLEN K.B.E.,
Inspector General of Customs,
PEKING.

*e.g. regarding periodicity of levies in certain cases, but not in rates, measurement, or other fundamentals.

2.

and there can be considered in the light of the experience gained. The Regulations to be interpreted liberally meantime. I gather this reasonable proposal will meet their wishes: and, in fact, it is no more than was contemplated when the Regulations were framed. The Fukien junk people who hitherto - unauthorisedly, by the Hu Shang Chü - have been exempted are also in a more chastened and conciliatory mood, and realise that the exemption they enjoyed hitherto is not viewed favourably by the Wenchow traders. They seem practically to have fallen into line and to be unlikely to create any more difficulty. The Regulations were operated on the due date - 1st October - and, so far, smoothly and without any incident. The Superintendent fully concurs with all arrangements made. I appreciate the position of the Central Government versus such like provincial questions: but the action of the petitioners - acting largely at the instance, I am informed, of disappointed agitators among the late

3.

late Hu Shang Chü and the Fishery Office - was calculated to complicate matters, which are now in all probability straightened out. It has also to be remembered that for some long while past - since the abolition of the Hu Shang Chü - no junks have been paying any dues at all, though they have had early notice of our intention to collect. Junk Dues can, of course, scarcely form a very potent means of revenue addition: we look chiefly to the cargo junks carry, and do not want to place on them a burden more than they can bear. While all this has been, and is being, considered I hope, nevertheless, that we shall be able to receive a reasonable annual sum from this source: though the few thousand taels we shall get each year from Junk Dues, important to the Wenchow Revenue in itself, is less important, perhaps than the hold we shall be enabled to have over junk movements. I am reporting officially and now write this in advance.

The

…cy.

…erty: Commissioner's
…e; Bunding; Examiners
…e, Tidewaiters'
…ters: in good order.

…nue: September
…ease.

The head of the lorcha guild informs me that a regular engagement took place lately in the neighbourhood of the Chusan Group between three gunboats specially sent by the Provincial Authorities and a lorcha in piratical possession. The gunboats were poorly handled, and their prey escaped them.

Our property here is now in good order, and Works Department operations have ceased; though the stone paving of the bunding remains over to be completed next year. I will shortly report officially on all the property work done here by the Works Department.

Our September Maritime Customs Collection shows an apparently satisfactory increase, which is, however, rather more apparent than real, as in September 1920 various typhoons hampered the Shipping.

Yours truly,

INSPECTORATE GENERAL OF CUSTOMS,

S/O.   PEKING, 31st October 1921.

Dear Mr. Alabaster,

I have duly received your S/O letter No. 234 of the 4th October.

<u>Junk Dues protests - matter being adjusted locally.</u>

I hope there will be no more trouble. We don't want to impose heavy burdens, but it is necessary to establish our control. Do you have any Junk Pass book system?

Yours truly,

E. Alabaster, Esquire,
    Wenchow.

S/O NO. 235.

CUSTOM HOUSE,

Wenchow, 19th October 1921

k Dues: Chamber of
nerce accepts
nissioner's
ommendations.

Dear Sir Francis,

  Since writing my last letter the Chamber of Commerce - which I have been expecting would sooner or later emerge - has held meetings and has accepted, through the Superintendent, my recommendations as set forth in S/O No. 234 and despatch No. 3618. It is a satisfaction to have, as we have at present at this Port, a Superintendency which co-operates well with the Commissioner. And I may also add that the Fukien Guild - a powerful interest here - displays a conciliatory and reasonable and even friendly attitude. I am glad to gather from local information that the agitators have not received any encouragement

from

FRANCIS A AGLEN K. B. E.,
Inspector General of Customs,
  PEKING.

2.

icials: return of
yin.

ing arrangements:
y to I.G. Circular
3205.

from the Ministry and Shui-wu Ch'u. Any necessary changes as regards the periodicity of the levy, and such like, can easily be adjusted after three months actual working.

The <u>taoyin</u> has returned here as foreshadowed in S/O No. 232. Besides the Superintendent, I have lately seen the Hangchow Salt Inspector.

I might have added in my Report that we invariably keep only small balances - and merely of an essential kind to meet necessary current expenses <u>e.g.</u> such portion of the salaries as are locally paid, etc. - in the local Branch of the Bank of China. This latter appears to be quite sound.

Yours truly,

[A.—42]

INSPECTORATE GENERAL OF CUSTOMS,

PEKING, 1/11/21 19 .

Dear Sir,

I am directed by the Inspector General to inform you that your S/O Letter No. 255, dated 19/10/21, has been duly received.

Yours truly,

B. Phillips Denham
Private Secretary.

Alabaster Esquire
Wenchow

CUSTOM HOUSE,

S/O NO. 236.　　　　　　Wenchow, 7th November 1921.

Dear Sir Francis,

Dues (reply to S/O of 31st ...ber).

There is no more trouble and all is going quite smoothly. Our first months Revenue shows something over Kpg.Tls.414.— scarcely a colossal amount. Trade may not be booming - though it is now better - but the merchants here certainly tried things on with Peking in this particular matter.

JUNK PASS BOOKS. There are none at present in use. We purpose introducing them later: please c/f despatch No. 3611 (paragraph 5).

...ard Oil Co.'s
...ene Oil Tank
...llation.

The Standard Oil Company have sent a representative, Mr. Corbett, here finally to arrange things with the territorial Authorities,

SIR FRANCIS A AGLEN K.B.E.,
　　Inspector General of Customs,
　　　　PEKING.

2.

Authorities, his instructions being to remain here until matters have been fixed. I fancy things have been pretty well adjusted locally: but as the affair has gone to Hangchow, some delay is yet certain. When, and if, the territorial matter is decided, I shall report certain details to you officially and apply for certain instructions.

f: Mr. Gaylard, stant Examiner B, with influenza: Cammiade, 1st Class aiter, arrived.

Mr. Gaylard, Assistant Examiner B, is down with influenza. Mr. Cammiade, 1st Class Tidewaiter, has arrived from Kiungchow, and I have put him to Maritime Customs work as a preliminary. I try to encourage them - especially, now, Mr. West (4th Class Tidewaiter) at Native Customs - in practical Chinese study: but it is not easy. A way we adopt here - one involving the least loss of effort - is the collection by the particular officer of all Chinese forms (in fact any document passing) at the Native Customs, kept in a portfolio with an analysis attached giving the various

characters,

3.

characters, their separate meanings, and those of any particular phrases: *translation of both, its use, etc. etc.* The portfolio is of course constantly added to, and constantly (a zealous man would do so daily for some months) gone over again and memory refreshed. In this way a practical and useful officer capable of real - and not blind - supervision is reasonably speedily evolved with the least expenditure of mental effort and loss of energy. I think it is advisable for young foreign Tidewaiters to spend some of their early years in mandarin speaking ports.

[margin: ...ing: new line ...mplated.]

I hear that a new Chinese line is shortly to place steamers on the run from Shanghai viâ Ningpo to this and on to Foochow. If this develops it will hit the C.M.S.N.Co. rather badly, but the latter will probably triumph in the end.

Considerable local activity in road making is taking actual shape. The tracing of the main trunk road contemplated - a widening of existing roads, with certain

changes -

changes - runs to the Fukien boundary to join up with the Fukien artery, north again viâ Taichow to Hangchow. The roads are being poorly constructed unfortunately, to judge from local efforts.

     Yours truly,

INSPECTORATE GENERAL OF CUSTOMS,

S/O. PEKING, 28th November 1921.

Dear Mr. Alabaster,

I have duly received your S/O letter No. 236 of the 7th November.

<u>Training of Outdoor Staff in Chinese- Commissioner's plan of collecting all Chinese forms and documents in one portfolio for reference and study.</u>

A good idea: let me know how it works.

<u>Roads - Commissioner writes that considerable local activity in road making is taking actual shape.</u>

China is gradually waking up!

Yours truly,

E. Alabaster, Esquire,
    Wenchow.

CUSTOM HOUSE,

S/O No. 237.   Wenchow, 25th November, 1921.

Dear Sir Francis,

Dues. Conference merchants.
      On receipt of your despatch No.1055 I sent for the junk representatives, and am conferring with them. The result will be reported to you. The merchants themselves, and their agent the Chamber of Commerce, have behaved very crookedly in this matter.

Mr. Hirano charge against Examiner.
      Mr. Hirano is sick with autumn fever, of which there is much about. An allegation has been made against one of our Native Customs Examiners (Chinese) of extortion: the accuser, I am almost sure, is a scoundrel; and bad temper, rigidity in examination, and ill-feeling are very

probably

FRANCIS A AGLEN K. B. E.,
Inspector General of Customs,
   PEKING.

2.

probably at the root of the accusation. The matter is being investigated

Yours truly,

[signature]

[.—42]

INSPECTORATE GENERAL OF CUSTOMS,

PEKING, 22/12/21 19.

ear Sir,

I am directed by the Inspector General

form you that your S/O Letter No. 257,

25/11/21, has been duly

ved.

Yours truly,

B. Phillipson Tinker
Private Secretary.

Alabaster, Lynn
Wombur

CUSTOM HOUSE,

S/O No. 238.

Wenchow, 11th December 1921.

Dues: revision of.

f: Mr. Hirano at
ghai for Chinese
ination: Native
oms Examiner,
ge against.

Dear Sir Francis,

You will receive my report on this subject with my proposals, in a few days.

Mr. Hirano leaves today for his Chinese examination. His illness proved to be influenza and he could not go to Shanghai when Mr. MacDonald arrived there first. He is quite well again, and wished to be examined now instead of later on. - I have not heard anything further as regards the accusation against the N.C. Examiner referred to in my last S/O: and it is possible that the matter will not develop. I will, in any case, report later.

This is proceeding quite rapidly and passes down river to the old Lower Anchorage.

FRANCIS A AGLEN K. B. E.,
Inspector General of Customs,
   P E K I N G.

Anchorage. The width is about 32 feet: bɩ too little stone is being used in the construction, and there will be a wash-out with the first heavy rains. The Taichow people are raising trouble as to their section of the work, across the river at the Lower Anchorage and up to Taichow.

Various items of work have rather been retarding me with this: but I am getting along and hope soon to report quicker progress.

At Xmas I propose to go up country in this district for a few days, including the holidays, and returning 26th.

Yours truly,

CUSTOM HOUSE,

S/O NO. 239.   Wenchow 28th December 1921

Dues (Wenchow
atch No.3637).

Dear Sir Francis,

What the merchants would like is that the Wenchow Native Customs should refrain from collecting Junk Dues, in which case the merchants would re-establish some office here under one name or another and do the collecting themselves, the former hu shang employés also receiving jobs. Consequently every expedient, open or otherwise, is being tried: and possibly it was thought that a long range bombardment of Peking with telegrams would be the most fruitful course. The origin of the abolition of the Hu Shang Chü by the Provincial Assembly lay in the fact that certain parties (timber merchants) felt aggrieved in that they did not receive shares in the undertaking, and thereafter

stirred

IR FRANCIS A AGLEN K. B. E.,
    Inspector General of Customs,
        PEKING.

Medical Officer.

...ials: change of
...intendent.

stirred up trouble with the assembly.

We are all well. — Dr. Stedeford, former Medical Officer, has returned from furlough. I hear he took a course in dentistry, which may be useful to us here.

I am sorry for this change: the Superintendent himself, of course, was always away: but his manager here is an unusually hardworking and obliging official.

I went up country for two days only at Xmas.

Yours truly,

E. Alabaster